DATE DUE			
Jun 7 '82			

THE NATURE
OF THE
PHYSICAL WORLD

THE NATURE
OF THE
PHYSICAL WORLD

by

A. S. EDDINGTON
M.A., LL.D., D.SC., F.R.S.

*Plumian Professor of Astronomy
in the
University of Cambridge*

THE
GIFFORD LECTURES
1927

NEW YORK:
THE MACMILLAN COMPANY

CAMBRIDGE, ENGLAND:
AT THE UNIVERSITY PRESS

1929

SET UP BY BROWN BROTHERS LINOTYPERS
PRINTED IN THE UNITED STATES OF AMERICA
BY THE FERRIS PRINTING COMPANY

PREFACE

This book is substantially the course of Gifford Lectures which I delivered in the University of Edinburgh in January to March 1927. It treats of the philosophical outcome of the great changes of scientific thought which have recently come about. The theory of relativity and the quantum theory have led to strange new conceptions of the physical world; the progress of the principles of thermodynamics has wrought more gradual but no less profound change. The first eleven chapters are for the most part occupied with the new physical theories, with the reasons which have led to their adoption, and especially with the conceptions which seem to underlie them. The aim is to make clear the scientific view of the world as it stands at the present day, and, where it is incomplete, to judge the direction in which modern ideas appear to be tending. In the last four chapters I consider the position which this scientific view should occupy in relation to the wider aspects of human experience, including religion. The general spirit of the inquiry followed in the lectures is stated in the concluding paragraph of the Introduction (p. xviii).

I hope that the scientific chapters may be read with interest apart from the later applications in the book; but they are not written quite on the lines that would have been adopted had they been wholly independent. It would not serve my purpose to give an easy introduction to the rudiments of the relativity and quantum theories; it was essential to reach the later and more recondite developments in which the conceptions of greatest philosophical significance are to be found. Whilst much of the book should prove fairly easy reading, arguments of considerable difficulty have to be taken in their turn.

My principal aim has been to show that these scientific developments provide new material for the philosopher. I have, however, gone beyond this and indicated how I myself think the material might be used. I realise that the philosophical views here put forward can only claim attention in so far as they are the direct outcome of a study and apprehension of modern scientific work. General ideas of the nature of things which I may have formed apart from this particular stimulus from science are of little moment to anyone but myself. But although the two sources of ideas were fairly distinct in my mind when I began to prepare these lectures they have become inextricably combined in the effort to reach a coherent outlook and to defend it from probable criticism. For that reason I would like to recall that the idealistic tinge in my conception of the physical world arose out of mathematical researches on the relativity theory. In so far as I had any earlier philosophical views, they were of an entirely different complexion.

From the beginning I have been doubtful whether it was desirable for a scientist to venture so far into extra-scientific territory. The primary justification for such an expedition is that it may afford a better view of his own scientific domain. In the oral lectures it did not seem a grave indiscretion to speak freely of the various suggestions I had to offer. But whether they should be recorded permanently and given a more finished appearance has been difficult to decide. I have much to fear from the expert philosophical critic, but I am filled with even more apprehension at the thought of readers who may look to see whether the book is "on the side of the angels" and judge its trustworthiness accordingly. During the year which has elapsed since the delivery of the lectures I have made many efforts to shape this and other parts of the book into something with which I might feel better content. I release it now with more diffidence than I have felt with regard to former books.

The conversational style of the lecture-room is generally considered rather unsuitable for a long book, but I decided not to modify it. A scientific writer, in forgoing the mathematical formulae which are his natural and clearest medium of expression, may perhaps claim some concession from the reader in return. Many parts of the subject are intrinsically so difficult that my only hope of being understood is to explain the points as I would were I face to face with an inquirer.

It may be necessary to remind the American reader that our nomenclature for large numbers differs from his, so that a billion here means a million million.

A. S. E.

August 1928

INTRODUCTION

I have settled down to the task of writing these lectures and have drawn up my chairs to my two tables. Two tables! Yes; there are duplicates of every object about me—two tables, two chairs, two pens.

This is not a very profound beginning to a course which ought to reach transcendent levels of scientific philosophy. But we cannot touch bedrock immediately; we must scratch a bit at the surface of things first. And whenever I begin to scratch the first thing I strike is—my two tables.

One of them has been familiar to me from earliest years. It is a commonplace object of that environment which I call the world. How shall I describe it? It has extension; it is comparatively permanent; it is coloured; above all it is *substantial*. By substantial I do not merely mean that it does not collapse when I lean upon it; I mean that it is constituted of "substance" and by that word I am trying to convey to you some conception of its intrinsic nature. It is a *thing*; not like space, which is a mere negation; nor like time, which is—Heaven knows what! But that will not help you to my meaning because it is the distinctive characteristic of a "thing" to have this substantiality, and I do not think substantiality can be described better than by saying that it is the kind of nature exemplified by an ordinary table. And so we go round in circles. After all if you are a plain commonsense man, not too much worried with scientific scruples, you will be confident that you understand the nature of an ordinary table. I have even heard of plain men who had the idea that they could better understand the mystery of their own nature if scientists would discover a way of explaining it in terms of the easily comprehensible nature of a table.

Table No. 2 is my scientific table. It is a more recent acquaintance and I do not feel so familiar with it. It does not belong to the world previously mentioned—that world which spontaneously appears around me when I open my eyes, though how much of it is objective and how much subjective I do not here consider. It is part of a world which in more devious ways has forced itself on my attention. My scientific table is mostly emptiness. Sparsely scattered in that emptiness are numerous electric charges rushing about with great speed; but their combined bulk amounts to less than a billionth of the bulk of the table itself. Notwithstanding its strange construction it turns out to be an entirely efficient table. It supports my writing paper as satisfactorily as table No. 1; for when I lay the paper on it the little electric particles with their headlong speed keep on hitting the underside, so that the paper is maintained in shuttlecock fashion at a nearly steady level. If I lean upon this table I shall not go through; or, to be strictly accurate, the chance of my scientific elbow going through my scientific table is so excessively small that it can be neglected in practical life. Reviewing their properties one by one, there seems to be nothing to choose between the two tables for ordinary purposes; but when abnormal circumstances befall, then my scientific table shows to advantage. If the house catches fire my scientific table will dissolve quite naturally into scientific smoke, whereas my familiar table undergoes a metamorphosis of its substantial nature which I can only regard as miraculous.

There is nothing *substantial* about my second table. It is nearly all empty space—space pervaded, it is true, by fields of force, but these are assigned to the category of "influences", not of "things". Even in the minute part which is not empty we must not transfer the old notion of substance. In dissecting matter into electric charges we have travelled far from that picture of it which first gave rise to the conception of substance, and the meaning of that conception—if it ever had any—has been lost by the way. The whole trend of modern scientific views is to break down the separate categories of "things", "influences", "forms", etc., and to substitute a common background of all experience. Whether we are studying a material object, a magnetic field, a geometrical figure, or a duration of time, our scientific information is summed up in measures; neither the apparatus of measurement nor the mode of using it suggests that there is anything essentially different in these problems. The measures themselves afford no ground for a classification by categories. We feel it necessary to concede some background to the measures—an external world; but the attributes of this world, except in so far as they are reflected in the measures, are outside scientific scrutiny. Science has at last revolted against attaching the exact knowledge contained in these measurements to a traditional picture-gallery of conceptions which convey no authentic information of the background and obtrude irrelevancies into the scheme of knowledge.

I will not here stress further the non-substantiality of electrons, since it is scarcely necessary to the present line of thought. Conceive them as substantially as you will, there is a vast difference between my scientific table with its substance (if any) thinly scattered in specks in a region mostly empty and the table of everyday conception which we regard as the type of solid reality

—an incarnate protest against Berkleian subjectivism. It makes all the difference in the world whether the paper before me is poised as it were on a swarm of flies and sustained in shuttlecock fashion by a series of tiny blows from the swarm underneath, or whether it is supported because there is substance below it, it being the intrinsic nature of substance to occupy space to the exclusion of other substance; all the difference in conception at least, but no difference to my practical task of writing on the paper.

I need not tell you that modern physics has by delicate test and remorseless logic assured me that my second scientific table is the only one which is really there—wherever "there" may be. On the other hand I need not tell you that modern physics will never succeed in exorcising that first table—strange compound of external nature, mental imagery and inherited prejudice—which lies visible to my eyes and tangible to my grasp. We must bid good-bye to it for the present for we are about to turn from the familiar world to the scientific world revealed by physics. This is, or is intended to be, a wholly external world.

"You speak paradoxically of two worlds. Are they not really two aspects or two interpretations of one and the same world?"

Yes, no doubt they are ultimately to be identified after some fashion. But the process by which the external world of physics is transformed into a world of familiar acquaintance in human consciousness is outside the scope of physics. And so the world studied according to the methods of physics remains detached from the world familiar to consciousness, until after the physicist has finished his labours upon it. Provisionally, therefore, we regard the table which is the subject of physical research as altogether separate from the familiar table, without prejudging the question of their ultimate identification. It is true that the whole scientific inquiry starts from the familiar world and in the end it must return to the familiar world; but the part of the journey over which the physicist has charge is in foreign territory.

Until recently there was a much closer linkage; the physicist used to borrow the raw material of his world from the familiar world, but he does so no longer. His raw materials are aether, electrons, quanta, potentials, Hamiltonian functions, etc., and he is nowadays scrupulously careful to guard these from contamination by conceptions borrowed from the other world. There is a familiar table parallel to the scientific table, but there is no familiar electron, quantum or potential parallel to the scientific electron, quantum or potential. We do not even desire to manufacture a familiar counterpart to these things or, as we should commonly say, to "explain" the electron. After the physicist has quite finished his world-building a linkage or identification is allowed; but premature attempts at linkage have been found to be entirely mischievous.

Science aims at constructing a world which shall be symbolic of the world of commonplace experience. It is not at all necessary that every individual symbol that is used should represent something in common experience or even something explicable in terms of common experience. The man in the street is always making this demand for concrete explanation of the things referred to in science; but of necessity he must be disappointed. It is like our experience in learning to read. That which is written in a book is symbolic of a story in real life. The whole intention of the book is that ultimately a reader will identify some symbol, say BREAD, with one of the conceptions of familiar life. But it is mischievous to attempt such identifications prematurely, before the letters are strung into words and the words into sentences. The symbol A is not the counterpart of anything in familiar life. To the child the letter A would seem horribly abstract; so we give him a familiar conception along with it. "A was an Archer who shot at a frog." This tides over his immediate difficulty; but he cannot make serious progress with word-building so long as Archers, Butchers, Captains, dance round the letters. The letters are abstract, and sooner or later he has to realise it. In physics we have outgrown archer and apple-pie definitions of the fundamental symbols. To a request to explain what an electron really is supposed to be we can only answer, "It is part of the A B C of physics".

The external world of physics has thus become a world of shadows. In removing our illusions we have removed the substance, for indeed we have seen that substance is one of the greatest of our illusions. Later perhaps we may inquire whether in our zeal to cut out all that is unreal we may not have used the knife too ruthlessly. Perhaps, indeed, reality is a child which cannot survive without its nurse illusion. But if so, that is of little concern to the scientist, who has good and sufficient reasons for pursuing his investigations in the world of shadows and is content to leave to the philosopher the determination of its exact status in regard to reality. In the world of physics we watch a shadowgraph performance of the drama of familiar life. The shadow of my elbow rests on the shadow table as the shadow ink flows over the shadow paper. It is all symbolic, and as a symbol the physicist leaves it. Then comes the alchemist Mind who transmutes the symbols. The sparsely spread nuclei of electric force become a tangible solid; their restless agitation becomes the warmth of summer; the octave of aethereal vibrations becomes a gorgeous rainbow. Nor does the alchemy stop here. In the transmuted world new significances arise which are scarcely to be traced in the world of symbols; so that it becomes a world of beauty and purpose—and, alas, suffering and evil.

The frank realisation that physical science is concerned with a world of shadows is one of the most significant of recent advances. I do not mean that physicists are to any extent preoccupied with the philosophical implications of this. From their point of view it is not so much a withdrawal of untenable claims as an assertion of freedom for autonomous development. At the moment I am not insisting on the shadowy and symbolic character of the world of physics because of its bearing on philosophy, but because the aloofness from familiar conceptions will be apparent in the scientific theories I have to describe. If you are not prepared for this aloofness you are likely to be out of sympathy with modern scientific theories, and may even think them ridiculous—as, I daresay, many people do.

It is difficult to school ourselves to treat the physical world as purely symbolic. We are always relapsing and mixing with the symbols incongruous conceptions taken from the world of consciousness. Untaught by long experience we stretch a hand to grasp the shadow, instead of accepting its shadowy nature. Indeed, unless we confine ourselves altogether to mathematical symbolism it is hard to avoid dressing our symbols in deceitful clothing. When I think of an electron there rises to my mind a hard, red, tiny ball; the proton simi-

larly is neutral grey. Of course the colour is absurd—
perhaps not more absurd than the rest of the conception—
but I am incorrigible. I can well understand that the
younger minds are finding these pictures too concrete
and are striving to construct the world out of Hamiltonian functions and symbols so far removed from
human preconception that they do not even obey
the laws of orthodox arithmetic. For myself I find some
difficulty in rising to that plane of thought; but I am
convinced that it has got to come.

In these lectures I propose to discuss some of the
results of modern study of the physical world which
give most food for philosophic thought. This will include
new conceptions in science and also new knowledge. In
both respects we are led to think of the material universe in a way very different from that prevailing at the
end of the last century. I shall not leave out of
sight the ulterior object which must be in the mind of
a Gifford Lecturer, the problem of relating these
purely physical discoveries to the wider aspects and
interests of our human nature. These relations cannot but have undergone change, since our whole conception of the physical world has radically changed. I am
convinced that a just appreciation of the physical
world as it is understood to-day carries with it a feeling
of open-mindedness towards a wider significance transcending scientific measurement, which might have
seemed illogical a generation ago; and in the later
lectures I shall try to focus that feeling and make
inexpert efforts to find where it leads. But I should
be untrue to science if I did not insist that its study is
an end in itself. The path of science must be pursued
for its own sake, irrespective of the views it may afford
of a wider landscape; in this spirit we must follow the

path whether it leads to the hill of vision or the tunnel of obscurity. Therefore till the last stage of the course is reached you must be content to follow with me the beaten track of science, nor scold me too severely for loitering among its wayside flowers. That is to be the understanding between us. Shall we set forth?

CONTENTS

THE NATURE
OF THE
PHYSICAL WORLD

Chapter I

THE DOWNFALL OF CLASSICAL PHYSICS

The Structure of the Atom.   Between 1905 and 1908 Einstein and Minkowski introduced fundamental changes in our ideas of time and space.   In 1911 Rutherford introduced the greatest change in our idea of matter since the time of Democritus.   The reception of these two changes was curiously different.   The new ideas of space and time were regarded on all sides as revolutionary; they were received with the greatest enthusiasm by some and the keenest opposition by others.   The new idea of matter underwent the ordinary experience of scientific discovery; it gradually proved its worth, and when the evidence became overwhelmingly convincing it quietly supplanted previous theories.   No great shock was felt. And yet when I hear to-day protests against the Bolshevism of modern science and regrets for the old-established order, I am inclined to think that Rutherford, not Einstein, is the real villain of the piece.   When we compare the universe as it is now supposed to be with the universe as we had ordinarily preconceived it, the most arresting change is not the rearrangement of space and time by Einstein but the dissolution of all that we regard as most solid into tiny specks floating in void.   That gives an abrupt jar to those who think that things are more or less what they seem.   The revelation by modern physics of the void within the atom is more disturbing than the revelation by astronomy of the immense void of interstellar space.

The atom is as porous as the solar system.   If we eliminated all the unfilled space in a man's body and

1

collected his protons and electrons into one mass, the man would be reduced to a speck just visible with a magnifying glass.

This porosity of matter was not foreshadowed in the atomic theory. Certainly it was known that in a gas like air the atoms are far separated, leaving a great deal of empty space; but it was only to be expected that material with the characteristics of air should have relatively little substance in it, and "airy nothing" is a common phrase for the insubstantial. In solids the atoms are packed tightly in contact, so that the old atomic theory agreed with our preconceptions in regarding solid bodies as mainly substantial without much interstice.

The electrical theory of matter which arose towards the end of the nineteenth century did not at first alter this view. It was known that the negative electricity was concentrated into unit charges of very small bulk; but the other constituent of matter, the positive electricity, was pictured as a sphere of jelly of the same dimensions as the atom and having the tiny negative charges embedded in it. Thus the space inside a solid was still for the most part well filled.

But in 1911 Rutherford showed that the positive electricity was also concentrated into tiny specks. His scattering experiments proved that the atom was able to exert large electrical forces which would be impossible unless the positive charge acted as a highly concentrated source of attraction; it must be contained in a nucleus minute in comparison with the dimensions of the atom. Thus for the first time the main volume of the atom was entirely evacuated, and a "solar system" type of atom was substituted for a substantial "billiard-ball". Two years later Niels Bohr developed his famous theory on the basis of the Rutherford atom, and since then rapid progress has been made. Whatever further changes of view are in prospect, a reversion to the old substantial atoms is unthinkable.

The accepted conclusion at the present day is that all varieties of matter are ultimately composed of two elementary constituents—protons and electrons. Electrically these are the exact opposites of one another, the proton being a charge of positive electricity and the electron a charge of negative electricity. But in other respects their properties are very different. The proton has 1840 times the mass of the electron, so that nearly all the mass of matter is due to its constituent protons. The proton is not found unadulterated except in hydrogen, which seems to be the most primitive form of matter, its atom consisting of one proton and one electron. In other atoms a number of protons and a lesser number of electrons are cemented together to form a nucleus; the electrons required to make up the balance are scattered like remote satellites of the nucleus, and can even escape from the atom and wander freely through the material. The diameter of an electron is about 1/50,000 of the diameter of an atom; that of the nucleus is not very much larger; an isolated proton is supposed to be much smaller still.

Thirty years ago there was much debate over the question of aether-drag—whether the earth moving round the sun drags the aether with it. At that time the solidity of the atom was unquestioned, and it was difficult to believe that matter could push its way through the aether without disturbing it. It was surprising and perplexing to find as the result of experiments that no convection of the aether occurred. But we now realise that the aether can slip through the atoms as easily as through the solar system, and our expectation is all the other way.

We shall return to the "solar system" atom in later chapters. For the present the two things which concern us are (1) its extreme emptiness, and (2) the fact that it is made up of electrical charges.

Rutherford's nuclear theory of the atom is not usually counted as one of the scientific revolutions of the present century. It was a far-reaching discovery, but a discovery falling within the classical scheme of physics. The nature and significance of the discovery could be stated in plain terms, i.e. in terms of conceptions already current in science. The epithet "revolutionary" is usually reserved for two great modern developments—the Relativity Theory and the Quantum Theory. These are not merely new discoveries as to the content of the world; they involve changes in our mode of thought about the world. They cannot be stated immediately in plain terms because we have first to grasp new conceptions undreamt of in the classical scheme of physics.

I am not sure that the phrase "classical physics" has ever been closely defined. But the general idea is that the scheme of natural law developed by Newton in the *Principia* provided a pattern which all subsequent developments might be expected to follow. Within the four corners of the scheme great changes of outlook were possible; the wave-theory of light supplanted the corpuscular theory; heat was changed from substance (caloric) to energy of motion; electricity from continuous fluid to nuclei of strain in the aether. But this was all allowed for in the elasticity of the original scheme. Waves, kinetic energy, and strain already had their place in the scheme; and the application of the same conceptions to account for a wider range of phenomena was a tribute to the comprehensiveness of Newton's original outlook.

We have now to see how the classical scheme broke down.

The FitzGerald Contraction. We can best start from the following fact. Suppose that you have a rod moving at very high speed. Let it first be pointing transverse to its line of motion. Now turn it through a right angle so that it is along the line of motion. The rod contracts. It is shorter when it is along the line of motion than when it is across the line of motion.

This contraction, known as the FitzGerald contraction, is exceedingly small in all ordinary circumstances. It does not depend at all on the material of the rod but only on the speed. For example, if the speed is 19 miles a second—the speed of the earth round the sun—the contraction of length is 1 part in 200,000,000, or 2½ inches in the diameter of the earth.

This is demonstrated by a number of experiments of different kinds of which the earliest and best known is the Michelson-Morley experiment first performed in 1887, repeated more accurately by Morley and Miller in 1905, and again by several observers within the last year or two. I am not going to describe these experiments except to mention that the convenient way of giving your rod a large velocity is to carry it on the earth which moves at high speed round the sun. Nor shall I discuss here how complete is the proof afforded by these experiments. It is much more important that you should realise that the contraction is just what would be expected from our current knowledge of a material rod.

You are surprised that the dimensions of a moving

rod can be altered merely by pointing it different ways. You expect them to remain unchanged. But which rod are you thinking of? (You remember my two tables.) If you are thinking of continuous substance, extending in space because it is the nature of substance to occupy space, then there seems to be no valid cause for a change of dimensions. But the scientific rod is a swarm of electrical particles rushing about and widely separated from one another. The marvel is that such a swarm should tend to preserve any definite extension. The particles, however, keep a certain average spacing so that the whole volume remains practically steady; they exert electrical forces on one another, and the volume which they fill corresponds to a balance between the forces drawing them together and the diverse motions tending to spread them apart. When the rod is set in motion these electrical forces change. Electricity in motion constitutes an electric current. But electric currents give rise to forces of a different type from those due to electricity at rest, viz. magnetic forces. Moreover these forces arising from the motion of electric charges will naturally be of different intensity in the directions along and across the line of motion.

By setting in motion the rod with all the little electric charges contained in it we introduce new magnetic forces between the particles. Clearly the original balance is upset, and the average spacing between the particles must alter until a new balance is found. And so the extension of the swarm of particles—the length of the rod—alters.

There is really nothing mysterious about the Fitz-Gerald contraction. It would be an unnatural property of a rod pictured in the old way as continuous substance occupying space in virtue of its substantiality; but it is

an entirely natural property of a swarm of particles held
in delicate balance by electromagnetic forces, and occupying space by buffeting away anything that tries to
enter. Or you may look at it this way: your expectation that the rod will keep its original length presupposes, of course, that it receives fair treatment and
is not subjected to any new stresses. But a rod in motion
is subjected to a new magnetic stress, arising not from
unfair outside tampering but as a necessary consequence
of its own electrical constitution; and under this stress
the contraction occurs. Perhaps you will think that if
the rod were rigid enough it might be able to resist the
compressing force. That is not so; the FitzGerald contraction is the same for a rod of steel and for a rod of
india-rubber; the rigidity and the compressing stress are
bound up with the constitution in such a way that if
one is large so also is the other. It is necessary to rid
our minds of the idea that this failure to keep a constant
length is an imperfection of the rod; it is only imperfect
as compared with an imaginary "something" which has
not this electrical constitution—and therefore is not
material at all. The FitzGerald contraction is not an
imperfection but a fixed and characteristic property of
matter, like inertia.

We have here drawn a qualitative inference from the
electrical structure of matter; we must leave it to the
mathematician to calculate the quantitative effect. The
problem was worked out by Lorentz and Larmor about
1900. They calculated the change in the average spacing
of the particles required to restore the balance after it
had been upset by the new forces due to the change of
motion of the charges. This calculation was found to
give precisely the FitzGerald contraction, i.e. the amount
already inferred from the experiments above mentioned.

Thus we have two legs to stand on. Some will prefer to trust the results because they seem to be well established by experiment; others will be more easily persuaded by the knowledge that the FitzGerald contraction is a necessary consequence of the scheme of electromagnetic laws universally accepted since the time of Maxwell. Both experiments and theories sometimes go wrong; so it is just as well to have both alternatives.

Consequences of the Contraction. This result alone, although it may not quite lead you to the theory of relativity, ought to make you uneasy about classical physics. The physicist when he wishes to measure a length— and he cannot get far in any experiment without measuring a length—takes a scale and turns it in the direction needed. It never occurred to him that in spite of all precautions the scale would change length when he did this; but unless the earth happens to be at rest a change must occur. The constancy of a measuring scale is the rock on which the whole structure of physics has been reared; and that rock has crumbled away. You may think that this assumption cannot have betrayed the physicist very badly; the changes of length cannot be serious or they would have been noticed. Wait and see.

Let us look at some of the consequences of the Fitz-Gerald contraction. First take what may seem to be a rather fantastic case. Imagine you are on a planet moving very fast indeed, say 161,000 miles a second. For this speed the contraction is one-half. Any solid contracts to half its original length when turned from across to along the line of motion. A railway journey between two towns which was 100 miles at noon is shortened to 50 miles at 6 p.m. when the planet has turned through a right angle. The inhabitants copy Alice in Wonderland; they pull out and shut up like a telescope.

I do not know of a planet moving at 161,000 miles a second, but I could point to a spiral nebula far away in space which is moving at 1000 miles a second. This may well contain a planet and (speaking unprofessionally) perhaps I shall not be taking too much licence if I place intelligent beings on it. At 1000 miles a second the contraction is not large enough to be appreciable in ordinary affairs; but it is quite large enough to be appreciable in measurements of scientific or even of engineering accuracy. One of the most fundamental procedures in physics is to measure lengths with a scale moved about in any way. Imagine the consternation of the physicists on this planet when they learn that they have made a mistake in supposing that their scale is a constant measure of length. What a business to go back over all the experiments ever performed, apply the corrections for orientation of the scale at the time, and then consider *de novo* the inferences and system of physical laws to be deduced from the amended data! How thankful our own physicists ought to be that they are not in this runaway nebula but on a decently slow-moving planet like the earth!

But stay a moment. Is it so certain that we are on a slow-moving planet? I can imagine the astronomers in that nebula observing far away in space an insignificant star attended by an insignificant planet called Earth. They observe too that it is moving with the huge velocity of 1000 miles a second; because naturally if we see them receding from us at 1000 miles a second they will see us receding from them at 1000 miles a second. "A thousand miles a second!" exclaim the nebular physicists, "How unfortunate for the poor

physicists on the Earth! The FitzGerald contraction
will be quite appreciable, and all their measures with
scales will be seriously wrong. What a weird system of
laws of Nature they will have deduced, if they have overlooked this correction!"

There is no means of deciding which is right—to
which of us the observed relative velocity of 1000
miles a second *really* belongs. Astronomically the galaxy of which the earth is a member does not seem to
be more important, more central, than the nebula.
The presumption that it is we who are the more nearly
at rest has no serious foundation; it is mere self-
flattery.

"But", you will say, "surely if these appreciable
changes of length occurred on the earth, we should
detect them by our measurements." That brings me to
the interesting point. We could not detect them by any
measurement; they may occur and yet pass quite un-
noticed. Let me try to show how this happens.

This room, we will say, is travelling at 161,000 miles
a second vertically upwards. That is my statement, and
it is up to you to prove it wrong. I turn my arm from
horizontal to vertical and it contracts to half its original
length. You don't believe me? Then bring a yard-
measure and measure it. First, horizontally, the result
is 30 inches; now vertically, the result is 30 half-inches.
You must allow for the fact that an inch-division of the
scale contracts to half an inch when the yard-measure
is turned vertically.

"But we can see that your arm does not become
shorter; can we not trust our own eyes?"

Certainly not, unless you remember that when you
got up this morning your retina contracted to half its
original width in the vertical direction; consequently it

is now exaggerating vertical distances to twice the scale of horizontal distances.

"Very well", you reply, "I will not get up. I will lie in bed and watch you go through your performance in an inclined mirror. Then my retina will be all right, but I know I shall still see no contraction."

But a moving mirror does not give an undistorted image of what is happening. The angle of reflection of light is altered by motion of a mirror, just as the angle of reflection of a billiard-ball would be altered if the cushion were moving. If you will work out by the ordinary laws of optics the effect of moving a mirror at 161,000 miles a second, you will find that it introduces a distortion which just conceals the contraction of my arm.

And so on for every proposed test. You cannot disprove my assertion, and, of course, I cannot prove it; I might equally well have chosen and defended any other velocity. At first this seems to contradict what I told you earlier—that the contraction had been proved and measured by the Michelson-Morley and other experiments—but there is really no contradiction. They were all *null* experiments, just as your experiment of watching my arm in an inclined mirror was a null experiment. Certain optical or electrical consequences of the earth's motion were looked for of the same type as the distortion of images by a moving mirror; these would have been observed unless a contraction occurred of just the right amount to compensate them. They were not observed; therefore the compensating contraction had occurred. There was just one alternative; the earth's true velocity through space might happen to have been nil. This was ruled out by repeating the experiment six months later, since the earth's motion could not be nil on both occasions. Thus the contraction was demonstrated and its law of dependence on velocity verified. But the actual amount of contraction on either occasion was unknown, since the earth's true velocity (as distinct from its orbital velocity with respect to the sun) was unknown. It remains unknown because the optical and electrical effects by which we might hope to measure it are always compensated by the contraction.

I have said that the constancy of a measuring scale is the rock on which the structure of physics has been reared. The structure has also been supported by supplementary props because optical and electrical devices can often be used instead of material scales to ascertain lengths and distances. But we find that all these are united in a conspiracy not to give one another away. The rock has crumbled and simultaneously all the other supports have collapsed.

Frames of Space. We can now return to the quarrel between the nebular physicists and ourselves. One of us has a large velocity and his scientific measurements are seriously affected by the contraction of his scales. Each has hitherto taken it for granted that it is the other fellow who is making the mistake. We cannot settle the dispute by appeal to experiment because in every *experiment* the mistake introduces two errors which just compensate one another.

It is a curious sort of mistake which always carries with it its own compensation. But remember that the compensation only applies to phenomena actually observed or capable of observation. The compensation does not apply to the intermediate part of our deduction—that system of inference from observation which forms the classical physical theory of the universe.

Suppose that we and the nebular physicists survey the world, that is to say we allocate the surrounding objects to their respective positions in space. One party, say the nebular physicists, has a large velocity; their yard-measures will contract and become less than a yard when they measure distances in a certain direction; consequently they will reckon distances in that direction too great. It does not matter whether they use a yard-measure, or a theodolite, or merely judge distances with the eye; all methods of measurement must agree. If motion caused a disagreement of any kind, we should be able to determine the motion by observing the amount of disagreement; but, as we have already seen, both theory and observation indicate that there is complete compensation. If the nebular physicists try to construct a square they will construct an oblong. No test can ever reveal to them that it is not a square; the greatest advance they can make is to recognise that there are people in another world who have got it into their heads that it is an oblong, and they may be broadminded enough to admit that this point of view, absurd as it seems, is really as defensible as their own. It is clear that their whole conception of space is distorted as compared with ours, and ours is distorted as compared with theirs. We are regarding the same universe, but we have arranged it in different spaces. The original quarrel as to whether they or we are moving with the speed of 1000 miles a second has made so deep a cleavage between us that we cannot even use the same space.

Space and time are words conveying more than one meaning. Space is an empty void; or it is such and such a number of inches, acres, pints. Time is an ever-rolling stream; or it is something signalled to us by wireless. The physicist has no use for vague conceptions; he often has them, alas! but he cannot make real use of them. So when he speaks of space it is always the inches or pints that he should have in mind. It is from this point of view that our space and the space of the nebular physicists are different spaces; the reckoning of inches and pints is different. To avoid possible misunderstanding it is perhaps better to say that we have different *frames of space*—different frames to which we refer the location of objects. Do not, however, think of a frame of space as something consciously artificial; the frame of space comes into our minds with our first perception of space. Consider, for example, the more extreme case when the FitzGerald contraction is one-half. If a man takes a rectangle $2'' \times 1''$ to be a square it is clear that space must have dawned on his intelligence in a way very different from that in which we have apprehended it.

The frame of space used by an observer depends only on his motion. Observers on different planets with the same velocity (i.e. having zero relative velocity) will agree as to the location of the objects of the universe; but observers on planets with different velocities have different frames of location. You may ask, How can I be so confident as to the way in which these imaginary beings will interpret their observations? If that objection is pressed I shall not defend myself; but those who dislike my imaginary beings must face the alternative of following the argument with mathematical symbols. Our purpose has been to express in a conveniently apprehensible form certain results which follow from terrestrial experiments and calculations as to the effect of motion on electrical, optical and metrical phenomena. So much careful work has been done on this subject that science is in a position to state what will be the consequence of making measurements with instruments travelling at high speed—whether instruments of a technical kind or, for example, a human retina. In only one respect do I treat my nebular observer as more than a piece of registering apparatus; I assume that he is subject to a common failing of human nature, viz. he takes it for granted that it was his planet that God chiefly had in mind when the universe was created. Hence he is (like my reader perhaps?) disinclined to take seriously the views of location of those people who are so misguided as to move at 1000 miles a second relatively to his parish pump.

An exceptionally modest observer might take some other planet than his own as the standard of rest. Then he would have to correct all his measurements for the FitzGerald contraction due to his own motion with respect to the standard, and the corrected measures would give the space-frame belonging to the standard planet as the original measures gave the space-frame of his own planet. For him the dilemma is even more pressing, for there is nothing to guide him as to the planet to be selected for the standard of rest. Once he gives up the naïve assumption that his own frame is the one and only right frame the question arises, Which then of the innumerable other frames is right? There is no answer, and so far as we can see no possibility of an answer. Meanwhile all his experimental measurements are waiting unreduced, because the corrections to be applied to them depend on the answer. I am afraid our modest observer will get rather left behind by his less humble colleagues.

The trouble that arises is not that we have found anything necessarily wrong with the frame of location that has been employed in our system of physics; it has not led to experimental contradictions. The only thing known to be "wrong" with it is that it is not unique. If we had found that our frame was unsatisfactory and another frame was preferable, that would not have caused a great revolution of thought; but to discover that ours is one of many frames, all of which are equally satisfactory, leads to a change of interpretation of the significance of a frame of location.

"Commonsense" Objections.   Before going further I must answer the critic who objects in the name of commonsense. Space—*his* space—is so vivid to him. "This object is obviously here; that object is just there. I know it; and I am not going to be shaken by any amount of scientific obscurantism about contraction of measuring rods."

We have certain preconceived ideas about location in space which have come down to us from ape-like ancestors. They are deeply rooted in our mode of thought, so that it is very difficult to criticise them impartially and to realise the very insecure foundation on which they rest. We commonly suppose that each of the objects surrounding us has a definite location in space and that we are *aware* of the right location. The objects in my study are actually in the positions where I am "aware" that they are; and if an observer (on another star) surveying the room with measuring rods, etc., makes out a different arrangement of location, he is merely spinning a scientific paradox which does not shake the real facts of location obvious to any man of commonsense. This attitude rejects with contempt the question, How am I aware of the location? If the location is determined by scientific measurements with elaborate precautions, we are ready enough to suggest all sorts of ways in which the apparatus might have misbehaved; but if the knowledge of location is obtained with no precautions, if it just comes into our heads unsought, then it is obviously true and to doubt it would be flying in the face of commonsense! We have a sort of impression (although we do not like to acknowledge it) that the mind puts out a feeler into space to ascertain directly where each familiar object is. That is nonsense; our commonsense knowledge of location is not obtained that way. Strictly it is *sense* knowledge, not *commonsense* knowledge. It is partly obtained by touch and locomotion; such and such an object is at arm's length or a few steps away. Is there any essential difference (other than its crudity) between this method and scientific measurements with a scale? It is partly obtained by vision—a crude version of scientific measurement with a theodolite. Our common knowledge of where things are is not a miraculous revelation of unquestionable authority; it is inference from observations of the same kind as, but cruder than, those made in a scientific survey. Within its own limits of accuracy the scheme of location of objects that I am instinctively "aware" of is the same as my scientific scheme of location, or frame of space.

When we use a carefully made telescope lens and a sensitised plate instead of the crystalline lens and retina of the eye we increase the accuracy but do not alter the character of our survey of space. It is by this increase of refinement that we have become "aware" of certain characteristics of space which were not known to our ape-like ancestor when he instituted the common ideas that have come down to us. His scheme of location works consistently so long as there is no important change in his motion (a few miles a second makes no appreciable difference); but a large change involves a transition to a different system of location which is likewise self-consistent, although it is inconsistent with the original one.   Having any number of these systems of location, or frames of space, we can no longer pretend that each of them indicates "just where things are". Location is not something supernaturally revealed to the mind; it is a kind of conventional summary of those properties or relations of objects which condition certain visual and tactual sensations.

Does not this show that "right" location in space cannot be nearly so important and fundamental as it is made out to be in the Newtonian scheme of things? The different observers are able to play fast and loose with it without ill effects.

Suppose that location is, I will not say entirely a myth, but not quite the definite thing it is made out to be in classical physics; that the Newtonian idea of location contains some truth and some padding, and it is not the truth but the padding that our observers are quarrelling over.   That would explain a great deal.   It would explain, for instance, why all the forces of Nature seem to have entered into a conspiracy to prevent our discovering the definite location of any object (its position in the "right" frame of space); naturally they cannot reveal it, if it does not exist.

This thought will be followed up in the next chapter. Meanwhile let us glance back over the arguments that have led to the present situation.   It arises from the failure of our much-trusted measuring scale, a failure which we can infer from strong experimental evidence or more simply as an inevitable consequence of accepting the electrical theory of matter.   This unforeseen be-haviour is a constant property of all kinds of matter and is even shared by optical and electrical measuring devices.

Thus it is not betrayed by any kind of discrepancy in applying the usual methods of measurement. The discrepancy is revealed when we change the standard motion of the measuring appliances, e.g. when we compare lengths and distances as measured by terrestrial observers with those which would be measured by observers on a planet with different velocity. Provisionally we shall call the measured lengths which contain this discrepancy "fictitious lengths".

According to the Newtonian scheme length is definite and unique; and each observer should apply corrections (dependent on his motion) to reduce his fictitious lengths to the unique Newtonian length. But to this there are two objections. The corrections to reduce to Newtonian length are indeterminate; we know the corrections necessary to reduce our own fictitious lengths to those measured by an observer with any other prescribed motion, but there is no criterion for deciding which system is the one intended in the Newtonian scheme. Secondly, the whole of present-day physics has been based on lengths measured by terrestrial observers without this correction, so that whilst its assertions ostensibly refer to Newtonian lengths they have actually been proved for fictitious lengths.

The FitzGerald contraction may seem a little thing to bring the whole structure of classical physics tumbling down. But few indeed are the experiments contributing to our scientific knowledge which would not be invalidated if our methods of measuring lengths were fundamentally unsound. We now find that there is no guarantee that they are not subject to a systematic kind of error. Worse still we do not know if the error occurs or not, and there is every reason to presume that it is impossible to know.

Chapter II

RELATIVITY

Einstein's Principle. The modest observer mentioned in the first chapter was faced with the task of choosing between a number of frames of space with nothing to guide his choice. They are different in the sense that they frame the material objects of the world, including the observer himself, differently; but they are indistinguishable in the sense that the world as framed in one space conducts itself according to precisely the same laws as the world framed in another space. Owing to the accident of having been born on a particular planet our observer has hitherto unthinkingly adopted one of the frames; but he realises that this is no ground for obstinately asserting that it must be the right frame. Which is the right frame?

At this juncture Einstein comes forward with a suggestion—

"You are seeking a frame of space which you call the *right* frame. In what does its *rightness* consist?"

You are standing with a label in your hand before a row of packages all precisely similar. You are worried because there is nothing to help you decide which of the packages it should be attached to. Look at the label and see what is written on it. Nothing.

"Right" as applied to frames of space is a blank label. It implies that there is something distinguishing a right frame from a wrong frame; but when we ask what is this distinguishing property, the only answer we receive is "Rightness", which does not make the meaning clearer or convince us that there is a meaning.

I am prepared to admit that frames of space in spite of their present resemblance may in the future turn out to be not entirely indistinguishable. (I deem it unlikely, but I do not exclude it.) The future physicist might find that the frame belonging to Arcturus, say, is unique as regards some property not yet known to science. Then no doubt our friend with the label will hasten to affix it. "I told you so. I knew I meant something when I talked about a right frame." But it does not seem a profitable procedure to make odd noises on the off-chance that posterity will find a significance to attribute to them. To those who now harp on a right frame of space we may reply in the words of Bottom the weaver—

"Who would set his wit to so foolish a bird? Who would give a bird the lie, though he cry 'cuckoo' never so?"

And so the position of Einstein's theory is that the question of a unique right frame of space does not arise. There is a frame of space *relative* to a terrestrial observer, another frame *relative* to the nebular observers, others *relative* to other stars. Frames of space are relative. Distances, lengths, volumes—all quantities of space-reckoning which belong to the frames—are likewise relative. A distance as reckoned by an observer on one star is as good as the distance reckoned by an observer on another star. We must not expect them to agree; the one is a distance relative to one frame, the other is a distance relative to another frame. Absolute distance, not relative to some special frame, is meaningless.

The next point to notice is that the other quantities of physics go along with the frame of space, so that they also are relative. You may have seen one of those tables of "dimensions" of physical quantities showing how they are all related to the reckoning of length, time and mass. If you alter the reckoning of length you alter the reckoning of other physical quantities.

Consider an electrically charged body at rest on the earth. Since it is at rest it gives an electric field but no magnetic field. But for the nebular physicist it is a charged body moving at 1000 miles a second. A moving charge constitutes an electric current which in accordance with the laws of electromagnetism gives rise to a magnetic field. How can the same body both give and not give a magnetic field? On the classical theory we should have had to explain one of these results as an illusion. (There is no difficulty in doing that; only there is nothing to indicate which of the two results is the one to be explained away.) On the relativity theory both results are accepted. Magnetic fields are relative. There is no magnetic field relative to the terrestrial frame of space; there is a magnetic field relative to the nebular frame of space. The nebular physicist will duly detect the magnetic field with his instruments although our instruments show no magnetic field. That is because he uses instruments at rest on his planet and we use instruments at rest on ours; or at least we correct our observations to accord with the indications of instruments at rest in our respective frames of space.

Is there *really* a magnetic field or not? This is like the previous problem of the square and the oblong. There is one specification of the field relative to one planet, another relative to another. There is no absolute specification.

It is not quite true to say that all the physical quantities are relative to frames of space. We can construct new physical quantities by multiplying, dividing, etc.; thus we multiply mass and velocity to give momentum, divide energy by time to give horse-power. We can set ourselves the mathematical problem of constructing in this way quantities which shall be invariant, that is to say, shall have the same measure whatever frame of space may be used. One or two of these invariants turn out to be quantities already recognised in pre-relativity physics; "action" and "entropy" are the best known. Relativity physics is especially interested in invariants, and it has discovered and named a few more. It is a common mistake to suppose that Einstein's theory of relativity asserts that everything is relative. Actually it says, "There are absolute things in the world but you must look deeply for them. The things that first present themselves to your notice are for the most part relative."

Relative and Absolute Quantities. I will try to make clear the distinction between absolute and relative quantities. Number (of discrete individuals) is absolute. It is the result of counting, and counting is an absolute operation. If two men count the number of people in this room and reach different results, one of them must be wrong.

The measurement of distance is not an absolute operation. It is possible for two men to measure the same distance and reach different results, and yet neither of them be wrong.

I mark two dots on the blackboard and ask two students to measure very accurately the distance between them. In order that there may be no possible doubt as to what I mean by distance I give them elaborate instructions as to the standard to be used and the precautions necessary to obtain an accurate measurement of distance. They bring me results which differ. I ask them to compare notes to find out which of them is wrong, and why? Presently they return and say: "It was your fault because in one respect your instructions were not explicit. You did not mention what motion the scale should have when it was being used." One of them without thinking much about the matter had kept the scale at rest on the earth. The other had reflected that the earth was a very insignificant planet of which the Professor had a low opinion. He thought it would be only reasonable to choose some more important body to regulate the motion of the scale, and so he had given it a motion agreeing with that of the enormous star Betelgeuse. Naturally the FitzGerald contraction of the scale accounted for the difference of results.

I am disinclined to accept this excuse. I say severely, "It is all nonsense dragging in the earth or Betelgeuse or any other body. You do not require any standard external to the problem. I told you to measure the distance of two points on the blackboard; you should have made the motion of the scale agree with that of the blackboard. Surely it is commonsense to make your measuring scale move with what you are measuring. Remember that next time."

A few days later I ask them to measure the wavelength of sodium light—the distance from crest to crest of the light waves. They do so and return in triumphal agreement: "The wave-length is infinite". I point out to them that this does not agree with the result given in the book (.000059 cm.). "Yes", they reply, "we noticed that; but the man in the book did not do it right. You told us always to make the measuring scale move with the thing to be measured. So at great trouble and expense we sent our scales hurtling through the laboratory at the same speed as the light." At this speed the FitzGerald contraction is infinite, the metre rods contract to nothing, and so it takes an infinite number of them to fill up the interval from crest to crest of the waves.

My supplementary rule was in a way quite a good rule; it would always give something absolute—something on which they would necessarily agree. Only unfortunately it would not give the length or distance. When we ask whether distance is absolute or relative, we must not first make up our minds that it ought to be absolute and then change the current significance of the term to make it so.

Nor can we altogether blame our predecessors for having stupidly made the word "distance" mean something relative when they might have applied it to a result of spatial measurement which was absolute and unambiguous. The suggested supplementary rule has one drawback. We often have to consider a system containing a number of bodies with different motions; it would be inconvenient to have to measure each body with apparatus in a different state of motion, and we should get into a terrible muddle in trying to fit the different measures together. Our predecessors were wise in referring all distances to a single frame of space, even though their expectation that such distances would be absolute has not been fulfilled.

As for the absolute quantity given by the proposed supplementary rule, we may set it alongside distances relative to the earth and distances relative to Betelgeuse, etc., as a quantity of some interest to study. It is called "proper-distance". Perhaps you feel a relief at getting hold of something absolute and would wish to follow it up. Excellent. But remember this will lead you away from the classical scheme of physics which has chosen the *relative* distances to build on. The quest of the absolute leads into the four-dimensional world.

A more familiar example of a relative quantity is "direction" of an object. There is a direction of Cambridge relative to Edinburgh and another direction relative to London, and so on. It never occurs to us to think of this as a discrepancy, or to suppose that there must be some direction of Cambridge (at present undiscoverable) which is absolute. The idea that there ought to be an absolute distance between two points contains the same kind of fallacy. There is, of course, a difference of detail; the relative direction above mentioned is relative to a particular position of the observer, whereas the relative distance is relative to a particular velocity of the observer. We can change position freely and so introduce large changes of relative direction; but we cannot change velocity appreciably—the 300 miles an hour attainable by our fastest devices being too insignificant to count. Consequently the relativity of distance is not a matter of common experience as the relativity of direction is. That is why we have unfortunately a rooted impression in our minds that distance ought to be absolute.

A very homely illustration of a relative quantity is afforded by the pound sterling. Whatever may have been the correct theoretical view, the man in the street until very recently regarded a pound as an absolute amount of wealth. But dire experience has now convinced us all of its relativity. At first we used to cling to the idea that there ought to be an absolute pound and struggle to express the situation in paradoxical statements—the pound had *really* become seven-and-sixpence. But we have grown accustomed to the situation and continue to reckon wealth in pounds as before,

merely recognising that the pound is relative and therefore must not be expected to have those properties that
we had attributed to it in the belief that it was absolute.

You can form some idea of the essential difference in
the outlook of physics before and after Einstein's
principle of relativity by comparing it with the difference
in economic theory which comes from recognising the
relativity of value of money. I suppose that in stable
times the practical consequences of this relativity are
manifested chiefly in the minute fluctuations of foreign
exchanges, which may be compared with the minute
changes of length affecting delicate experiments like the
Michelson-Morley experiment. Occasionally the consequences may be more sensational—a mark-exchange
soaring to billions, a high-speed β particle contracting
to a third of its radius. But it is not these casual mani-
festations which are the main outcome. Clearly an
economist who believes in the absoluteness of the pound
has not grasped the rudiments of his subject. Similarly
if we have conceived the physical world as intrinsically
constituted out of those distances, forces and masses
which are now seen to have reference only to our own
special reference frame, we are far from a proper understanding of the nature of things.

Nature's Plan of Structure. Let us now return to the
observer who was so anxious to pick out a "right"
frame of space. I suppose that what he had in mind
was to find Nature's own frame—the frame on which
Nature based her calculations when she poised the
planets under the law of gravity, or the reckoning of
symmetry which she used when she turned the electrons
on her lathe. But Nature has been too subtle for him;
she has not left anything to betray the frame which she

used.   Or perhaps the concealment is not any particular subtlety; she may have done her work without employing a frame of space.   Let me tell you a parable.

There was once an archaeologist who used to compute the dates of ancient temples from their orientation. He found that they were aligned with respect to the rising of particular stars.   Owing to precession the star no longer rises in the original line, but the date when it was rising in the line of the temple can be calculated, and hence the epoch of construction of the temple is discovered.   But there was one tribe for which this method would not work; they had built only circular temples.   To the archaeologist this seemed a manifestation of extraordinary subtlety on their part; they had hit on a device which would conceal entirely the date when their temples were constructed.   One critic, however, made the ribald suggestion that perhaps this particular tribe was not enthusiastic about astronomy.

Like the critic I do not think Nature has been particularly subtle in concealing which frame she prefers. It is just that she is not enthusiastic about frames of space.   They are a method of partition which we have found useful for reckoning, but they play no part in the architecture of the universe.   Surely it is absurd to suppose that the universe is planned in such a way as to conceal its plan.   It is like the schemes of the White Knight—

> But I was thinking of a plan
> To dye one's whiskers green,
> And always use so large a fan
> That they could not be seen.

If this is so we shall have to sweep away the frames of space before we can see Nature's plan in its real significance. She herself has paid no attention to them, and they can only obscure the simplicity of her scheme. I do not mean to suggest that we should entirely rewrite physics, eliminating all reference to frames of space or any quantities referred to them; science has many tasks to perform, besides that of apprehending the ultimate plan of structure of the world. But if we do wish to have insight on this latter point, then the first step is to make an escape from the irrelevant space-frames.

This will involve a great change from classical conceptions, and important developments will follow from our change of attitude. For example, it is known that both gravitation and electric force follow approximately the law of inverse-square of the distance. This law appeals strongly to us by its simplicity; not only is it mathematically simple but it corresponds very naturally with the weakening of an effect by spreading out in three dimensions. We suspect therefore that it is likely to be the exact law of gravitational and electric fields. But although it is simple for us it is far from simple for Nature. Distance refers to a space-frame; it is different according to the frame chosen. We cannot make sense of the law of inverse-square of the distance unless we have first fixed on a frame of space; but Nature has not fixed on any one frame. Even if by some self-compensation the law worked out so as to give the same observable consequences whatever space-frame we might happen to choose (which it does not) we should still be misapprehending its real mode of operation. In chapter VI we shall try to gain a new insight into the law (which for most practical applications is so nearly expressed by the inverse-square) and obtain a picture of its working which does not drag in an irrelevant frame of space. The recognition of relativity leads us to seek a new way of unravelling the complexity of natural phenomena.

Velocity through the Aether. The theory of relativity is evidently bound up with the impossibility of detecting absolute velocity; if in our quarrel with the nebular physicists one of us had been able to claim to be absolutely at rest, that would be sufficient reason for preferring the corresponding frame. This has something in common with the well-known philosophic belief that motion must necessarily be relative. Motion is change of position relative to *something*; if we try to think of change of position relative to *nothing* the whole conception fades away. But this does not completely settle the physical problem. In physics we should not be quite so scrupulous as to the use of the word absolute. Motion with respect to aether or to any universally significant frame would be called absolute.

No aethereal frame has been found. We can only discover motion relative to the material landmarks scattered casually about the world; motion with respect to the universal ocean of aether eludes us. We say, "Let V be the velocity of a body through the aether", and form the various electromagnetic equations in which V is scattered liberally. Then we insert the observed values, and try to eliminate everything that is unknown except V. The solution goes on famously; but just as we have got rid of the other unknowns, behold! V disappears as well, and we are left with the indisputable but irritating conclusion—

$$0 = 0.$$

This is a favourite device that mathematical equations resort to, when we propound stupid questions. If we tried to find the latitude and longitude of a point north-east from the north pole we should probably receive the same mathematical answer. "Velocity through aether" is as meaningless as "north-east from the north pole".

This does not mean that the aether is abolished. We need an aether. The physical world is not to be analysed into isolated particles of matter or electricity with featureless interspace. We have to attribute as much character to the interspace as to the particles, and in present-day physics quite an army of symbols is required to describe what is going on in the interspace. We postulate aether to bear the characters of the interspace as we postulate matter or electricity to bear the characters of the particles. Perhaps a philosopher might question whether it is not possible to admit the characters alone without picturing anything to support them—thus doing away with aether and matter at one stroke. But that is rather beside the point.

In the last century it was widely believed that aether was a kind of matter, having properties such as mass, rigidity, motion, like ordinary matter. It would be difficult to say when this view died out. It probably lingered longer in England than on the continent, but I think that even here it had ceased to be the orthodox view some years before the advent of the relativity theory. Logically it was abandoned by the numerous nineteenth-century investigators who regarded matter as vortices, knots, squirts, etc., in the aether; for clearly they could not have supposed that aether consisted of vortices in the aether. But it may not be safe to assume that the authorities in question were logical.

Nowadays it is agreed that aether is not a kind of matter. Being non-material, its properties are *sui generis*. We must determine them by experiment; and since we

aetherial

have no ground for any preconception, the experimental conclusions can be accepted without surprise or misgiving. Characters such as mass and rigidity which we meet with in matter will naturally be absent in aether; but the aether will have new and definite characters of its own. In a material ocean we can say that a particular particle of water which was here a few moments ago is now over there; there is no corresponding assertion that can be made about the aether. If you have been thinking of the aether in a way which takes for granted this property of permanent identification of its particles, you must revise your conception in accordance with the modern evidence. We cannot find our velocity through the aether; we cannot say whether the aether now in this room is flowing out through the north wall or the south wall. The question would have a meaning for a material ocean, but there is no reason to expect it to have a meaning for the non-material ocean of aether.

The aether itself is as much to the fore as ever it was, in our present scheme of the world. But *velocity through aether* has been found to resemble that elusive lady Mrs. Harris; and Einstein has inspired us with the daring scepticism—"I don't believe there's no sich a person".

Is the FitzGerald Contraction Real? I am often asked whether the FitzGerald contraction really occurs. It was introduced in the first chapter before the idea of relativity was mentioned, and perhaps it is not quite clear what has become of it now that the theory of relativity has given us a new conception of what is going on in the world. Naturally my first chapter, which describes the phenomena according to the ideas of classical physics in order to show the need for a new theory, contains many statements which we should express differently in relativity physics.

Is it really true that a moving rod becomes shortened in the direction of its motion? It is not altogether easy to give a plain answer. I think we often draw a distinction between what is *true* and what is *really true*. A statement which does not profess to deal with anything except appearances may be *true*; a statement which is not only true but deals with the realities beneath the appearances is *really true*.

You receive a balance-sheet from a public company and observe that the assets amount to such and such a figure. Is this true? Certainly; it is certified by a chartered accountant. But is it *really* true? Many questions arise; the real values of items are often very different from those which figure in the balance-sheet. I am not especially referring to fraudulent companies. There is a blessed phrase "hidden reserves"; and generally speaking the more respectable the company the more widely does its balance-sheet deviate from reality. This is called sound finance. But apart from deliberate use of the balance-sheet to conceal the actual situation, it is not well adapted for exhibiting realities, because the main function of a balance-sheet is to balance and everything else has to be subordinated to that end.

The physicist who uses a frame of space has to account for every millimetre of space—in fact to draw up a balance-sheet, *and make it balance*. Usually there is not much difficulty. But suppose that he happens to be concerned with a man travelling at 161,000 miles a second. The man is an ordinary 6-foot man. So far as reality is concerned the proper entry in the balance-sheet would appear to be 6 feet. But then the balance-sheet would not balance. In accounting for the rest of space there is left only 3 feet between the crown of his head and the soles of his boots. His balance-sheet length is therefore "written down" to 3 feet.

The writing-down of lengths for balance-sheet purposes is the FitzGerald contraction. The shortening of the moving rod is *true*, but it is not *really true*. It is not a statement about reality (the absolute) but it is a true statement about appearances in our frame of reference.* An object has different lengths in the different space-frames, and any 6-foot man will have a length 3 feet in some frame or other. The statement that the length of the rapid traveller is 3 feet is true, but it does not indicate any special peculiarity about the man; it only indicates that our adopted frame is the one in which his length is 3 feet. If it hadn't been ours, it would have been some-one else's.

Perhaps you will think we ought to alter our method of keeping the accounts of space so as to make them directly represent the realities. That would be going to a lot of trouble to provide for what are after all rather rare transactions. But as a matter of fact we have managed to meet your desire. Thanks to Minkowski a way of keeping accounts has been found which exhibits realities (absolute things) *and balances*. There has been no great rush to adopt it for ordinary purposes because it is a four-dimensional balance-sheet.

Let us take a last glance back before we plunge into

---

*The proper-length (p. 25) is unaltered; but the relative length is shortened. We have already seen that the word "length" as currently used refers to relative length, and in confirming the statement that the moving rod changes its length we are, of course, assuming that the word is used with its current meaning.

four dimension

four dimensions. We have been confronted with something not contemplated in classical physics—a multiplicity of frames of space, each one as good as any other. And in place of a distance, magnetic force, acceleration, etc., which according to classical ideas must necessarily be definite and unique, we are confronted with different distances, etc., corresponding to the different frames, with no ground for making a choice between them. Our simple solution has been to give up the idea that one of these is right and that the others are spurious imitations, and to accept them *en bloc*; so that distance, magnetic force, acceleration, etc., are relative quantities, comparable with other relative quantities already known to us such as direction or velocity. In the main this leaves the structure of our physical knowledge unaltered; only we must give up certain expectations as to the behaviour of these quantities, and certain tacit assumptions which were based on the belief that they are absolute. In particular a law of Nature which seemed simple and appropriate for absolute quantities may be quite inapplicable to relative quantities and therefore require some tinkering. Whilst the structure of our physical knowledge is not much affected, the change in the underlying conceptions is radical. We have travelled far from the old standpoint which demanded mechanical models of everything in Nature, seeing that we do not now admit even a definite unique distance between two points. The relativity of the current scheme of physics invites us to search deeper and find the absolute scheme underlying it, so that we may see the world in a truer perspective.

Chapter III

TIME

Astronomer Royal's Time. I have sometimes thought it would be very entertaining to hear a discussion between the Astronomer Royal and, let us say, Prof. Bergson on the nature of time. Prof. Bergson's authority on the subject is well known; and I may remind you that the Astronomer Royal is entrusted with the duty of finding out time for our everyday use, so presumably he has some idea of what he has to find. I must date the discussion some twenty years back, before the spread of Einstein's ideas brought about a *rapprochement*. There would then probably have been a keen disagreement, and I rather think that the philosopher would have had the best of the verbal argument. After showing that the Astronomer Royal's idea of time was quite nonsensical, Prof. Bergson would probably end the discussion by looking at his watch and rushing off to catch a train which was starting by the Astronomer Royal's time.

Whatever may be time *de jure*, the Astronomer Royal's time is time *de facto*. His time permeates every corner of physics. It stands in no need of logical defence; it is in the much stronger position of a vested interest. It has been woven into the structure of the classical physical scheme. "Time" in physics means Astronomer Royal's time. You may be aware that it is revealed to us in Einstein's theory that time and space are mixed up in a rather strange way. This is a great stumbling-block to the beginner. He is inclined to say, "That is impossible. I feel it in my bones that time and space must be of entirely different nature. They cannot possibly be mixed up." The Astronomer Royal complacently retorts, "It is not impossible. *I* have mixed them up." Well, that settles it. If the Astronomer Royal has mixed them, then his mixture will be the groundwork of present-day physics.

We have to distinguish two questions which are not necessarily identical. First, what is the true nature of time? Second, what is the nature of that quantity which has under the name of time become a fundamental part of the structure of classical physics? By long history of experiment and theory the results of physical investigation have been woven into a scheme which has on the whole proved wonderfully successful. Time—the Astronomer Royal's time—has its importance from the fact that it is a constituent of that scheme, the binding material or mortar of it. That importance is not lessened if it should prove to be only imperfectly representative of the time familiar to our consciousness. We therefore give priority to the second question.

But I may add that Einstein's theory, having cleared up the second question, having found that physical time is incongruously mixed with space, is able to pass on to the first question. There *is* a quantity, unrecognised in pre-relativity physics, which more directly represents the time known to consciousness. This is called proper-time or *interval*. It is definitely separate from and unlike proper-space. Your protest in the name of commonsense against a mixing of time and space is a feeling which I desire to encourage. Time and space ought to be separated. The current representation of the enduring world as a three-dimensional space leaping from instant to instant through time is an *unsuccessful* attempt to separate them. Come back with me into the virginal four-dimensional world and we will carve it anew on a plan which keeps them entirely distinct. We can then resurrect the almost forgotten time of consciousness and find that it has a gratifying importance in the absolute scheme of Nature.

But first let us try to understand why physical time has come to deviate from time as immediately perceived. We have jumped to certain conclusions about time and have come to regard them almost as axiomatic, although they are not really justified by anything in our immediate perception of time. Here is one of them.

If two people meet twice they must have lived the same time between the two meetings, even if one of them has travelled to a distant part of the universe and back in the interim.

An absurdly impossible experiment, you will say. Quite so; it is outside all experience. Therefore, may I suggest that you are not appealing to your experience of time when you object to a theory which denies the above statement? And yet if the question is pressed most people would answer impatiently that of course the statement is true. They have formed a notion of time rolling on outside us in a way which makes this seem inevitable. They do not ask themselves whether this conclusion is warranted by anything in their actual experience of time.

Although we cannot try the experiment of sending a man to another part of the universe, we have enough scientific knowledge to compute the rates of atomic and other physical processes in a body at rest and a body travelling rapidly. We can say definitely that the bodily processes in the traveller occur more slowly than the corresponding processes in the man at rest (i.e. more slowly according to the Astronomer Royal's time). This is not particularly mysterious; it is well known both from theory and experiment that the mass or inertia of matter increases when the velocity increases. The retardation is a natural consequence of the greater inertia. Thus so far as bodily processes are concerned the fast-moving traveller lives more slowly. His cycle of digestion and fatigue; the rate of muscular response to stimulus; the development of his body from youth to age; the material processes in his brain which must more or less keep step with the passage of thoughts and emotions; the watch which ticks in his waistcoat pocket; all these must be slowed down in the same ratio. If the speed of travel is very great we may find that, whilst the stay-at-home individual has aged 70 years, the traveller has aged 1 year. He has only found appetite for 365 breakfasts, lunches, etc.; his intellect, clogged by a slow-moving brain, has only traversed the amount of thought appropriate to one year of terrestrial life. His watch, which gives a more accurate and scientific reckoning, confirms this. Judging by the time which consciousness attempts to measure after its own rough fashion—and, I repeat, this is the only reckoning of time which we have a right to expect to be distinct from space—the two men have not *lived* the same time between the two meetings.

Reference to time as estimated by consciousness is complicated by the fact that the reckoning is very erratic. "I'll tell you who Time ambles withal, who Time trots withal, who Time gallops withal, and who he stands still withal." I have not been referring to these subjective variations. I do not very willingly drag in so unsatisfactory a time-keeper; only I have to deal with the critic who tells me what "he feels in his bones" about time, and I would point out to him that the basis of that feeling is time *lived*, which we have just seen may be 70 years for one individual and 1 year for another between their two meetings. We can reckon "time lived" quite scientifically, e.g. by a watch travelling with the individual concerned and sharing his changes of inertia with velocity. But there are obvious drawbacks to the general adoption of "time lived". It might be useful for each individual to have a private time exactly proportioned to his time lived; but it would be extremely inconvenient for making appointments. Therefore the Astronomer Royal has adopted a universal time-reckoning which does not follow at all strictly the time lived. According to it the time-lapse does not depend on how the object under consideration has moved in the meanwhile. I admit that this reckoning is a little hard on our returned traveller, who will be counted by it as an octogenarian although he is to all appearances still a boy in his teens. But sacrifices must be made for the general benefit. In practice we have not to deal with human beings travelling at any great speed; but we have to deal with atoms and electrons travelling at terrific speed, so that the question of private time-reckoning *versus* general time-reckoning is a very practical one.

Thus in physical time (or Astronomer Royal's time) two people are deemed to have lived the same time between two meetings, whether or not that accords with their actual experience. The consequent deviation from the time of experience is responsible for the mixing up of time and space, which, of course, would be impossible if the time of direct experience had been rigidly adhered to. Physical time is, like space, a kind of frame in which we locate the events of the external world. We are now going to consider how in practice external events are located in a frame of space and time. We have seen that there is an infinite choice of alternative frames; so, to be quite explicit, I will tell you how *I* locate events in *my* frame.

Location of Events. In Fig. 1 you see a collection of events, indicated by circles. They are not at present in

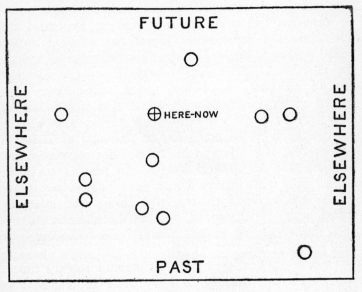

Fig. 1

their right places; that is the job before me—to put them into proper location in my frame of space and time. Among them I can immediately recognise and label the event Here-Now, viz. that which is happening in this room at this moment. The other events are at varying degrees of remoteness from Here-Now, and it is obvious to me that the remoteness is not only of different degrees but of different kinds. Some events spread away towards what in a general way I call the Past; I can contemplate others which are distant in the Future; others are remote in another kind of way towards China or Peru, or in general terms Elsewhere. In this picture I have only room for one dimension of Elsewhere; another dimension sticks out at right angles to the paper; and you must imagine the third dimension as best you can.

Now we must pass from this vague scheme of location to a precise scheme. The first and most important thing is to put Myself into the picture. It sounds egotistical; but, you see, it is *my* frame of space that will be used, so it all hangs round *me*. Here I am—a kind of four-dimensional worm (Fig. 2). It is a correct portrait; I have considerable extension towards the Past and presumably towards the Future, and only a moderate extension towards Elsewhere. The "instantaneous me", i.e. myself at this instant, coincides with the event Here-Now. Surveying the world from Here-Now, I can see many other events happening now. That puts it into my head that the instant of which I am conscious here must be extended to include them; and I jump to the conclusion that Now is not confined to Here-Now. I therefore draw the instant Now, running as a clean section across the world of events, in order to accommodate all the distant events which are happening now. I select the events which I see happening now and place them on this section, which I call a moment of time or an "instantaneous state of the world". I locate them on Now because they seem to be Now.

This method of location lasted until the year 1667, when it was found impossible to make it work consistently. It was then discovered by the astronomer Roemer that what is seen now cannot be placed on the instant Now. (In ordinary parlance—light takes time to travel.) That was really a blow to the whole system of world-wide instants, which were specially invented to accommodate these events. We had been mixing up two distinct

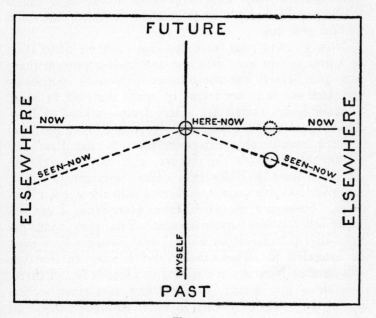

Fig. 2

events; there was the original event somewhere out in the external world and there was a second event, viz. the *seeing* by us of the first event. The second event was in our bodies Here-Now; the first event was neither Here nor Now. The experience accordingly gives no indication of a Now which is not Here; and we might

well have abandoned the idea that we have intuitive
recognition of a Now other than Here-Now, which was
the original reason for postulating world-wide instants
Now.

However, having become accustomed to world-wide
instants, physicists were not ready to abandon them.
And, indeed, they have considerable usefulness provided that we do not take them too seriously. They were
left in as a feature of the picture, and two Seen-Now
lines were drawn, sloping backwards from the Now line,
on which events seen now could be consistently placed.
The cotangent of the angle between the Seen-Now lines
and the Now line was interpreted as the velocity of light.

Accordingly when I see an event in a distant part of
the universe, e.g. the outbreak of a new star, I locate it
(quite properly) on the Seen-Now line. Then I make a
certain calculation from the measured parallax of the
star and draw my Now line to pass, say, 300 years in
front of the event, and my Now line of 300 years ago
to pass through the event. By this method I trace the
course of my Now lines or world-wide instants among
the events, and obtain a frame of time-location for
external events. The auxiliary Seen-Now lines, having
served their purpose, are rubbed out of the picture.

That is how *I* locate events; how about *you?* We
must first put You into the picture (Fig. 3). We shall
suppose that you are on another star moving with
different velocity but passing close to the earth at the
present moment. You and I were far apart in the past
and will be again in the future, but we are both Here-
Now. That is duly shown in the picture. We survey
the world from Here-Now, and of course we both see
the same events simultaneously. We may receive rather
different impressions of them; our different motions

will cause different Doppler effects, FitzGerald contractions, etc. There may be slight misunderstandings until we realise that what you describe as a red square is what I would describe as a green oblong, and so on. But, allowing for this kind of difference of description,

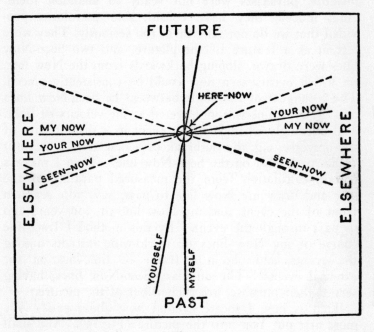

Fig. 3

it will soon become clear that we are looking at the same events, and we shall agree entirely as to how the Seen-Now lines lie with respect to the events. Starting from our common Seen-Now lines, you have next to make the calculations for drawing your Now line among the events, and you trace it as shown in Fig. 3.

How is it that, starting from the same Seen-Now lines, you do not reproduce my Now line? It is because a certain measured quantity, viz. the velocity of light, has to be employed in the calculations; and naturally you trust to your measures of it as I trust to mine. Since our instruments are affected by different Fitz-Gerald contractions, etc., there is plenty of room for divergence. Most surprisingly we both find the same velocity of light, 299,796 kilometres per second. But this apparent agreement is really a disagreement; because you take this to be the velocity relative to your planet and I take it to be the velocity relative to mine.* Therefore our calculations are not in accord, and your Now line differs from mine.

If we believe our world-wide instants or Now lines to be something inherent in the world outside us, we shall quarrel frightfully. To my mind it is ridiculous that you should take events on the right of the picture which have not happened yet and events on the left which are already past and call the combination an instantaneous condition of the universe. You are equally scornful of my grouping. We can never agree. Certainly it looks from the picture as though my instants were more natural than yours; but that is because *I* drew the picture. You, of course, would redraw it with your Now lines at right angles to yourself.

---

* The measured velocity of light is the average to-and-fro velocity. The velocity in one direction singly cannot be measured until *after* the Now lines have been laid down and therefore cannot be used in laying down the Now lines. Thus there is a deadlock in drawing the Now lines which can only be removed by an arbitrary assumption or convention. The convention actually adopted is that (relative to the observer) the velocities of light in the two opposite directions are equal. The resulting Now lines must therefore be regarded as equally conventional.

But we need not quarrel if the Now lines are merely reference lines drawn across the world for convenience in locating events—like the lines of latitude and longitude on the earth. There is then no question of a right way and a wrong way of drawing the lines; we draw them as best suits our convenience. World-wide instants are not natural cleavage planes of time; there is nothing equivalent to them in the absolute structure of the world; they are imaginary partitions which we find it convenient to adopt.

We have been accustomed to regard the world—the enduring world—as *stratified* into a succession of instantaneous states. But an observer on another star would make the strata run in a different direction from ours. We shall see more clearly the real mechanism of the physical world if we can rid our minds of this illusion of stratification. The world that then stands revealed, though strangely unfamiliar, is actually much simpler. There is a difference between simplicity and familiarity. A pig may be most familiar to us in the form of rashers, but the unstratified pig is a simpler object to the biologist who wishes to understand how the animal functions.

Absolute Past and Future. Let us now try to attain this absolute view. We rub out all the Now lines. We rub out Yourself and Myself, since we are no longer essential to the world. But the Seen-Now lines are left. They are absolute, since all observers from Here-Now agree about them. The flat picture is a section; you must imagine it rotated (twice rotated in fact, since there are two more dimensions outside the picture). The Seen-Now locus is thus really a cone; or by taking account of the prolongation of the lines into the future a double cone or hour-glass figure (Fig. 4). These hour-glasses (drawn through each point of the world considered in turn as a Here-Now) embody what we know of the absolute structure of the world so far as space and time are concerned. They show how the "grain" of the world runs.

Father Time has been pictured as an old man with a scythe and an hour-glass. We no longer permit him to mow instants through the world with his scythe; but we leave him his hour-glass.

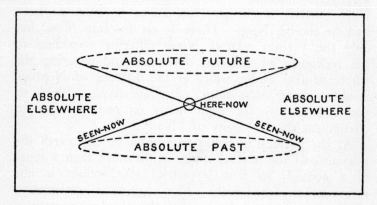

Fig. 4

Since the hour-glass is absolute its two cones provide respectively an Absolute Future and an Absolute Past for the event Here-Now. They are separated by a wedge-shaped neutral zone which (absolutely) is neither past nor future. The common impression that relativity turns past and future altogether topsy-turvy is quite false. But, unlike the relative past and future, the absolute past and future are not separated by an infinitely narrow present. It suggests itself that the neutral wedge might be called the Absolute Present; but I do not think that is a good nomenclature. It is much better described as Absolute Elsewhere. We have abolished the Now lines, and in the absolute world the present (Now) is restricted to Here-Now.

Perhaps I may illustrate the peculiar conditions arising from the wedge-shaped neutral zone by a rather hypothetical example. Suppose that you are in love with a lady on Neptune and that she returns the sentiment. It will be some consolation for the melancholy separation if you can say to yourself at some—possibly pre-arranged—moment, "She is thinking of me now". Unfortunately a difficulty has arisen because we have had to abolish Now. There is no absolute Now, but only the various relative Nows differing according to the reckoning of different observers and covering the whole neutral wedge which at the distance of Neptune is about eight hours thick. She will have to think of you continuously for eight hours on end in order to circumvent the ambiguity of "Now".

At the greatest possible separation on the earth the thickness of the neutral wedge is no more than a tenth of a second; so that terrestrial synchronism is not seriously interfered with. This suggests a qualification of our previous conclusion that the absolute present is confined to Here-Now. It is true as regards instantaneous events (point-events). But in practice the events we notice are of more than infinitesimal duration. If the duration is sufficient to cover the width of the neutral zone, then the event taken as a whole may fairly be considered to be Now absolutely. From this point of view the "nowness" of an event is like a shadow cast by it into space, and the longer the event the farther will the umbra of the shadow extend.

As the speed of matter approaches the speed of light its mass increases to infinity, and therefore it is impossible to make matter travel faster than light. This conclusion is deduced from the classical laws of physics, and the increase of mass has been verified by experiment up to very high velocities. In the absolute world this means that a particle of matter can only proceed from Here-Now into the absolute future—which, you will agree, is a reasonable and proper restriction. It cannot travel into the neutral zone; the limiting cone is the track of light or of anything moving with the speed of light. We ourselves are attached to material bodies, and therefore we can only go on into the absolute future.

Events in the absolute future are not absolutely Elsewhere. It would be possible for an observer to travel from Here-Now to the event in question in time to experience it, since the required velocity is less than that of light; relative to the frame of such an observer the event would be Here. No observer can reach an event in the neutral zone, since the required speed is too great. The event is not Here for any observer (from Here-Now); therefore it is absolutely Elsewhere.

The Absolute Distinction of Space and Time. By dividing the world into Absolute Past and Future on the one hand and Absolute Elsewhere on the other hand, our hour-glasses have restored a fundamental differentiation between time and space. It is not a distinction between time and space as they appear in a space-time frame, but a distinction between temporal and spatial relations. Events can stand to us in a temporal relation (absolutely past or future) or a spatial relation (absolutely elsewhere), but not in both. The temporal relations radiate into the past and future cones and the spatial relations into the neutral wedge; they are kept absolutely separated by the Seen-Now lines which we have identified with the grain of absolute structure in the world. We have recovered the distinction which the Astronomer Royal confused when he associated time with the merely artificial Now lines.

I would direct your attention to an important difference in our apprehension of time-extension and space-extension. As already explained our course through the world is into the absolute future, i.e. along a sequence of time-relations. We can never have a similar experience of a sequence of space-relations because that would involve travelling with velocity greater than light. Thus we have immediate experience of the time-relation but not of the space-relation. Our knowledge of space-relations is indirect, like nearly all our knowledge of the external world—a matter of inference and interpretation of the impressions which reach us through our sense-organs. We have similar indirect knowledge of the time-relations existing between the events in the world outside us; but in addition we have direct experience of the time-relations that we ourselves are traversing—a knowledge of time not coming through external sense-organs, but taking a short cut into our consciousness. When I close my eyes and retreat into my inner mind, I feel myself *enduring,* I do not feel myself *extensive.* It is this feeling of time as affecting ourselves and not merely as existing in the relations of external events which is so peculiarly characteristic of it; space on the other hand is always appreciated as something external.

That is why time seems to us so much more mysterious than space. We know nothing about the intrinsic nature of space, and so it is quite easy to conceive it satisfactorily. We have intimate acquaintance with the nature of time and so it baffles our comprehension. It is the same paradox which makes us believe we understand the nature of an ordinary table whereas the nature of human personality is altogether mysterious. We never have that intimate contact with space and tables which would make us realise how mysterious they are; we have direct knowledge of time and of the human spirit which makes us reject as inadequate that merely symbolic conception of the world which is so often mistaken for an insight into its nature.

The Four-Dimensional World. I do not know whether you have been keenly alive to the fact that for some time now we have been immersed in a four-dimensional world. The fourth dimension required no introduction; as soon as we began to consider *events* it was there. Events obviously have a fourfold order which we can dissect into right or left, behind or in front, above or below, sooner or later—or into many alternative sets of fourfold specification. The fourth dimension is not a difficult conception. It is not difficult to conceive of events as ordered in four dimensions; it is impossible to conceive them otherwise. The trouble begins when we continue farther along this line of thought, because by long custom we have divided the world of events into three-dimensional sections or instants, and regarded the piling of the instants as something distinct from a dimension. That gives us the usual conception of a three-dimensional world floating in the stream of time. This pampering of a particular dimension is not entirely without foundation; it is our crude appreciation of the absolute separation of space-relations and time-relations by the hour-glass figures. But the crude discrimination has to be replaced by a more accurate discrimination.

The supposed planes of structure represented by Now lines separated one dimension from the other three; but the cones of structure given by the hour-glass figures keep the four dimensions firmly pinned together.*

We are accustomed to think of a man apart from his duration. When I portrayed "Myself" in Fig. 2, you were for the moment surprised that I should include my boyhood and old age. But to think of a man without his duration is just as abstract as to think of a man without his inside. Abstractions are useful, and a man without his inside (that is to say, a *surface*) is a well-known geometrical conception. But we ought to realise what is an abstraction and what is not. The "four-dimensional worms" introduced in this chapter seem to many people terribly abstract. Not at all; they are un-familiar conceptions but not abstract conceptions. It is the section of the worm (the man Now) which is an abstraction. And as sections may be taken in somewhat different directions, the abstraction is made differently by different observers who accordingly attribute different FitzGerald contractions to it. The non-abstract man enduring through time is the common source from which the different abstractions are made.

The appearance of a four-dimensional world in this subject is due to Minkowski. Einstein showed the rela-tivity of the familiar quantities of physics; Minkowski showed how to recover the absolute by going back to their four-dimensional origin and searching more deeply.

---

* In Fig. 4 the scale is such that a second of time corresponds to 70,000 miles of space. If we take a more ordinary scale of experience, say a second to a yard, the Seen-Now lines become almost horizontal; and it will easily be understood why the cones which pin the four dimensions together have generally been mistaken for sections separating them.

The Velocity of Light. A feature of the relativity theory which seems to have aroused special interest among philosophers is the absoluteness of the velocity of light. In general velocity is relative. If I speak of a velocity of 40 kilometres a second I must add "relative to the earth", "relative to Arcturus", or whatever reference body I have in mind. No one will understand anything from my statement unless this is added or implied. But it is a curious fact that if I speak of a velocity of 299,796 kilometres a second it is unnecessary to add the explanatory phrase. Relative to what? Relative to any and every star or particle of matter in the universe.

It is no use trying to overtake a flash of light; however fast you go it is always travelling away from you at 186,000 miles a second. Now from one point of view this is a rather unworthy deception that Nature has practised upon us. Let us take our favourite observer who travels at 161,000 miles a second and send him in pursuit of the flash of light. It is going 25,000 miles a second faster than he is; but that is not what he will report. Owing to the contraction of his standard scale his miles are only half-miles; owing to the slowing down of his clocks his seconds are double-seconds. His measurements would therefore make the speed 100,000 miles a second (really half-miles per double-second). He makes a further mistake in synchronising the clocks with which he records the velocity. (You will remember that he uses a different Now line from ours.) This brings the speed up to 186,000 miles a second. From his own point of view the traveller is lagging hopelessly behind the light; he does not realise what a close race he is making of it, because his measuring appliances have been upset. You will note that the evasiveness of the light-flash is not in the least analogous to the evasiveness of the rainbow.

But although this explanation may help to reconcile us to what at first seems a blank impossibility, it is not really the most penetrating. You will remember that a Seen-Now line, or track of a flash of light, represents the *grain* of the world-structure. Thus the peculiarity of a velocity of 299,796 kilometres a second is that it coincides with the grain of the world. The four-dimensional worms representing material bodies must necessarily run across the grain into the future cone, and we have to introduce some kind of reference frame to describe their course. But the flash of light is exactly along the grain, and there is no need of any artificial system of partitions to describe this fact.

The number 299,796 (kilometres per second) is, so to speak, a code-number for the grain of the wood. Other code-numbers correspond to the various worm-holes which may casually cross the grain. We have different codes corresponding to different frames of space and time; the code-number of the grain of the wood is the only one which is the same in all codes. This is no accident; but I do not know that any deep inference is to be drawn from it, other than that our measure-codes have been planned rationally so as to turn on the essential and not on the casual features of world-structure.

The speed of 299,796 kilometres per second which occupies a unique position in every measure-system is commonly referred to as the speed of light. But it is much more than that; it is the speed at which the mass of matter becomes infinite, lengths contract to zero, clocks stand still. Therefore it crops up in all kinds of problems whether light is concerned or not.

The scientist's interest in the absoluteness of this velocity is very great; the philosopher's interest has been, I think, largely a mistaken interest. In asserting its absoluteness scientists mean that they have assigned the same number to it in every measure-system; but that is a private arrangement of their own—an unwitting compliment to its universal importance.* Turning from the measure-numbers to the thing described by them, the "grain" is certainly an absolute feature of the wood, but so also are the "worm-holes" (material particles). The difference is that the grain is essential and universal, the worm-holes casual. Science and philosophy have often been at cross-purposes in discussing the Absolute—a misunderstanding which is I am afraid chiefly the fault of the scientists. In science we are chiefly concerned with the absoluteness or relativity of the *descriptive terms* we employ; but when the term absolute is used with reference to *that which is being described* it has generally the loose meaning of "universal" as opposed to "casual".

Another point on which there has sometimes been a misunderstanding is the existence of a superior limit to velocity. It is not permissible to say that no velocity can exceed 299,796 kilometres per second. For example, imagine a search-light capable of sending an accurately parallel beam as far as Neptune. If the search-light is made to revolve once a minute, Neptune's end of the beam will move round a circle with velocity far greater than the above limit. This is an example of our habit of creating velocities by a mental association of states

* In the general relativity theory (chapter VI) measure-systems are employed in which the velocity of light is no longer assigned the same constant value, but it continues to correspond to the grain of absolute world-structure.

which are not themselves in direct causal connection. The assertion made by the relativity theory is more restricted, viz.——

Neither *matter,* nor *energy,* nor anything capable of being used as a *signal* can travel faster than 299,796 kilometres per second, provided that the velocity is referred to one of the frames of space and time considered in this chapter.*

The velocity of light in matter can under certain circumstances (in the phenomenon of anomalous dispersion) exceed this value. But the higher velocity is only attained after the light has been passing through the matter for some moments so as to set the molecules in sympathetic vibration. An unheralded light-flash travels more slowly. The speed, exceeding 299,796 kilometres a second, is, so to speak, achieved by prearrangement, and has no application in signalling.

We are bound to insist on this limitation of the speed of signalling. It has the effect that it is only possible to signal into the Absolute Future. The consequences of being able to transmit messages concerning events Here-Now into the neutral wedge are too bizarre to contemplate. Either the part of the neutral wedge that can be reached by the signals must be restricted in a way which violates the principle of relativity; or it will be possible to arrange for a confederate to receive the messages which we shall send him to-morrow, and to retransmit them to us so that we receive them to-day. The limit to the velocity of signals is our bulwark

* Some proviso of this kind is clearly necessary. We often employ for special purposes a frame of reference rotating with the earth; in this frame the stars describe circles once a day, and are therefore ascribed enormous velocities.

against that topsy-turvydom of past and future, of which Einstein's theory is sometimes wrongfully accused.

Expressed in the conventional way this limitation of the speed of signalling to 299,796 kilometres a second seems a rather arbitrary decree of Nature. We almost feel it as a challenge to find something that goes faster. But if we state it in the absolute form that signalling is only possible along a track of temporal relation and not along a track of spatial relation the restriction seems rational. To violate it we have not merely to find something which goes just 1 kilometre per second better, but something which overleaps that distinction of time and space—which, we are all convinced, ought to be maintained in any sensible theory.

Practical Applications. In these lectures I am concerned more with the ideas of the new theories than with their practical importance for the advancement of science. But the drawback of dwelling solely on the underlying conceptions is that it is likely to give the impression that the new physics is very much "up in the air". That is by no means true, and the relativity theory is used in a businesslike way in the practical problems to which it applies. I can only consider here quite elementary problems which scarcely do justice to the power of the new theory in advanced scientific research. Two examples must suffice.

1. It has often been suggested that the stars will be retarded by the back-pressure of their own radiation. The idea is that since the star is moving forward the emitted radiation is rather heaped up in front of it and thinned out behind. Since radiation exerts pressure the pressure will be stronger on the front surface than on the rear. Therefore there is a force retarding the star

tending to bring it gradually to rest. The effect might be of great importance in the study of stellar motions; it would mean that on the average old stars must have lower speeds than young stars—a conclusion which, as it happens, is contrary to observation.

But according to the theory of relativity "coming to rest" has no meaning. A decrease of velocity relative to one frame is an increase relative to another frame. There is no absolute velocity and no absolute rest for the star to come to. The suggestion may therefore be at once dismissed as fallacious.

2. The β particles shot out by radioactive substances are electrons travelling at speeds not much below the speed of light. Experiment shows that the mass of one of these high-speed electrons is considerably greater than the mass of an electron at rest. The theory of relativity predicts this increase and provides the formula for the dependence of mass on velocity. The increase arises solely from the fact that mass is a relative quantity depending by definition on the relative quantities length and time.

Let us look at a β particle from its own point of view. It is an ordinary electron in no wise different from any other. But it is travelling with unusually high speed? "No", says the electron, "That is *your* point of view. I contemplate with amazement your extraordinary speed of 100,000 miles a second with which you are shooting past me. I wonder what it feels like to move so quickly. However, it is no business of mine." So the β particle, smugly thinking itself at rest, pays no attention to our goings on, and arranges itself with the usual mass, radius and charge. It has just the standard mass of an electron, 9.10^{-28} grams. But mass and radius are relative quantities, and in this case the frame to which they are referred is evidently the frame appropriate to an electron engaged in self-contemplation, viz. the frame in which it is at rest. But when we talk about mass we refer it to the frame in which *we* are at rest. By the geometry of the four-dimensional world we can calculate the formulae for the change of reckoning of mass in two different frames, which is consequential on the change of reckoning of length and time; we find in fact that the mass is increased in the same ratio as the length is diminished (FitzGerald factor). The increase of mass that we observe arises from the change of reckoning between the electron's own frame and our frame.

All electrons are alike from their own point of view. The apparent differences arise in fitting them into our own frame of reference which is irrelevant to their structure. Our reckoning of their mass is higher than their own reckoning, and increases with the difference between our respective frames, i.e. with the relative velocity between us.

We do not bring forward these results to demonstrate or confirm the *truth* of the theory, but to show the *use* of the theory. They can both be deduced from the classical electromagnetic theory of Maxwell coupled (in the second problem) with certain plausible assumptions as to the conditions holding at the surface of an electron. But to realise the advantage of the new theory we must consider not what *could have been* but what *was* deduced from the classical theory. The historical fact is that the conclusions of the classical theory as to the first problem were wrong; an important compensating factor escaped notice. Its conclusions as to the second problem were (after some false starts) entirely correct numerically. But since the result was deduced from the electromagnetic equations of the electron it was thought that it depended on the fact that an electron is an electrical structure; and the agreement with observation was believed to confirm the hypothesis that an electron is pure electricity and nothing else. Our treatment above makes no reference to any electrical properties of the electron, the phenomenon having been found to arise solely from the relativity of mass. Hence, although there may be other good reasons for believing that an electron consists solely of negative electricity, the increase of mass with velocity is no evidence one way or the other.

In this chapter the idea of a multiplicity of frames of space has been extended to a multiplicity of frames of space and time. The system of location in space, called a frame of space, is only a part of a fuller system of location of events in space and time. Nature provides no indication that one of these frames is to be preferred to the others. The particular frame in which we are relatively at rest has a symmetry with respect to us which other frames do not possess, and for this reason we have drifted into the common assumption that it is the only reasonable and proper frame; but this egocentric outlook should now be abandoned, and all frames treated as on the same footing. By considering time and space together we have been able to understand how the multiplicity of frames arises. They correspond to different directions of section of the four-dimensional world of events, the sections being the "world-wide instants". Simultaneity (Now) is seen to be relative. The denial of absolute simultaneity is intimately connected with the denial of absolute velocity; knowledge of absolute velocity would enable us to assert that certain events in the past or future occur Here but not Now; knowledge of absolute simultaneity would tell us that certain events occur Now but not Here. Removing these artificial sections, we have had a glimpse of the absolute world-structure with its grain diverging and interlacing after the plan of the hour-glass figures. By reference to this structure we discern an absolute distinction between space-like and time-like separation of events—a distinction which justifies and explains our instinctive feeling that space and time are fundamentally different. Many of the important applications of the new conceptions to the practical problems of physics are too technical to be considered in this book; one of the simpler applications is to determine the changes of the physical properties of objects due to rapid motion. Since the motion can equally well be described as a motion of ourselves relative to the object or of the object relative to ourselves, it cannot influence the absolute behaviour of the object. The apparent changes in the length, mass, electric and magnetic fields, period of vibration, etc., are merely a change of reckoning introduced in passing from the frame in which the object is at rest to the frame in which the observer is at rest. Formulae for calculating the change of reckoning of any of these quantities are easily deduced now that the geometrical relation of the frames has been ascertained.

Chapter IV

THE RUNNING-DOWN OF THE UNIVERSE

Shuffling. The modern outlook on the physical world is not composed exclusively of conceptions which have arisen in the last twenty-five years; and we have now to deal with a group of ideas dating far back in the last century which have not essentially altered since the time of Boltzmann. These ideas display great activity and development at the present time. The subject is relevant at this stage because it has a bearing on the deeper aspects of the problem of Time; but it is so fundamental in physical theory that we should be bound to deal with it sooner or later in any comprehensive survey.

If you take a pack of cards as it comes from the maker and shuffle it for a few minutes, all trace of the original systematic order disappears. The order will never come back however long you shuffle. Something has been done which cannot be undone, namely, the introduction of a random element in place of arrangement.

Illustrations may be useful even when imperfect, and therefore I have slurred over two points, which affect the illustration rather than the application which we are about to make. It was scarcely true to say that the shuffling cannot be undone. *You* can sort out the cards into their original order if you like. But in considering the shuffling which occurs in the physical world we are not troubled by a *deus ex machina* like you. I am not prepared to say how far the human mind is bound by the conclusions we shall reach. So I exclude you—at least I exclude that activity of your mind which you employ

63

in sorting the cards.   I allow you to shuffle them because you can do that *absent-mindedly*.

Secondly, it is not quite true that the original order never comes back.   There is a ghost of a chance that some day a thoroughly shuffled pack will be found to have come back to the original order.   That is because of the comparatively small number of cards in the pack. In our applications the units are so numerous that this kind of contingency can be disregarded.

We shall put forward the contention that—

Whenever anything happens which cannot be undone, it is always reducible to the introduction of a random element analogous to that introduced by shuffling.

Shuffling is the only thing which Nature cannot undo.

When Humpty Dumpty had a great fall—

> All the king's horses and all the king's men
> Cannot put Humpty Dumpty together again.

Something had happened which could not be undone. The fall could have been undone.   It is not necessary to invoke the king's horses and the king's men; if there had been a perfectly elastic mat underneath, that would have sufficed.   At the end of his fall Humpty Dumpty had kinetic energy which, properly directed, was just sufficient to bounce him back on to the wall again.   But, the elastic mat being absent, an irrevocable event happened at the end of the fall—namely, the introduction of a *random element* into Humpty Dumpty.

But why should we suppose that shuffling is the *only* process that cannot be undone?

> The Moving Finger writes; and, having writ,
> Moves on: nor all thy Piety and Wit
> Can lure it back to cancel half a Line.

When there is no shuffling, is the Moving Finger stayed? The answer of physics is unhesitatingly Yes. To judge of this we must examine those operations of Nature in which no increase of the random element can possibly occur. These fall into two groups. Firstly, we can study those laws of Nature which control the behaviour of a single unit. Clearly no shuffling can occur in these problems; you cannot take the King of Spades away from the pack and shuffle him. Secondly, we can study the processes of Nature in a crowd which is already so completely shuffled that there is no room for any further increase of the random element. If our contention is right, everything that occurs in these conditions is capable of being undone. We shall consider the first condition immediately; the second must be deferred until p. 78.

Any change occurring to a body which can be treated as a single unit can be undone. The laws of Nature admit of the undoing as easily as of the doing. The earth describing its orbit is controlled by laws of motion and of gravitation; these admit of the earth's actual motion, but they also admit of the precisely opposite motion. In the same field of force the earth could retrace its steps; it merely depends on how it was started off. It may be objected that we have no right to dismiss the starting-off as an inessential part of the problem; it may be as much a part of the coherent scheme of Nature as the laws controlling the subsequent motion. Indeed, astronomers have theories explaining why the eight planets all started to move the same way round the sun. But that is a problem of eight planets, not of a single individual—a problem of the pack, not of the isolated card. So long as the earth's motion is treated as an isolated problem, no one would dream of putting into the laws of Nature a clause requiring that it must go *this* way round and not the opposite.

There is a similar reversibility of motion in fields of electric and magnetic force. Another illustration can be given from atomic physics. The quantum laws admit of the emission of certain kinds and quantities of light from an atom; these laws also admit of absorption of the same kinds and quantities, i.e. the undoing of the emission. I apologise for an apparent poverty of illustration; it must be remembered that many properties of a body, e.g. temperature, refer to its constitution as a large number of separate atoms, and therefore the laws controlling temperature cannot be regarded as controlling the behaviour of a single individual.

The common property possessed by laws governing the individual can be stated more clearly by a reference to time. A certain sequence of states running from past to future is the *doing* of an event; the same sequence running from future to past is the *undoing* of it—because in the latter case we turn round the sequence so as to view it in the accustomed manner from past to future. So if the laws of Nature are indifferent as to the doing and undoing of an event, they must be indifferent as to a direction of time from past to future. That is their common feature, and it is seen at once when (as usual) the laws are formulated mathematically. There is no more distinction between past and future than between right and left. In algebraic symbolism, left is $-x$, right is $+x$; past is $-t$, future is $+t$. This holds for all laws of Nature governing the behaviour of non-composite individuals—the "primary laws", as we shall call them. There is only one law of Nature—the second law of thermodynamics—which recognises a distinction between past and future more profound than the difference of plus and minus. It stands aloof from all the rest. But this law has no application to the behaviour of a single individual, and as we shall see later its subject-matter is the random element in a crowd.

Whatever the primary laws of physics may say, it is obvious to ordinary experience that there is a distinction between past and future of a different kind from the distinction of left and right. In *The Plattner Story* H. G. Wells relates how a man strayed into the fourth dimension and returned with left and right interchanged. But we notice that this interchange is not the theme of the story; it is merely a corroborative detail to give an air of verisimilitude to the adventure. In itself the change is so trivial that even Mr. Wells cannot weave a romance out of it. But if the man had come back with past and future interchanged, then indeed the situation would have been lively. Mr. Wells in *The Time-Machine* and Lewis Carroll in *Sylvie and Bruno* give us a glimpse of the absurdities which occur when time runs backwards. If space is "looking-glassed" the world continues to make sense; but looking-glassed time has an inherent absurdity which turns the world-drama into the most nonsensical farce.

Now the primary laws of physics taken one by one all declare that they are entirely indifferent as to which way you consider time to be progressing, just as they are indifferent as to whether you view the world from the right or the left. This is true of the classical laws, the relativity laws, and even of the quantum laws. It is not an accidental property; the reversibility is inherent in the whole conceptual scheme in which these laws find a place. Thus the question whether the world does or does not "make sense" is outside the range of these laws. We have to appeal to the one outstanding law—

the second law of thermodynamics—to put some sense into the world. It opens up a new province of knowledge, namely, the study of organisation; and it is in connection with organisation that a direction of time-flow and a distinction between doing and undoing appears for the first time.

Time's Arrow. The great thing about time is that it goes on. But this is an aspect of it which the physicist sometimes seems inclined to neglect. In the four-dimensional world considered in the last chapter the events past and future lie spread out before us as in a map. The events are there in their proper spatial and temporal relation; but there is no indication that they undergo what has been described as "the formality of taking place", and the question of their doing or undoing does not arise. We see in the map the path from past to future or from future to past; but there is no signboard to indicate that it is a one-way street. Something must be added to the geometrical conceptions comprised in Minkowski's world before it becomes a complete picture of the world as we know it. We may appeal to consciousness to suffuse the whole—to turn *existence* into *happening, being* into *becoming.* But first let us note that the picture as it stands is entirely adequate to represent those primary laws of Nature which, as we have seen, are indifferent to a direction of time. Objection has sometimes been felt to the relativity theory because its four-dimensional picture of the world seems to overlook the directed character of time. The objection is scarcely logical, for the theory is in this respect no better and no worse than its predecessors. The classical physicist has been using without misgiving a system of laws which do not recognise a directed time; he is shocked that the new picture should expose this so glaringly.

Without any mystic appeal to consciousness it is possible to find a direction of time on the four-dimensional map by a study of organisation. Let us draw an arrow arbitrarily. If as we follow the arrow we find more and more of the random element in the state of the world, then the arrow is pointing towards the future; if the random element decreases the arrow points towards the past. That is the only distinction known to physics. This follows at once if our fundamental contention is admitted that the introduction of randomness is the only thing which cannot be undone.

I shall use the phrase "time's arrow" to express this one-way property of time which has no analogue in space. It is a singularly interesting property from a philosophical standpoint. We must note that—

(1) It is vividly recognised by consciousness.

(2) It is equally insisted on by our reasoning faculty, which tells us that a reversal of the arrow would render the external world nonsensical.

(3) It makes no appearance in physical science except in the study of organisation of a number of individuals. Here the arrow indicates the direction of progressive increase of the random element.

Let us now consider in detail how a random element brings the irrevocable into the world. When a stone falls it acquires kinetic energy, and the amount of the energy is just that which would be required to lift the stone back to its original height. By suitable arrangements the kinetic energy can be made to perform this task; for example, if the stone is tied to a string it can alternately fall and reascend like a pendulum. But if the stone hits an obstacle its kinetic energy is converted into heat-energy. There is still the same quantity of energy, but even if we could scrape it together and put it through an engine we could not lift the stone back with it. What has happened to make the energy no longer serviceable?

Looking microscopically at the falling stone we see an enormous multitude of molecules moving downwards with equal and parallel velocities—an organised motion like the march of a regiment. We have to notice two things, the *energy* and the *organisation of the energy*. To return to its original height the stone must preserve both of them.

When the stone falls on a sufficiently elastic surface the motion may be reversed without destroying the organisation. Each molecule is turned backwards and the whole array retires in good order to the starting-point—

> The famous Duke of York
> With twenty thousand men,
> He marched them up to the top of the hill
> And marched them down again.

History is not made that way. But what usually happens at the impact is that the molecules suffer more or less random collisions and rebound in all directions. They no longer conspire to make progress in any one direction; they have lost their organisation. Afterwards they continue to collide with one another and keep changing their directions of motion, but they never again find a common purpose. Organisation cannot be brought about by continued shuffling. And so, although the energy remains quantitatively sufficient (apart from unavoidable leakage which we suppose made good), it cannot lift the stone back. To restore the stone we must supply extraneous energy which has the required amount of organisation.

Here a point arises which unfortunately has no analogy in the shuffling of a pack of cards. No one (except a conjurer) can throw two half-shuffled packs into a hat and draw out one pack in its original order and one pack fully shuffled. But we can and do put partly disorganised energy into a steam-engine, and draw it out again partly as fully organised energy of motion of massive bodies and partly as heat-energy in a state of still worse disorganisation. Organisation of energy is negotiable, and so is the disorganisation or random element; disorganisation does not for ever remain attached to the particular store of energy which first suffered it, but may be passed on elsewhere. We cannot here enter into the question why there should be a difference between the shuffling of energy and the shuffling of material objects; but it is necessary to use some caution in applying the analogy on account of this difference. As regards heat-energy the temperature is the measure of its degree of organisation; the lower the temperature, the greater the disorganisation.

Coincidences. There are such things as chance coincidences; that is to say, chance can deceive us by bringing about conditions which look very unlike chance. In particular chance might imitate organisation, whereas we have taken organisation to be the antithesis of chance or, as we have called it, the "random element". This threat to our conclusions is, however, not very serious. *There is safety in numbers.*

Suppose that you have a vessel divided by a partition into two halves, one compartment containing air and the other empty. You withdraw the partition. For the moment all the molecules of air are in one half of the vessel; a fraction of a second later they are spread over the whole vessel and remain so ever afterwards. The molecules will not return to one half of the vessel; the spreading cannot be undone—unless other material is introduced into the problem to serve as a scapegoat for the disorganisation and carry off the random element elsewhere. This occurrence can serve as a criterion to distinguish past and future time. If you observe first the molecules spread through the vessel and (as it seems to you) an instant later the molecules all in one half of it—then your consciousness is going backwards, and you had better consult a doctor.

Now each molecule is wandering round the vessel with no preference for one part rather than the other. On the average it spends half its time in one compartment and half in the other. There is a faint possibility that at one moment all the molecules might in this way happen to be visiting the one half of the vessel. You will easily calculate that if n is the number of molecules (roughly a quadrillion) the chance of this happening is $(\frac{1}{2})^n$. The reason why we ignore this chance may be seen by a rather classical illustration. If I let my fingers wander idly over the keys of a typewriter it *might* happen that my screed made an intelligible sentence. If an army of monkeys were strumming on typewriters they *might* write all the books in the British Museum. The chance of their doing so is decidedly more favourable than the chance of the molecules returning to one half of the vessel.

When numbers are large, chance is the best warrant for certainty. Happily in the study of molecules and energy and radiation in bulk we have to deal with a vast population, and we reach a certainty which does not always reward the expectations of those who court the fickle goddess.

In one sense the chance of the molecules returning to one half of the vessel is too absurdly small to think about. Yet in science we think about it a great deal, because it gives a measure of the irrevocable mischief we did when we casually removed the partition. Even if we had good reasons for wanting the gas to fill the vessel there was no need to waste the organisation; as we have mentioned, it is negotiable and might have been passed on somewhere where it was useful.* When the gas was released and began to spread across the vessel, say from left to right, there was no immediate increase of the random element. In order to spread from left to right, left-to-right velocities of the molecules must have preponderated, that is to say the motion was partly organised. Organisation of position was replaced by organisation of motion. A moment later the molecules struck the farther wall of the vessel and the random element began to increase. But, before it was destroyed, the left-to-right organisation of molecular velocities was the exact numerical equivalent of the lost organisation in space. By that we mean that the chance against the left-to-right preponderance of velocity occurring by accident is the same as the chance against segregation in one half of the vessel occurring by accident.

The adverse chance here mentioned is a preposterous number which (written in the usual decimal notation) would fill all the books in the world many times over. We are not interested in it as a practical contingency; but we are interested in the fact that it is definite. It raises "organisation" from a vague descriptive epithet to one of the measurable quantities of exact science. We are confronted with many kinds of organisation.

---

* If the gas in expanding had been made to move a piston, the organisation would have passed into the motion of the piston.

The uniform march of a regiment is not the only form of organised motion; the organised evolutions of a stage chorus have their natural analogue in sound waves. A common measure can now be applied to all forms of organisation. Any loss of organisation is equitably measured by the chance against its recovery by an accidental coincidence. The chance is absurd regarded as a contingency, but it is precise as a measure.

The practical measure of the random element which can increase in the universe but can never decrease is called *entropy*. Measuring by entropy is the same as measuring by the chance explained in the last paragraph, only the unmanageably large numbers are transformed (by a simple formula) into a more convenient scale of reckoning. Entropy continually increases. We can, by isolating parts of the world and postulating rather idealised conditions in our problems, arrest the increase, but we cannot turn it into a decrease. That would involve something much worse than a violation of an ordinary law of Nature, namely, an improbable coincidence. The law that entropy always increases—the second law of thermodynamics—holds, I think, the supreme position among the laws of Nature. If someone points out to you that your pet theory of the universe is in disagreement with Maxwell's equations—then so much the worse for Maxwell's equations. If it is found to be contradicted by observation—well, these experimentalists do bungle things sometimes. But if your theory is found to be against the second law of thermodynamics I can give you no hope; there is nothing for it but to collapse in deepest humiliation. This exaltation of the second law is not unreasonable. There are other laws which we have strong reason to believe in, and we feel that a hypothesis which violates them is highly improbable; but the improbability is vague and does not confront us as a paralysing array of figures, whereas the chance against a breach of the second law (i.e. against a decrease of the random element) can be stated in figures which are overwhelming.

I wish I could convey to you the amazing power of this conception of entropy in scientific research. From the property that entropy must always increase, practical methods of measuring it have been found. The chain of deductions from this simple law have been almost illimitable; and it has been equally successful in connection with the most recondite problems of theoretical physics and the practical tasks of the engineer. Its special feature is that the conclusions are independent of the nature of the microscopical processes that are going on. It is not concerned with the nature of the individual; it is interested in him only as a component of a crowd. Therefore the method is applicable in fields of research where our ignorance has scarcely begun to lift, and we have no hesitation in applying it to problems of the quantum theory, although the mechanism of the individual quantum process is unknown and at present unimaginable.

Primary and Secondary Law. I have called the laws controlling the behaviour of single individuals "primary laws", implying that the second law of thermodynamics, although a recognised law of Nature, is in some sense a secondary law. This distinction can now be placed on a regular footing. Some things never happen in the physical world because they are *impossible*; others because they are *too improbable*. The laws which forbid the first are the primary laws; the laws which forbid the second are the secondary laws. It has been the conviction of nearly all physicists* that at the root of everything there is a complete scheme of primary law governing the career of every particle or constituent of the world with an iron determinism. This primary scheme is all-sufficing, for, since it fixes the history of every constituent of the world, it fixes the whole world-history.

But for all its completeness primary law does not answer every question about Nature which we might reasonably wish to put. Can a universe evolve backwards, i.e. develop in the opposite way to our own system? Primary law, being indifferent to a time-direction, replies, "Yes, it is not impossible". Secondary law replies, "No, it is too improbable". The answers are not really in conflict; but the first, though true, rather misses the point. This is typical of some much more commonplace queries. If I put *this* saucepan of water on *this* fire, will the water boil? Primary law can answer definitely if it is given the chance; but it must be understood that "this" translated into mathematics means a specification of the positions, motions, etc., of some quadrillions of particles and elements of energy. So in practice the question answered is not quite the one that is asked: If I put *a* saucepan resembling this one in a few major respects on *a* fire, will the water boil? Primary law replies, "It may boil; it may freeze; it may do pretty well anything. The details given are insufficient to exclude any result as impossible." Secondary law replies plainly, "It will boil because it is too improbable that it should do anything else." Secondary law is not in conflict with primary law, nor can we regard it as essential to complete a scheme of law already

* There are, however, others beside myself who have recently begun to question it.

complete in itself. It results from a different (and rather more practical) conception of the aim of our traffic with the secrets of Nature.

The question whether the second law of thermodynamics and other statistical laws are mathematical deductions from the primary laws, presenting their results in a conveniently usable form, is difficult to answer; but I think it is generally considered that there is an unbridgeable hiatus. At the bottom of all the questions settled by secondary law there is an elusive conception of "*a priori* probability of states of the world" which involves an essentially different attitude to knowledge from that presupposed in the construction of the scheme of primary law.

Thermodynamical Equilibrium. Progress of time introduces more and more of the random element into the constitution of the world. There is less of chance about the physical universe to-day than there will be to-morrow. It is curious that in this very matter-of-fact branch of physics, developed primarily because of its importance for engineers, we can scarcely avoid expressing ourselves in teleological language. We admit that the world contains both chance and design, or at any rate chance and the antithesis of chance. This antithesis is emphasised by our method of measurement of entropy; we assign to the organisation or non-chance element a measure which is, so to speak, proportional to the strength of our disbelief in a chance origin for it. "A fortuitous concourse of atoms"—that bugbear of the theologian—has a very harmless place in orthodox physics. The physicist is acquainted with it *as a much-prized rarity*. Its properties are very distinctive, and unlike those of the physical world in general. The scientific name for a fortuitous concourse of atoms is "thermodynamical equilibrium".

Thermodynamical equilibrium is the other case which we promised to consider in which no increase in the random element can occur, namely, that in which the shuffling is already as thorough as possible. We must isolate a region of the universe, arranging that no energy can enter or leave it, or at least that any boundary effects are precisely compensated. The conditions are ideal, but they can be reproduced with sufficient approximation to make the ideal problem relevant to practical experiment. A region in the deep interior of a star is an almost perfect example of thermodynamical equilibrium. Under these isolated conditions the energy will be shuffled as it is bandied from matter to aether and back again, and very soon the shuffling will be complete.

The possibility of the shuffling becoming complete is significant. If after shuffling the pack you tear each card in two, a further shuffling of the half-cards becomes possible. Tear the cards again and again; each time there is further scope for the random element to increase. With infinite divisibility there can be no end to the shuffling. The experimental fact that a definite state of equilibrium is rapidly reached indicates that energy is not infinitely divisible, or at least that it is not infinitely divided in the natural processes of shuffling. Historically this is the result from which the quantum theory first arose. We shall return to it in a later chapter.

In such a region we lose time's arrow. You remember that the arrow points in the direction of increase of the random element. When the random element has reached its limit and become steady the arrow does not know which way to point. It would not be true to say that such a region is timeless; the atoms vibrate as usual like little clocks; by them we can measure speeds and durations. Time is still there and retains its ordinary properties, but it has lost its arrow; like space it extends, but it does not "go on".

This raises the important question, Is the random element (measured by the criterion of probability already discussed) the only feature of the physical world which can furnish time with an arrow? Up to the present we have concluded that no arrow can be found from the behaviour of isolated individuals, but there is scope for further search among the properties of crowds beyond the property represented by entropy. To give an illustration which is perhaps not quite so fantastic as it sounds, Might not the assemblage become more and more *beautiful* (according to some agreed aesthetic standard) as time proceeds?* The question is answered by another important law of Nature which runs—

Nothing in the statistics of an assemblage can distinguish a direction of time when entropy fails to distinguish one.

I think that although this law was only discovered in the last few years there is no serious doubt as to its truth. It is accepted as fundamental in all modern studies of atoms and radiation and has proved to be one of the most powerful weapons of progress in such researches. It is, of course, one of the secondary laws. It does not seem to be rigorously deducible from the second law of thermodynamics, and presumably must be regarded as an additional secondary law.†

* In a kaleidoscope the shuffling is soon complete and all the patterns are equal as regards random element, but they differ greatly in elegance.

† The law is so much disguised in the above enunciation that I must explain to the advanced reader that I am referring to "the Principle of

The conclusion is that whereas other statistical characters besides entropy might perhaps be used to discriminate time's arrow, they can only succeed when it succeeds and they fail when it fails. Therefore they cannot be regarded as independent tests. So far as physics is concerned time's arrow is a property of entropy alone.

Are Space and Time Infinite? I suppose that everyone has at some time plagued his imagination with the question, Is there an end to space? If space comes to an end, what is beyond the end? On the other hand the idea that there is no end, but space beyond space for ever, is inconceivable. And so the imagination is tossed to and fro in a dilemma. Prior to the relativity theory the orthodox view was that space is infinite. No one can conceive infinite space; we had to be content to admit in the physical world an inconceivable conception—disquieting but not necessarily illogical. Einstein's theory now offers a way out of the dilemma. Is space infinite, or does it come to an end? Neither. Space is finite but it has no end; "finite but unbounded" is the usual phrase.

Infinite space cannot be conceived by anybody; finite but unbounded space is difficult to conceive but not impossible. I shall not expect you to conceive it; but you can try. Think first of a circle; or, rather, not

Detailed Balancing." This principle asserts that to every type of process (however minutely particularised) there is a converse process, and in thermodynamical equilibrium direct and converse processes occur with equal frequency. Thus every statistical enumeration of the processes is unaltered by reversing the time-direction, i.e. interchanging direct and converse processes. Hence there can be no statistical criterion for a direction of time when there is thermodynamical equilibrium, i.e. when entropy is steady and ceases to indicate time's arrow.

the circle, but the line forming its circumference. This is a finite but endless line. Next think of a sphere—the surface of a sphere—that also is a region which is finite but unbounded. The surface of this earth never comes to a boundary; there is always some country beyond the point you have reached; all the same there is not an infinite amount of room on the earth. Now go one dimension more; circle, sphere—the next thing. Got that? Now for the real difficulty. Keep a tight hold of the skin of this hypersphere and imagine that the inside is not there at all—that the skin exists without the inside. That is finite but unbounded space.

No; I don't think you have quite kept hold of the conception. You overbalanced just at the end. It was not the adding of one more dimension that was the real difficulty; it was the final taking away of a dimension that did it. I will tell you what is stopping you. You are using a conception of space which must have originated many million years ago and has become rather firmly embedded in human thought. But the space of physics ought not to be dominated by this creation of the dawning mind of an enterprising ape. Space is not necessarily like this conception; it is like—whatever we find from experiment it is like. Now the features of space which we discover by experiment are extensions, i.e. lengths and distances. So space is *like* a network of distances. Distances are linkages whose intrinsic nature is inscrutable; we do not deny the inscrutability when we apply measure numbers to them —2 yards, 5 miles, etc.—as a kind of code distinction. We cannot predict out of our inner consciousness the laws by which code-numbers are distributed among the different linkages of the network, any more than we can predict how the code-numbers for electromagnetic force are distributed. Both are a matter for experiment.

If we go a very long way to a point A in one direction through the universe and a very long way to a point B in the opposite direction, it is believed that between A and B there exists a linkage of the kind indicated by a very small code-number; in other words these points reached by travelling vast distances in opposite directions would be found experimentally to be close together. Why not? This happens when we travel east and west on the earth. It is true that our traditional inflexible conception of space refuses to admit it; but there was once a traditional conception of the earth which refused to admit circumnavigation. In our approach to the conception of spherical space the difficult part was to destroy the inside of the hypersphere leaving only its three-dimensional surface existing. I do not think that is so difficult when we conceive space as a network of distances. The network over the surface constitutes a self-supporting system of linkage which can be contemplated without reference to extraneous linkages. We can knock away the constructional scaffolding which helped us to approach the conception of this kind of network of distances without endangering the conception.

We must realise that a scheme of distribution of inscrutable relations linking points to one another is not bound to follow any particular preconceived plan, so that there can be no obstacle to the acceptance of any scheme indicated by experiment.

We do not yet know what is the radius of spherical space; it must, of course, be exceedingly great compared with ordinary standards. On rather insecure evidence it has been estimated to be not many times greater than the distance of the furthest known nebulae. But the boundlessness has nothing to do with the bigness. Space is boundless by re-entrant form not by great extension. *That which is* is a shell floating in the infinitude of *that which is not*. We say with Hamlet, "I could be bounded in a nutshell and count myself a king of infinite space".

But the nightmare of infinity still arises in regard to time. The world is closed in its space dimensions like a sphere, but it is open at both ends in the time dimension. There is a bending round by which East ultimately becomes West, but no bending by which Before ultimately becomes After.

I am not sure that I am logical but I cannot feel the difficulty of an infinite future time very seriously. The difficulty about A.D. ∞ will not happen until we reach A.D. ∞, and presumably in order to reach A.D. ∞ the difficulty must first have been surmounted. It should also be noted that according to the second law of thermodynamics the whole universe will reach thermodynamical equilibrium at a not infinitely remote date in the future. Time's arrow will then be lost altogether and the whole conception of progress towards a future fades away.

But the difficulty of an infinite past is appalling. It is inconceivable that we are the heirs of an infinite time of preparation; it is not less inconceivable that there was once a moment with no moment preceding it.

This dilemma of the beginning of time would worry us more were it not shut out by another overwhelming difficulty lying between us and the infinite past. We have been studying the running-down of the universe; if our views are right, somewhere between the beginning of time and the present day we must place the winding up of the universe.

Travelling backwards into the past we find a world with more and more organisation. If there is no barrier to stop us earlier we must reach a moment when the energy of the world was wholly organised with none of the random element in it. It is impossible to go back any further under the present system of natural law. I do not think the phrase "wholly organised" begs the question. The organisation, we are concerned with is exactly definable, and there is a limit at which it becomes perfect. There is not an infinite series of states of higher and still higher organisation; nor, I think, is the limit one which is ultimately approached more and more slowly. Complete organisation does not tend to be more immune from loss than incomplete organisation.

There is no doubt that the scheme of physics as it has stood for the last three-quarters of a century postulates a date at which either the entities of the universe were created in a state of high organisation, or pre-existing entities were endowed with that organisation which they have been squandering ever since. Moreover, this organisation is admittedly the antithesis of chance. It is something which could not occur fortuitously.

This has long been used as an argument against a too aggressive materialism. It has been quoted as scientific proof of the intervention of the Creator at a time not infinitely remote from to-day. But I am not advocating that we drew any hasty conclusions from it. Scientists and theologians alike must regard as somewhat crude the naïve theological doctrine which (suitably disguised) is at present to be found in every textbook of thermodynamics, namely that some billions of years ago God wound up the material universe and has left it to chance ever since. This should be regarded as the working-hypothesis of thermodynamics rather than its declaration of faith. It is one of those conclusions from which we can see no logical escape—only it suffers from the drawback that it is incredible. As a scientist I simply do not believe that the present order of things started off with a bang; unscientifically I feel equally unwilling to accept the implied discontinuity in the divine nature. But I can make no suggestion to evade the deadlock.

Turning again to the other end of time, there is one school of thought which finds very repugnant the idea of a wearing out of the world. This school is attracted by various theories of rejuvenescence. Its mascot is the Phoenix. Stars grow cold and die out. May not two dead stars collide, and be turned by the energy of the shock into fiery vapour from which a new sun—with planets and with life—is born? This theory very prevalent in the last century is no longer contemplated seriously by astronomers. There is evidence that the present stars at any rate are products of one evolutionary process which swept across primordial matter and caused it to aggregate; they were not formed individually by haphazard collisions having no particular time connection with one another. But the Phoenix complex is still active. Matter, we believe, is gradually destroyed and its energy set free in radiation. Is there no counter-process by which radiation collects in space, evolves into electrons and protons, and begins star-building all over again? This is pure speculation and there is not much to be said on one side or the other as to its truth. But I would mildly criticise the mental outlook which *wishes* it to be true. However much we eliminate the minor extravagances of Nature, we do not by these theories stop the inexorable running-down of the world by loss of organisation and increase of the random element. Whoever wishes for a universe which can continue indefinitely in 'activity must lead a crusade against the second law of thermodynamics; the possibility of re-formation of matter from radiation is not crucial and we can await conclusions with some indifference.

At present we can see no way in which an attack on the second law of thermodynamics could possibly succeed, and I confess that personally I have no great desire that it should succeed in averting the final running-down of the universe. I am no Phoenix worshipper. This is a topic on which science is silent, and all that one can say is prejudice. But since prejudice in favour of a never-ending cycle of rebirth of matter and worlds is often vocal, I may perhaps give voice to the opposite prejudice. I would feel more content that the universe should accomplish some great scheme of evolution and, having achieved whatever may be achieved, lapse back into chaotic changelessness, than that its purpose should be banalised by continual repetition. I am an Evolutionist, not a Multiplicationist. It seems rather stupid to keep doing the same thing over and over again.

Chapter V

"BECOMING"

Linkage of Entropy with Becoming. When you say to yourself, "Every day I grow better and better", science churlishly replies—

"I see no signs of it. I see you extended as a four-dimensional worm in space-time; and, although goodness is not strictly within my province, I will grant that one end of you is better than the other. But whether you *grow* better or worse depends on which way up I hold you. There is in your consciousness an idea of growth or 'becoming' which, if it is not illusory, implies that you have a label 'This side up'. I have searched for such a label all through the physical world and can find no trace of it, so I strongly suspect that the label is non-existent in the world of reality."

That is the reply of science comprised in primary law. Taking account of secondary law, the reply is modified a little, though it is still none too gracious—

"I have looked again and, in the course of studying a property called entropy, I find that the physical world is marked with an arrow which may possibly be intended to indicate which way up it should be regarded. With that orientation I find that you really do grow better. Or, to speak precisely, your good end is in the part of the world with most entropy and your bad end in the part with least. Why this arrangement should be considered more creditable than that of your neighbour who has his good and bad ends the other way round, I cannot imagine."

A problem here rises before us concerning the

linkage of the symbolic world of physics to the world of familiar experience. As explained in the Introduction this question of linkage remains over at the end of the strictly physical investigations. Our present problem is to understand the linkage between entropy which provides time's arrow in the symbolic world and the experience of growing or becoming which is the interpretation of time's arrow in the familiar world. We have, I think, shown exhaustively in the last chapter that the former is the only scientific counterpart to the latter.

But in treating change of entropy as a symbolic equivalent for the moving on of time familiar to our minds a double difficulty arises. Firstly, the symbol seems to be of inappropriate nature; it is an elaborate mathematical construct, whereas we should expect so fundamental a conception as "becoming" to be among the elementary indefinables—the A B C of physics. Secondly, a symbol does not seem to be quite what is wanted; we want a significance which can scarcely be conveyed by a symbol of the customary metrical type— the recognition of a dynamic quality in external Nature. We do not "put sense into the world" merely by recognising that one end of it is more random than the other; we have to put a genuine significance of "becoming" into it and not an artificial symbolic substitute.

The linkage of entropy-change to "becoming" presents features unlike every other problem of parallelism of the scientific and familiar worlds. The usual relation is illustrated by the familiar perception of colour and its scientific equivalent electromagnetic wavelength. Here there is no question of resemblance between the underlying physical cause and the mental sensation which arises. All that we can require of the symbolic counterpart of colour is that it shall be competent to pull the trigger of a (symbolic) nerve. The physiologist can trace the nerve mechanism up to the brain; but ultimately there is a hiatus which no one professes to fill up. Symbolically we may follow the influences of the physical world up to the door of the mind; they ring the door-bell and depart.

But the association of "becoming" with entropy-change is not to be understood in the same way. It is clearly not sufficient that the change in the random element of the world should deliver an impulse at the end of a nerve, leaving the mind to create in response to this stimulus the fancy that it is turning the reel of a cinematograph. Unless we have been altogether misreading the significance of the world outside us— by interpreting it in terms of evolution and progress, instead of a static extension—we must regard the feeling of "becoming" as (in some respects at least) a true mental insight into the physical condition which determines it. It is true enough that whether we are dealing with the experience of "becoming" or with the more typical sense-experiences of light, sound, smell, etc., there must always be some point at which we lose sight of the physical entities ere they arise in new dress above our mental horizon. But if there is any experience in which this mystery of mental recognition can be interpreted as *insight* rather than *image-building*, it should be the experience of "becoming"; because in this case the elaborate nerve mechanism does not intervene. That which consciousness is reading off when it feels the passing moments lies just outside its door. Whereas, even if we had reason to regard our vivid impression of colour as insight, it could not be insight into the electric waves, for these terminate at the retina far from the seat of consciousness.

I am afraid that the average reader will feel impatient with the long-winded discussion I am about to give concerning the dynamic character of the external world. "What is all the bother about? Why not make at once the hypothesis that 'becoming' is a kind of one-way texture involved fundamentally in the structure of Nature? The mind is cognisant of this texture (as it is cognisant of other features of the physical world) and apprehends it as the passing on of time—a fairly correct appreciation of its actual nature. As a result of this one-way texture the random element increases steadily in the direction of the grain, and thus conveniently provides the physicist with an experimental criterion for determining the way of the grain; but it is the grain and not this particular consequence of it which is the direct physical counterpart of 'becoming'. It may be difficult to find a rigorous proof of this hypothesis; but after all we have generally to be content with hypotheses that rest only on plausibility."

This is in fact the kind of idea which I wish to advocate; but the "average reader" has probably not appreciated that before the physicist can admit it, a delicate situation concerning the limits of scientific method and the underlying basis of physical law has to be faced. It is one thing to introduce a plausible hypothesis in order to explain observational phenomena; it is another thing to introduce it in order to give the world outside us a significant or purposive meaning, however strongly that meaning may be insisted on by something in our conscious nature. From the side of scientific investigation we recognise only the progressive change in the random element from the end of the world with least randomness to the end with most; that in itself gives no ground for suspecting any kind of dynamical meaning. The view here advocated is tantamount to an admission that consciousness, looking out through a private door, can learn by direct insight an underlying character of the world which physical measurements do not betray.

In any attempt to bridge the domains of experience belonging to the spiritual and physical sides of our nature, Time occupies the key position. I have already referred to its dual entry into our consciousness—through the sense organs which relate it to the other entities of the physical world, and directly through a kind of private door into the mind. The physicist, whose method of inquiry depends on sharpening up our sense organs by auxiliary apparatus of precision, naturally does not look kindly on private doors, through which all forms of superstitious fancy might enter unchecked. But is he ready to forgo that knowledge of the going on of time which has reached us through the door, and content himself with the time inferred from sense-impressions which is emaciated of all dynamic quality?

No doubt some will reply that they are content; to these I would say—Then show your good faith by reversing the dynamic quality of time (which you may freely do if it has no importance in Nature), and, just for a change, give us a picture of the universe passing from the more random to the less random state, each step showing a gradual victory of antichance over chance. If you are a biologist, teach us how from Man and a myriad other primitive forms of life, Nature in the course of ages achieved the sublimely simple structure of the amoeba. If you are an astronomer, tell how waves of light hurry in from the depths of space and condense on to the stars; how the complex solar system unwinds itself into the evenness of a nebula. Is this the

enlightened outlook which you wish to substitute for
the first chapter of Genesis? If you genuinely believe
that a contra-evolutionary theory is just as true and as
significant as an evolutionary theory, surely it is time that
a protest should be made against the entirely one-sided
version currently taught.

Dynamic Quality of the External World. But for our
ulterior conviction of the dynamic quality of time, it
would be possible to take the view that "becoming" is
purely subjective—that there is no "becoming" in the
external world which lies passively spread out in the
time-dimension as Minkowski pictured it. My consciousness then invents its own serial order for the sense
impressions belonging to the different view-points along
the track in the external world, occupied by the four-
dimensional worm who is in some mysterious way
Myself; and in focussing the sensations of a particular
view-point I get the illusion that the corresponding
external events are "taking place". I suppose that this
would be adequate to account for the observed phenomena. The objections to it hinge on the fact that it
leaves the external world without any dynamic quality
intrinsic to it.

It is useful to recognise how some of our most elementary reasoning tacitly assumes the existence of this
dynamic quality or trend; to eradicate it would almost
paralyse our faculties of inference. In the operation of
shuffling cards it seems axiomatic that the cards must
be in greater disarrangement at a *later* instant. Can
you conceive Nature to be such that this is not obviously
true? But what do we here mean by "later"? So far
as the axiomatic character of the conclusion is concerned

(not its experimental verification) we cannot mean "later" as judged by consciousness; its obviousness is not bound up with any speculations as to the behaviour of consciousness. Do we then mean "later" as judged by the physical criterion of time's arrow, i.e. corresponding to a greater proportion of the random element? But that would be tautological—the cards are more disarranged when there is more of the random element. We did not mean a tautology; we unwittingly accepted as a basis for our thought about the question an unambiguous trend from past to future in the space-time where the operation of shuffling is performed.

The crux of the matter is that, although a change described as sorting is the exact opposite to a change described as shuffling we cannot imagine a cause of sorting to be the exact opposite of a cause of shuffling. Thus a reversal of the time-direction which turns shuffling into sorting does not make the appropriate transformation of their causes. Shuffling can have inorganic causes, but sorting is the prerogative of mind or instinct. We cannot believe that it is merely an orientation with respect to the time-direction which differentiates us from inorganic nature. Shuffling is related to sorting (so far as the change of configuration is concerned) as plus is to minus; but to say that the cause of shuffling is related to the cause of sorting in the same way would seem equivalent to saying that the activities of matter and mind are related like plus and minus—which surely is nonsense. Hence if we view the world from future to past so that shuffling and sorting are interchanged, their causes do not follow suit, and the rational connection is broken. To restore coherency we must postulate that by this change of direction something else has been reversed, viz. the trend in world-texture

spoken of above; "becoming" has been turned into
"unbecoming". If we like we can now go on to account,
not for things *becoming unshuffled,* but for their *unbecoming shuffled*—and, if we wish to pursue this aspect
further, we must discuss not the causes but the un-
causes. But, without tying ourselves into verbal knots,
the meaning evidently is that "becoming" gives a
texture to the world which it is illegitimate to reverse.

Objectivity of Becoming. In general we should describe
the familiar world as subjective and the scientific world
as objective. Take for instance our former example of
parallelism, viz. colour in the familiar world and its
counterpart electromagnetic wave-length in the scientific
world. Here we have little hesitation in describing the
waves as objective and the colour as subjective. The
wave is the reality—or the nearest we can get to a
description of reality; the colour is mere mind-spinning.
The beautiful hues which flood our consciousness under
stimulation of the waves have no relevance to the objective reality. For a colour-blind person the hues are
different; and although persons of normal sight make
the same distinctions of colour, we cannot ascertain
whether their consciousness of red, blue, etc. is just like
our own. Moreover, we recognise that the longer and
shorter electromagnetic waves which have no visual
effect associated with them are just as real as the coloured waves. In this and other parallelisms we find the
objective in the scientific world and the subjective in the
familiar world.

But in the parallelism between entropy-gradient and
"becoming" the subjective and objective seem to have
got on to the wrong sides. Surely "becoming" is a
reality—or the nearest we can get to a description of

reality.   We are convinced that a dynamic character must be attributed to the external world; making all allowance for mental imagery, I do not see how the essence of "becoming" can be much different from what it appears to us to be.   On the other side we have entropy which is frankly of a much more subjective nature than most of the ordinary physical qualities. Entropy is an appreciation of arrangement and organisation; it is subjective in the same sense that the constellation Orion is subjective.   That which is arranged is objective, so too are the stars composing the constellation; but the association is the contribution of the mind which surveys.   If colour is mind-spinning, so also is entropy a mind-spinning—of the statistician.   It has about as much objectivity as a batting average.

Whilst the physicist would generally say that the matter of this familiar table is *really* a curvature of space, and its colour is *really* electromagnetic wavelength, I do not think he would say that the familiar moving on of time is *really* an entropy-gradient.   I am quoting a rather loose way of speaking; but it reveals that there is a distinct difference in our attitude towards the last parallelism.   Having convinced ourselves that the two things are connected, we must conclude that there is something as yet ungrasped behind the notion of entropy—some mystic interpretation, if you like— which is not apparent in the definition by which we introduced it into physics.   In short we strive to see that entropy-gradient may *really* be the moving on of time (instead of *vice versa*).

Before passing on I would note that this exceptional appearance of subjective and objective apparently in their wrong worlds gives food for thought.   It may prepare us for a view of the scientific world adopted in the later chapters which is much more subjective than that usually held by science.

The more closely we examine the association of entropy with "becoming" the greater do the obstacles appear. If entropy were one of the elementary indefinables of physics there would be no difficulty. Or if the moving on of time were something of which we were made aware through our sense organs there would be no difficulty. But the actual combination which we have to face seems to be unique in its difficulty.

Suppose that we had had to identify "becoming" with electrical potential-gradient instead of with entropy-change. We discover potential through the readings of a voltmeter. The numerical reading stands for something in the condition of the world, but we form no picture of what that something is. In scientific researches we only make use of the numerical value— a code-number attached to a background outside all conception. It would be very interesting if we could relate this mysterious potential to any of our familiar conceptions. Clearly, if we could identify the change of potential with the familiar moving on of time, we should have made a great step towards grasping its intrinsic nature. But turning from supposition to fact, we have to identify potential-gradient with force. Now it is true that we have a familiar conception of force— a sensation of muscular effort. But this does not give us any idea of the intrinsic nature of potential-gradient; the sensation is mere mind-spinning provoked by nervous impulses which have travelled a long way from the seat of the force. That is the way with all physical entities which affect the mind through the sense organs. The interposed nerve-mechanism would prevent any close association of the mental image with the physical cause, even if we were disposed to trust our mental insight when it has a chance of operating directly.

Or suppose that we had had to identify force with entropy-gradient. That would only mean that entropy-gradient is a condition which stimulates a nerve, which thereupon transmits an impulse to the brain, out of which the mind weaves its own peculiar impression of force. No one would feel intuitive objection to the hypothesis that the muscular sensation of force is associated with change of organisation of the molecules of the muscle.

Our trouble is that we have to associate two things, both of which we more or less understand, and, so far as we understand them, they are utterly different. It is absurd to pretend that we are in ignorance of the nature of organisation in the external world in the same way that we are ignorant of the intrinsic nature of potential. It is absurd to pretend that we have no justifiable conception of "becoming" in the external world. That dynamic quality—that significance which makes a development from past to future reasonable and a development from future to past farcical—has to do much more than pull the trigger of a nerve. It is so welded into our consciousness that a moving on of time is a condition of consciousness. We have direct insight into "becoming" which sweeps aside all symbolic knowledge as on an inferior plane. If I grasp the notion of existence because I myself exist, I grasp the notion of becoming because I myself become. It is the innermost Ego of all which *is* and *becomes*.

The incongruity of symbolising this fundamental intuition by a property of arrangement of the microscopic constituents of the world, is evident. What this difficulty portends is still very obscure. But it is not irrelevant to certain signs of change which we may discern in responsible scientific opinion with regard to the question of primary and secondary law. The cast-iron determinism of primary law is, I think, still widely accepted but no longer unquestioningly. It now seems clear that we have not yet got hold of *any* primary law —that all those laws at one time supposed to be primary are in reality statistical. No doubt it will be said that that was only to be expected; we must be prepared for a very long search before we get down to ultimate foundations, and not be disappointed if new discoveries reveal unsuspected depths beneath. But I think it might be said that Nature has been caught using rather unfair dodges to prevent our discovering primary law—that kind of artfulness which frustrated our efforts to discover velocity relative to the aether.* I believe that Nature is honest at heart, and that she only resorts to these apparent shifts of concealment when we are looking for something which is not there. It is difficult to see now any justification for the strongly rooted conviction in the ultimate re-establishment of a deterministic scheme of law except a supposed necessity of thought. Thought has grown accustomed to doing without a great many "necessities" in recent years.

One would not be surprised if in the reconstruction of the scheme of physics which the quantum theory is now pressing on us, secondary law becomes the basis and primary law is discarded. In the reconstructed world nothing is impossible though many things are improbable. The effect is much the same, but the kind of machinery that we must conceive is altogether different. We shall have further glimpses of this problem and I will not here pursue it. Entropy, being a quantity

* See p. 221.

introduced in connection with secondary law will now exist, so to speak, in its own right instead of by its current representation as arrangement of the quantities in the abandoned primary scheme; and in that right it may be more easily accepted as the symbol for the dynamic quality of the world. I cannot make my meaning more precise, because I am speaking of a still hypothetical change of ideas which no one has been able to bring about.

Our Dual Recognition of Time. Another curiosity which strikes us is the divorce in physics between time and time's arrow. A being from another world who wishes to discover the temporal relation of two events in this world has to read two different indicators. He must read a clock in order to find out *how much* later one event is than the other, and he must read some arrangement for measuring the disorganisation of energy (e.g. a thermometer) in order to discover *which* event is the later.* The division of labour is especially striking when we remember that our best clocks are those in which all processes such as friction, which introduce disorganisation of energy, are eliminated as far as possible. The more perfect the instrument as a measurer of time, the more completely does it conceal time's arrow.

* To make the test strictly from another world he must not assume that the figures marked on the clock-dial necessarily go the right way round; nor must he assume that the progress of his consciousness has any relation to the flow of time in our world. He has, therefore, merely two dial-readings for the two events without knowing whether the difference should be reckoned plus or minus. The thermometer would be used in conjunction with a hot and cold body in contact. The difference of the thermometer readings for the two bodies would be taken at the moment of each event. The event for which the difference is smaller is the later.

This paradox seems to be explained by the fact pointed out in chapter III that time comes into our consciousness by two routes. We picture the mind like an editor in his sanctum receiving through the nerves scrappy messages from all over the outside world, and making a story of them with, I fear, a good deal of editorial invention. Like other physical quantities time enters in that way as a particular measurable relation between events in the outside world; but it comes in without its arrow. In addition our editor himself experiences a time in his consciousness—the temporal relation along his own track through the world. This experience is immediate, not a message from outside, but the editor realises that what he is experiencing is equivalent to the time described in the messages. Now consciousness declares that this private time possesses an arrow, and so gives a hint to search further for the missing arrow among the messages. The curious thing is that, although the arrow is ultimately found among the messages from outside, it is not found in the messages from clocks, but in messages from thermometers and the like instruments which do not ordinarily pretend to measure time.

Consciousness, besides detecting time's arrow, also roughly measures the passage of time. It has the right idea of time-measurement, but is a bit of a bungler in carrying it out. Our consciousness somehow manages to keep in close touch with the material world, and we must suppose that its record of the flight of time is the reading of some kind of a clock in the material of the brain—possibly a clock which is a rather bad time-keeper. I have generally had in mind in this connection an analogy with the clocks of physics designed for good time-keeping; but I am now inclined to think that a better analogy would be an entropy-clock, i.e. an instrument designed primarily for measuring the rate of disorganisation of energy, and only very roughly keeping pace with time.

A typical entropy-clock might be designed as follows. An electric circuit is composed of two different metals with their two junctions embedded respectively in a hot and cold body in contact. The circuit contains a galvanometer which constitutes the dial of the entropy-clock. The thermoelectric current in the circuit is proportional to the difference of temperature of the two bodies; so that as the shuffling of energy between them proceeds, the temperature difference decreases and the galvanometer reading continually decreases. This clock will infallibly tell an observer from another world which of two events is the later. We have seen that no ordinary clock can do this. As to its time-keeping qualities we can only say that the motion of the galvanometer needle has some connection with the rate of passage of time—which is perhaps as much as can be said for the time-keeping qualities of consciousness.

It seems to me, therefore, that consciousness with its insistence on time's arrow and its rather erratic ideas of time measurement may be guided by entropy-clocks in some portion of the brain. That avoids the unnatural assumption that we consult two different cells of the material brain in forming our ideas of duration and of becoming, respectively. Entropy-gradient is then the direct equivalent of the time of consciousness in both its aspects. Duration measured by physical clocks (time-like interval) is only remotely connected.

Let us try to clear up our ideas of time by a summary of the position now reached. Firstly, *physical time* is a system of partitions in the four-dimensional world (world-wide instants). These are artificial and relative and by no means correspond to anything indicated to us by the time of consciousness. Secondly, we recognise in the relativity theory something called a *temporal relation* which is absolutely distinct from a spatial relation. One consequence of this distinction is that the mind attached to a material body can only traverse a temporal relation; so that, even if there is no closer connection, there is at least a one-to-one correspondence between the sequence of phases of the mind and a sequence of points in temporal relation. Since the mind interprets its own sequence as a *time of consciousness,* we can at least say that the temporal relation in physics has a connection with the time of consciousness which the spatial relation does not possess. I doubt if the connection is any closer. I do not think the mental sequence is a "reading off" of the physical temporal relation, because in physics the temporal relation is arrowless. I think it is a reading off of the physical entropy-gradient, since this has the necessary arrow. Temporal relation and entropy-gradient, both rigorously defined in physics, are entirely distinct and in general are not numerically related. But, of course, other things besides time can "keep time"; and there is no reason why the generation of the random element in a special locality of the brain should not proceed fairly uniformly. In that case there will not be too great a divergence between the passage of time in consciousness and the length of the corresponding temporal relation in the physical world.

The Scientific Reaction from Microscopic Analysis. From the point of view of philosophy of science the conception associated with entropy must I think be ranked as the great contribution of the nineteenth century to scientific thought. It marked a reaction from the view that everything to which science need pay attention is discovered by a microscopic dissection of objects. It provided an alternative standpoint in which the centre of interest is shifted from the entities reached by the customary analysis (atoms, electric potentials, etc.) to qualities possessed by the system as a whole, which cannot be split up and located—a little bit here, and a little bit there. The artist desires to convey significances which cannot be told by microscopic detail and accordingly he resorts to impressionist painting. Strangely enough the physicist has found the same necessity; but his impressionist scheme is just as much exact science and even more practical in its application than his microscopic scheme.

Thus in the study of the falling stone the microscopic analysis reveals myriads of separate molecules. The energy of the stone is distributed among the molecules, the sum of the energies of the molecules making up the energy of the stone. But we cannot distribute in that way the organisation or the random element in the motions. It would be meaningless to say that a particular fraction of the organisation is located in a particular molecule.

There is one ideal of survey which would look into each minute compartment of space in turn to see what it may contain and so make what it would regard as a complete inventory of the world. But this misses any world-features which are not located in minute compartments. We often think that when we have completed our study of *one* we know all about *two*, because "two" is "one and one". We forget that we have still to make a study of "and". Secondary physics is the study of "and"—that is to say, of organisation.

Thanks to clear-sighted pioneers in the last century science became aware that it was missing something of practical importance by following the inventory method of the primary scheme of physics. Entropy became recognised although it was not found in any of the compartments. It was discovered and exalted because it was essential to practical applications of physics, not to satisfy any philosophic hungering. But by it science has been saved from a fatal narrowness. If we had kept entirely to the inventory method, there would have been nothing to represent "becoming" in the physical world. And science, having searched high and low, would doubtless have reported that "becoming" is an unfounded mental illusion—like beauty, life, the soul, and other things which it is unable to inventory.

I think that doubts might well have been entertained as to whether the newcomer was strictly scientific. Entropy was not in the same category as the other physical quantities recognised in science, and the extension—as we shall presently see—was in a very dangerous direction. Once you admit attributes of arrangement as subject-matter of physics, it is difficult to draw the line. But entropy had secured a firm place in physics before it was discovered that it was a measure of the random element in arrangement. It was in great favour with the engineers. Their sponsorship was the highest testimonial to its good character; because at that time it was the general assumption that the Creation was the work of an engineer (not of a mathematician, as is the fashion nowadays).

Suppose that we were asked to arrange the following in two categories—

distance, mass, electric force, entropy, beauty, melody.

I think there are the strongest grounds for placing entropy alongside beauty and melody and not with the first three. Entropy is only found when the parts are viewed in association, and it is by viewing or hearing the parts in association that beauty and melody are discerned. All three are features of arrangement. It is a pregnant thought that one of these three associates should be able to figure as a commonplace quantity of science. The reason why this stranger can pass itself off among the aborigines of the physical world is, that it is able to speak their language, viz. the language of arithmetic. It has a measure-number associated with it and so is made quite at home in physics. Beauty and melody have not the arithmetical pass-word and so are barred out. This teaches us that what exact science looks out for is not entities of some particular category, but entities with a metrical aspect. We shall see in a later chapter that when science admits them it really admits only their metrical aspect and occupies itself solely with that. It would be no use for beauty, say, to fake up a few numerical attributes (expressing for instance the ideal proportions of symmetry) in the hope of thereby gaining admission into the portals of science and carrying on an aesthetic crusade within. It would find that the numerical aspects were duly admitted, but the aesthetic significance of them left outside. So also entropy is admitted in its numerical aspect; if it has as we faintly suspect some deeper significance touching that which appears in our consciousness as *purpose* (opposed to *chance*), that significance is left outside. These fare no worse than mass, distance, and the like which surely must have some significance beyond mere numbers; if so, that significance is lost on their incorporation into the scientific scheme—the world of shadows.

You may be inclined to regard my insistence that entropy is something excluded from the inventory of microscopic contents of the world as word-splitting. If you have all the individuals before you, their associations, arrangement and organisation are automatically before you. If you have the stars, you have the constellations. Yes; but if you have the stars, you do not take the constellations seriously. It had become the regular outlook of science, closely associated with its materialistic tendencies, that constellations are not to be taken seriously, until the constellation of entropy made a solitary exception. When we analyse the picture into a large number of particles of paint, we lose the aesthetic significance of the picture. The particles of paint go into the scientific inventory, and it is claimed that *everything that there really was* in the picture is kept. But this way of keeping a thing may be much the same as losing it. The essence of a picture (as distinct from the paint) is arrangement. Is arrangement kept or lost? The current answer seems inconsistent. In so far as arrangement signifies a picture, it is lost; science has to do with paint, not pictures. In so far as arrangement signifies organisation it is kept; science has much to do with organisation. Why should we (speaking now as philosophers, not scientists) make a discrimination between these two aspects of arrangement? The discrimination is made because the picture is no use to the scientist—he cannot get further with it. As impartial judges it is our duty to point out that likewise entropy is no use to the artist—he cannot develop his outlook with it.

I am not trying to argue that there is in the external world an objective entity which is the picture as distinct from the myriads of particles into which science has analysed it. I doubt if the statement has any meaning; nor, if it were true, would it particularly enhance my esteem of the picture. What I would say is this: There is a side of our personality which impels us to dwell on beauty and other aesthetic significances in Nature, and in the work of man, so that our environment means to us much that is not warranted by anything found in the scientific inventory of its structure. An overwhelming feeling tells us that this is right and indispensable to the purpose of our existence. But is it rational? How can reason regard it otherwise than as a perverse misrepresentation of what is after all only a collection of atoms, aether-waves and the like, going about their business? If the physicist as advocate for reason takes this line, just whisper to him the word Entropy.

Insufficiency of Primary Law. I daresay many of my physical colleagues will join issue with me over the status I have allowed to entropy as something foreign to the microscopic scheme, but essential to the physical world. They would regard it rather as a labour-saving device, useful but not indispensable. Given any practical problem ordinarily solved by introducing the conception of entropy, precisely the same result could be reached (more laboriously) by following out the motion of each individual particle of matter or quantum of energy under the primary microscopic laws without any reference to entropy explicit or implicit. Very well; let us try. *There's* a problem for you—

[A piece of chalk was thrown on the lecture table where it rolled and broke into two pieces.]

You are given the instantaneous position and velocity*
of every molecule, or if you like every proton and
electron, in those pieces of chalk and in as much of the
table and surrounding air as concerns you. Details of
the instantaneous state of every element of energy are
also given. By the microscopic (primary) laws of motion you can trace the state from instant to instant.
You can trace how the atoms moving aimlessly within
the lumps of chalk gradually form a conspiracy so that
the lumps begin to move as a whole. The lumps bounce
a little and roll on the table; they come together and
join up; then the whole piece of chalk rises gracefully
in the air, describes a parabola, and comes to rest between my fingers. I grant that you can do all that without requiring entropy or anything outside the limits of
microscopic physics. You have solved the problem.
But, have you quite got hold of the significance of your
solution? Is it quite a negligible point that what you
have described from your calculations is an *unhappening*? There is no need to alter a word of your description so far as it goes; but it does seem to need an
addendum which would discriminate between a trick
worthy of Mr. Maskelyne and an ordinary everyday
unoccurrence.

The physicist may say that the addendum asked for
relates to *significance,* and he has nothing to do with
significances; he is only concerned that his calculations
shall agree with observation. He cannot tell me whether
the phenomenon has the significance of a happening or
an unhappening; but if a clock is included in the

---

* Velocities are relative to a frame of space and time. Indicate which
frame you prefer, and you will be given velocity relative to that frame.
(This throws on you the responsibility for any labelling of the frame—
left, right, past, future, etc.)

problem he can give the readings of the clock at each stage. There is much to be said for excluding the whole field of significance from physics; it is a healthy reaction against mixing up with our calculations mystic conceptions that (officially) we know nothing about. I rather envy the pure physicist his impregnable position. But if he rules significances entirely outside his scope, *somebody* has the job of discovering whether the physical world of atoms, aether and electrons has any significance whatever. Unfortunately for me I am expected in these lectures to say how the plain man ought to regard the scientific world when it comes into competition with other views of our environment. Some of my audience may not be interested in a world invented as a mere calculating device. Am I to tell them that the scientific world has no claim on their consideration when the eternal question surges in the mind, What is it all about? I am sure my physical colleagues will expect me to put up some defence of the scientific world in this connection. I am ready to do so; only I must insist as a preliminary that we should settle which is the right way up of it. I cannot read any significance into a physical world when it is held before me upside down, as happened just now. For that reason I am interested in entropy not only because it shortens calculations which can be made by other methods, but because it determines an orientation which cannot be found by other methods.

The scientific world is, as I have often repeated, a shadow-world, shadowing a world familiar to our consciousness. Just how much do we expect it to shadow? We do not expect it to shadow all that is in our mind, emotions, memory, etc. In the main we expect it to shadow impressions which can be traced to external sense-organs. But time makes a dual entry and thus forms an intermediate link between the internal and the external. This is shadowed partially by the scientific world of primary physics (which excludes time's arrow), but fully when we enlarge the scheme to include entropy. Therefore by the momentous departure in the nineteenth century the scientific world is not confined to a static extension around which the mind may spin a romance of activity and evolution; it shadows that dynamic quality of the familiar world which cannot be parted from it without disaster to its significance.

In sorting out the confused data of our experience it has generally been assumed that the object of the quest is to find out all that really exists. There is another quest not less appropriate to the nature of our experience —to find out all that really becomes.

Chapter VI

GRAVITATION—THE LAW

You sometimes speak of gravity as essential and inherent to matter. Pray do not ascribe that notion to me; for the cause of gravity is what I do not pretend to know, and therefore would take more time to consider of it. . . .

Gravity must be caused by some agent acting constantly according to certain laws; but whether this agent be material or immaterial I have left to the consideration of my readers.

NEWTON, *Letters to Bentley.*

The Man in the Lift. About 1915 Einstein made a further development of his theory of relativity extending it to non-uniform motion. The easiest way to approach this subject is by considering the Man in the Lift.

Suppose that this room is a lift. The support breaks and down we go with ever-increasing velocity, falling freely.

Let us pass the time by performing physical experiments. The lift is our laboratory and we shall start at the beginning and try to discover all the laws of Nature —that is to say, Nature as interpreted by the Man in the Lift. To a considerable extent this will be a repetition of the history of scientific discovery already made in the laboratories on *terra firma*. But there is one notable difference.

I perform the experiment of dropping an apple held in the hand. The apple cannot fall any more than it was doing already. You remember that our lift and all things contained in it are falling freely. Consequently the apple remains poised by my hand. There is one incident in the history of science which will not repeat itself to the men in the lift, viz. Newton and the apple tree. The magnificent conception that the agent which guides the stars in their courses is the same as that which in our common experience causes apples to drop, breaks down because it is our common experience *in the lift* that apples do not drop.

I think we have now sufficient evidence to prove that in all other respects the scientific laws determined in the lift will agree with those determined under more orthodox conditions. But for this one omission the men in the lift will derive all the laws of Nature with which we are acquainted, and derive them in the same form that we have derived them. Only the force which causes apples to fall is not present in their scheme.

I am crediting our observers in the lift with the usual egocentric attitude, viz. the aspect of the world to *me* is its natural one. It does not strike them as odd to spend their lives falling in a lift; they think it much more odd to be perched on the earth's surface. Therefore although they perhaps have calculated that to beings supported in this strange way apples would seem to have a perplexing habit of falling, they do not take our experience of the ways of apples any more seriously than we have hitherto taken theirs.

Are we to take their experience seriously? Or to put it another way—What is the comparative importance to be attached to a scheme of natural laws worked out by observers in the falling lift and one worked out by observers on *terra firma*? Is one truer than the other? Is one superior to the other? Clearly the difference if any arises from the fact that the schemes are referred to different frames of space and time. Our frame is a frame in which the solid ground is at rest; similarly their frame is a frame in which their lift is at rest. We have had examples before of observers using different frames, but those frames differed by a *uniform velocity*. The velocity of the lift is ever-increasing—accelerated. Can we extend to accelerated frames our principle that Nature is indifferent to frames of space and time, so that no one frame is superior to any other? I think we can. The only doubt that arises is whether we should not regard the frame of the man in the lift as superior to, instead of being merely coequal with, our usual frame.

When we stand on the ground the molecules of the ground support us by hammering on the soles of our boots with force equivalent to some ten stone weight. But for this we should sink through the interstices of the floor. *We are being continuously and vigorously buffeted.* Now this can scarcely be regarded as the ideal condition for a judicial contemplation of our natural surroundings, and it would not be surprising if our senses suffering from this treatment gave a jaundiced view of the world. Our bodies are to be regarded as scientific instruments used to survey the world. We should not willingly allow anyone to hammer on a galvanometer when it was being used for observation; and similarly it is preferable to avoid a hammering on one's body when it is being used as a channel of scientific knowledge. We get rid of this hammering when we cease to be supported.

Let us then take a leap over a precipice so that we may contemplate Nature undisturbed. Or if that seems to you an odd way of convincing yourself that bodies do not fall,* let us enter the runaway lift again. Here nothing need be supported; our bodies, our galvano-

* So far as I can tell (without experimental trial) the man who jumped over a precipice would soon lose all conception of falling; he would only notice that the surrounding objects were impelled past him with ever-increasing speed.

meters, and all measuring apparatus are relieved of hammering and their indications can be received without misgiving. The space- and time-frame of the falling lift is the frame natural to observers who are unsupported; and the laws of Nature determined in these favourable circumstances should at least have not inferior status to those established by reference to other frames.

I perform another experiment. This time I take two apples and drop them at opposite ends of the lift. What will happen? Nothing much at first; the apples remain poised where they were let go. But let us step outside the lift for a moment to watch the experiment. The two apples are pulled by gravity towards the centre of the earth. As they approach the centre their paths converge and they will meet at the centre. Now step back into the lift again. To a first approximation the apples remain poised above the floor of the lift; but presently we notice that they are drifting towards one another, and they will meet at the moment when (according to an outside observer) the lift is passing through the centre of the earth. Even though apples (in the lift) do not tend to fall to the floor there is still a mystery about their behaviour; and the Newton of the lift may yet find that the agent which guides the stars in their courses is to be identified with the agent which plays these tricks with apples nearer home.

It comes to this. There are both relative and absolute features about gravitation. The feature that impresses us most is relative—relative to a frame that has no special importance apart from the fact that it is the one commonly used by us. This feature disappears altogether in the frame of the man in the lift and we ought to disregard it in any attempt to form an absolute picture of gravitation. But there always remains something absolute, of which we must try to devise an appropriate picture. For reasons which I shall presently explain we find that it can be pictured as a curvature of space and time.

A New Picture of Gravitation. The Newtonian picture of gravitation is a *tug* applied to the body whose path is disturbed. I want to explain why this picture must be superseded. I must refer again to the famous incident in which Newton and the apple-tree were concerned. The classical conception of gravitation is based on Newton's account of what happened; but it is time to hear what the apple had to say. The apple with the usual egotism of an observer deemed itself to be at rest; looking down it saw the various terrestrial objects including Newton rushing upwards with accelerated velocity to meet it. Does it invent a mysterious agency or tug to account for their conduct? No; it points out that the cause of their acceleration is quite evident. Newton is being hammered by the molecules of the ground underneath him. This hammering is absolute—no question of frames of reference. With a powerful enough magnifying appliance anyone can see the molecules at work and count their blows. According to Newton's own law of motion this must give him an acceleration, which is precisely what the apple has observed. Newton had to postulate a mysterious invisible force pulling the apple down; the apple can point to an evident cause propelling Newton up.

The case for the apple's view is so overwhelming that I must modify the situation a little in order to give Newton a fair chance; because I believe the apple is making too much of a merely accidental advantage. I will place Newton at the centre of the earth where gravity vanishes, so that he can remain at rest without support—without hammering. He looks up and sees apples falling at the surface of the earth, and as before ascribes this to a mysterious tug which he calls gravitation. The apple looks down and sees Newton approaching it; but this time it cannot attribute Newton's acceleration to any evident hammering. It also has to invent a mysterious tug acting on Newton.

We have two frames of reference. In one of them Newton is at rest and the apple is accelerated; in the other the apple is at rest and Newton accelerated. In neither case is there a visible cause for the acceleration; in neither is the object disturbed by extraneous hammering. The reciprocity is perfect and there is no ground for preferring one frame rather than the other. We must devise a picture of the disturbing agent which will not favour one frame rather than the other. In this impartial humour a tug will not suit us, because if we attach it to the apple we are favouring Newton's frame and if we attach it to Newton we are favouring the apple's frame.* The essence or absolute part of gravitation cannot be a force on a body, because we are entirely vague as to the body to which it is applied. We must picture it differently.

* It will probably be objected that since the phenomena here discussed are evidently associated with the existence of a massive body (the earth), and since Newton makes his tugs occur symmetrically about that body whereas the apple makes its tugs occur unsymmetrically (vanishing where the apple is, but strong at the antipodes), therefore Newton's frame is clearly to be preferred. It would be necessary to go deeply into the theory to explain fully why we do not regard this symmetry as of first importance; we can only say here that the criterion of symmetry proves to be insufficient to pick out a unique frame and does not draw a sharp dividing line between the frames that it would admit and those it would have us reject. After all we can appreciate that certain frames are more symmetrical than others without insisting on calling the symmetrical ones "right" and unsymmetrical ones "wrong".

The ancients believed that the earth was flat. The small part which they had explored could be represented without serious distortion on a flat map. When new countries were discovered it would be natural to think that they could be added on to the flat map. A familiar example of such a flat map is Mercator's projection, and you will remember that in it the size of Greenland appears absurdly exaggerated. (In other projections directions are badly distorted.) Now those who adhered to the flat-earth theory must suppose that the map gives the true size of Greenland—that the distances shown in the map are the true distances. How then would they explain that travellers in that country reported that the distances seemed to be much shorter than they "really" were? They would, I suppose, invent a theory that there was a demon living in Greenland who helped travellers on their way. Of course no scientist would use so crude a word; he would invent a Graeco-Latin polysyllable to denote the mysterious agent which made the journeys seem so short; but that is only camouflage. But now suppose the inhabitants of Greenland have developed their own geography. They find that the most important part of the earth's surface (Greenland) can be represented without serious distortion on a flat map. But when they put in distant countries such as Greece the size must be exaggerated; or, as they would put it, there is a demon active in Greece who makes the journeys there seem different from what the flat map clearly shows them to be. The demon is never where you are; it is always the other fellow who is haunted by him. We now understand that the true explanation is that the earth is curved, and the apparent activities of the demon arise from forcing the curved surface into a flat map and so distorting the simplicity of things.

What has happened to the theory of the earth has happened also to the theory of the world of space-time. An observer at rest at the earth's centre represents what is happening in a frame of space and time constructed on the usual conventional principles which give what is called a *flat* space-time. He can locate the events in his neighbourhood without distorting their natural simplicity. Objects at rest remain at rest; objects in uniform motion remain in uniform motion unless there is some evident cause of disturbance such as hammering; light travels in straight lines. He extends this flat frame to the surface of the earth where he encounters the phenomenon of falling apples. This new phenomenon has to be accounted for by an intangible agency or demon called *gravitation* which persuades the apples to deviate from their proper uniform motion. But we can also start with the frame of the falling apple or of the man in the lift. In the lift-frame bodies at rest remain at rest; bodies in uniform motion remain in uniform motion. But, as we have seen, even at the corners of the lift this simplicity begins to fail; and looking further afield, say to the centre of the earth, it is necessary to postulate the activity of a demon urging unsupported bodies upwards (relatively to the lift-frame). As we change from one observer to another—from one flat space-time frame to another—the scene of activity of the demon shifts. It is never where our observer is, but always away yonder. Is not the solution now apparent? The demon is simply the complication which arises when we try to fit a curved world into a flat frame. In referring the world to a flat frame of space-time we distort it so that the phenomena do not appear in their original simplicity. Admit a curvature of the world and the mysterious agency disappears. Einstein has exorcised the demon.

Do not imagine that this preliminary change of conception carries us very far towards an *explanation* of gravitation. We are not seeking an explanation; we are seeking a picture. And this picture of world-curvature (hard though it may seem) is more graspable than an elusive tug which flits from one object to another according to the point of view chosen.

A New Law of Gravitation. Having found a new picture of gravitation, we require a new law of gravitation; for the Newtonian law told us the amount of the tug and there is now no tug to be considered. Since the phenomenon is now pictured as curvature the new law must say something about curvature. Evidently it must be a law governing and limiting the possible curvature of space-time.

There are not many things which *can* be said about curvature—not many of a general character. So that when Einstein felt this urgency to say something about curvature, he almost automatically said the right thing. I mean that there was only one limitation or law that suggested itself as reasonable, and that law has proved to be right when tested by observation.

Some of you may feel that you could never bring your minds to conceive a curvature of space, let alone of space-time; others may feel that, being familiar with the bending of a two-dimensional surface, there is no insuperable difficulty in imagining something similar for three or even four dimensions. I rather think that the former have the best of it, for at least they escape being misled by their preconceptions. I have spoken of a "picture", but it is a picture that has to be described analytically rather than conceived vividly. Our ordinary conception of curvature is derived from surfaces, i.e.

two-dimensional manifolds embedded in a three-dimensional space. The absolute curvature at any point is measured by a single quantity called the radius of spherical curvature. But space-time is a four-dimensional manifold embedded in—well, as many dimensions as it can find new ways to twist about in. Actually a four-dimensional manifold is amazingly ingenious in discovering new kinds of contortion, and its invention is not exhausted until it has been provided with six extra dimensions, making ten dimensions in all. Moreover, twenty distinct measures are required at each point to specify the particular sort and amount of twistiness there. These measures are called coefficients of curvature. Ten of the coefficients stand out more prominently than the other ten.

Einstein's law of gravitation asserts that the ten principal coefficients of curvature are zero in empty space.

If there were no curvature, i.e. if *all* the coefficients were zero, there would be no gravitation. Bodies would move uniformly in straight lines. If curvature were unrestricted, i.e. if *all* the coefficients had unpredictable values, gravitation would operate arbitrarily and without law. Bodies would move just anyhow. Einstein takes a condition midway between; ten of the coefficients are zero and the other ten are arbitrary. That gives a world containing gravitation limited by a law. The coefficients are naturally separated into two groups of ten, so that there is no difficulty in choosing those which are to vanish.

To the uninitiated it may seem surprising that an exact law of Nature should leave some of the coefficients arbitrary. But we need to leave something over to be settled when we have specified the particulars of the problem to which it is proposed to apply the law. A

general law covers an infinite number of special cases.
The vanishing of the ten principal coefficients occurs
everywhere in empty space whether there is one gravi-
tating body or many. The other ten coefficients vary
according to the special case under discussion. This may
remind us that after reaching Einstein's law of gravitation and formulating it mathematically, it is still a very
long step to reach its application to even the simplest
practical problem. However, by this time many hun-
dreds of readers must have gone carefully through the
mathematics; so we may rest assured that there has
been no mistake. After this work has been done it
becomes possible to verify that the law agrees with
observation. It is found that it agrees with Newton's
law to a very close approximation so that the main
evidence for Einstein's law is the same as the evidence
for Newton's law; but there are three crucial astronomical phenomena in which the difference is large
enough to be observed. In these phenomena the observations support Einstein's law against Newton's.*

It is essential to our faith in a theory that its predictions should accord with observation, unless a reasonable
explanation of the discrepancy is forthcoming; so that
it is highly important that Einstein's law should have
survived these delicate astronomical tests in which Newton's law just failed. But our main reason for rejecting Newton's law is not its imperfect accuracy as shown
by these tests; it is because it does not contain the
kind of information about Nature that we want to
know now that we have an ideal before us which was
not in Newton's mind at all. We can put it this way.

---

* One of the tests—a shift of the spectral lines to the red in the sun
and stars as compared with terrestrial sources—is a test of Einstein's
theory rather than of his *law*.

Astronomical observations show that within certain limits of accuracy both Einstein's and Newton's laws are true. In confirming (approximately) Newton's law, we are confirming a statement as to what the appearances would be when referred to one particular space-time frame. No reason is given for attaching any fundamental importance to this frame. In confirming (approximately) Einstein's law, we are confirming a statement about the absolute properties of the world, true for all space-time frames. For those who are trying to get beneath the appearances Einstein's statement necessarily supersedes Newton's; it extracts from the observations a result with physical meaning as opposed to a mathematical curiosity. That Einstein's law has proved itself the better approximation encourages us in our opinion that the quest of the absolute is the best way to understand the relative appearances; but had the success been less immediate, we could scarcely have turned our back on the quest.

I cannot but think that Newton himself would rejoice that after 200 years the "ocean of undiscovered truth" has rolled back another stage. I do not think of him as censorious because we will not blindly apply his formula regardless of the knowledge that has since accumulated and in circumstances that he never had the opportunity of considering.

I am not going to describe the three tests here, since they are now well known and will be found in any of the numerous guides to relativity; but I would refer to the action of gravitation on light concerned in one of them. Light-waves in passing a massive body such as the sun are deflected through a small angle. This is additional evidence that the Newtonian picture of gravitation as a tug is inadequate. You cannot deflect *waves* by tugging at them, and clearly another representation of the agency which deflects them must be found.

The Law of Motion. I must now ask you to let your mind revert to the time of your first introduction to mechanics before your natural glimmerings of the truth were sedulously uprooted by your teacher. You were taught the First Law of Motion—

"Every body continues in its state of rest or uniform motion in a straight line, except in so far as it may be compelled to change that state by impressed forces."

Probably you had previously supposed that motion was something which would exhaust itself; a bicycle stops of its own accord if you do not impress force to keep it going. The teacher rightly pointed out the resisting forces which tend to stop the bicycle; and he probably quoted the example of a stone skimming over ice to show that when these interfering forces are reduced the motion lasts much longer. But even ice offers some frictional resistance. Why did not the teacher do the thing thoroughly and abolish resisting forces altogether, as he might easily have done by projecting the stone into empty space? Unfortunately in that case its motion is not uniform and rectilinear; the stone describes a parabola. If you raised that objection you would be told that the projectile was compelled to change its state of uniform motion by an invisible force called gravitation. How do we know that this invisible force exists? Why! because if the force did not exist the projectile would move uniformly in a straight line.

The teacher is not playing fair. He is determined to have his uniform motion in a straight line, and if we point out to him bodies which do not follow his rule he blandly invents a new force to account for the deviation. We can improve on his enunciation of the First Law of Motion. What he really meant was—

"Every body continues in its state of rest or uniform motion in a straight line, except in so far as it doesn't."

Material frictions and reactions are visible and absolute interferences which can change the motion of a body. I have nothing to say against them. The molecular battering can be recognised by anyone who looks deeply into the phenomenon no matter what his frame of reference. But when there is no such indication of disturbance the whole procedure becomes arbitrary. On no particular grounds the motion is divided into two parts, one of which is attributed to a passive tendency of the body called inertia and the other to an interfering field of force. The suggestion that the body really wanted to go straight but some mysterious agent made it go crooked is picturesque but unscientific. It makes two properties out of one; and then we wonder why they are always proportional to one another—why the gravitational force on different bodies is proportional to their inertia or mass. The dissection becomes untenable when we admit that all frames of reference are on the same footing. The projectile which describes a parabola relative to an observer on the earth's surface describes a straight line relative to the man in the lift. Our teacher will not easily persuade the man in the lift who sees the apple remaining where he released it, that the apple *really* would of its own initiative rush upwards were it not that an invisible tug exactly counteracts this tendency.*

Einstein's Law of Motion does not recognise this dissection. There are certain curves which can be

* The reader will verify that this is the doctrine the teacher would have to inculcate if he went as a missionary to the men in the lift.

defined on a curved surface without reference to any frame or system of partitions, viz. the geodesics or shortest routes from one point to another. The geodesics of our curved space-time supply the natural tracks which particles pursue if they are undisturbed.

We observe a planet wandering round the sun in an elliptic orbit. A little consideration will show that if we add a fourth dimension (time), the continual moving on in the time-dimension draws out the ellipse into a helix. Why does the planet take this spiral track instead of going straight? It is because it is following the shortest track; and in the distorted geometry of the curved region round the sun the spiral track is shorter than any other between the same points. You see the great change in our view. The Newtonian scheme says that the planet tends to move in a straight line, but the sun's gravity pulls it away. Einstein says that the planet tends to take the shortest route *and does take it*.

That is the general idea, but for the sake of accuracy I must make one rather trivial correction. The planet takes the *longest* route.

You may remember that points along the track of any material body (necessarily moving with a speed less than the velocity of light) are in the absolute past or future of one another; they are not absolutely "elsewhere". Hence the length of the track in four dimensions is made up of time-like relations and must be measured in time-units. It is in fact the number of seconds recorded by a clock carried on a body which describes the track.* This may be different from the time re-

---

* It may be objected that you cannot make a clock follow an arbitrary curved path without disturbing it by impressed forces (e.g. molecular hammering). But this difficulty is precisely analogous to the difficulty of measuring the length of a curve with a rectilinear scale, and is surmounted in the same way. The usual theory of "rectification of curves" applies to these time-tracks as well as to space-curves.

corded by a clock which has taken some other route between the same terminal points. On p. 39 we considered two individuals whose tracks had the same terminal points; one of them remained at home on the earth and the other travelled at high speed to a distant part of the universe and back. The first recorded a lapse of 70 years, the second of one year. Notice that it is the man who follows the undisturbed track of the earth who records or lives the longest time. The man whose track was violently dislocated when he reached the limit of his journey and started to come back again lived only one year. There is no limit to this reduction; as the speed of the traveller approaches the speed of light the time recorded diminishes to zero. There is no unique shortest track; but the longest track is unique. If instead of pursuing its actual orbit the earth made a wide sweep which required it to travel with the velocity of light, the earth could get from 1 January 1927 to 1 January 1928 in no time, i.e. no time as recorded by an observer or clock travelling with it, though it would be reckoned as a year according to "Astronomer Royal's time". The earth does not do this, because it is a rule of the Trade Union of matter that the longest possible time must be taken over every job.

Thus in calculating astronomical orbits and in similar problems two laws are involved. We must first calculate the curved form of space-time by using Einstein's law of gravitation, viz. that the ten principal curvatures are zero. We next calculate how the planet moves through the curved region by using Einstein's law of motion, viz. the law of the longest track. Thus far the procedure is analogous to calculations made with Newton's law of gravitation and Newton's law of motion. But there is a remarkable addendum which applies only to Einstein's laws. *Einstein's law of motion can be deduced from his law of gravitation.* The prediction of the track of a planet although divided into two stages for convenience rests on a single law.

I should like to show you in a general way how it is possible for a law controlling the curvature of empty space to determine the tracks of particles without being supplemented by any other conditions. Two "particles" in the four-dimensional world are shown in Fig. 5, namely *yourself* and *myself.* We are not empty space so there is

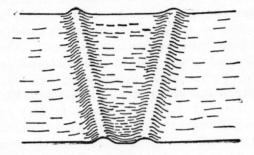

Fig. 5

no limit to the kind of curvature entering into our composition; in fact our unusual sort of curvature is what distinguishes us from empty space. We are, so to speak, ridges in the four-dimensional world where it is gathered into a pucker. The pure mathematician in his unflattering language would describe us as "singularities". These two non-empty ridges are joined by empty space, which must be free from those kinds of curvature described by the ten principal coefficients. Now it is common experience that if we introduce local puckers into the material of a garment, the remainder has a certain obstinacy and will not lie as smoothly as we might wish. You will realise the possibility that, given two ridges as in Fig. 5, it may be impossible to join them by an intervening valley without the illegal kind of curvature. That turns out to be the case. Two perfectly straight ridges alone in the world cannot be properly joined by empty space and therefore they cannot occur alone. But if they bend a little towards one another the connecting region can lie smoothly and satisfy the law of curvature. If they bend too much the illegal puckering reappears. The law of gravitation is a fastidious tailor who will not tolerate wrinkles (except of a limited approved type) in the main area of the garment; so that the seams are required to take courses which will not cause wrinkles. You and I have to submit to this and so our tracks curve towards each other. An onlooker will make the comment that here is an illustration of the law that two massive bodies attract each other.

We thus arrive at another but equivalent conception of how the earth's spiral track through the four-dimensional world is arrived at. It is due to the necessity of arranging two ridges (the solar track and the earth's track) so as not to involve a wrong kind of curvature in the empty part of the world. The sun as the more pronounced ridge takes a nearly straight track; but the earth as a minor ridge on the declivities of the solar ridge has to twist about considerably.

Suppose the earth were to defy the tailor and take a straight track. That would make a horrid wrinkle in the garment; and since the wrinkle is inconsistent with the laws of empty space, *something* must be there—where the wrinkle runs. This "something" need not be matter in the restricted sense. The things which can occupy space so that it is not empty in the sense intended in

Einstein's law, are *mass* (or its equivalent *energy*) *momentum* and *stress* (pressure or tension). In this case the wrinkle might correspond to stress. That is reasonable enough. If left alone the earth must pursue its proper curved orbit; but if some kind of stress or pressure were inserted between the sun and earth, it might well take another course. In fact if we were to observe one of the planets rushing off in a straight track, Newtonians and Einsteinians alike would infer that there existed a stress causing this behaviour. It is true that causation has apparently been turned topsy-turvy; according to our theory the stress seems to be caused by the planet taking the wrong track, whereas we usually suppose that the planet takes the wrong track because it is acted on by the stress. But that is a harmless accident common enough in primary physics. The discrimination between cause and effect depends on time's arrow and can only be settled by reference to entropy. We need not pay much attention to suggestions of causation arising in discussions of primary laws which, as likely as not, are contemplating the world upside down.

Although we are here only at the beginning of Einstein's general theory I must not proceed further into this very technical subject. The rest of this chapter will be devoted to elucidation of more elementary points.

Relativity of Acceleration. The argument in this chapter rests on *the relativity of acceleration.* The apple had an acceleration of 32 feet per second per second relative to the ordinary observer, but zero acceleration relative to the man in the lift. We ascribe to it one acceleration or the other according to the frame we happen to be using, but neither is to be singled out and labelled "true" or absolute acceleration. That led us to reject the

Newtonian conception which singled out 32 feet per second per second as the true acceleration and invented a disturbing agent of this particular degree of strength.

It will be instructive to consider an objection brought, I think, originally by Lenard. A train is passing through a station at 60 miles an hour. Since velocity is relative, it does not matter whether we say that the train is moving at 60 miles an hour past the station or the station is moving at 60 miles an hour past the train. Now suppose, as sometimes happens in railway accidents, that this motion is brought to a standstill in a few seconds. There has been a change of velocity or acceleration—a term which includes deceleration. If acceleration is relative this may be described indifferently as an acceleration of the train (relative to the station) or an acceleration of the station (relative to the train). Why then does it injure the persons in the train and not those in the station?

Much the same point was put to me by one of my audience. "You must find the journey between Cambridge and Edinburgh very tiring. I can understand the fatigue, if you travel to Edinburgh; but why should you get tired if Edinburgh comes to you?" The answer is that the fatigue arises from being shut up in a box and jolted about for nine hours; and it makes no difference whether in the meantime I move to Edinburgh or Edinburgh moves to me. Motion does not tire anybody. With the earth as our vehicle we are travelling at 20 miles a second round the sun; the sun carries us at 12 miles a second through the galactic system; the galactic system bears us at 250 miles a second amid the spiral nebulae; the spiral nebulae. . . . If motion could tire, we ought to be dead tired.

Similarly change of motion or acceleration does not

injure anyone, even when it is (according to the Newtonian view) an absolute acceleration. We do not even
feel the change of motion as our earth takes the curve
round the sun. We feel something when a railway train
takes a curve, but what we feel is not the change of
motion nor anything which invariably accompanies
change of motion; it is something incidental to the
curved track of the train but not to the curved track of
the earth. The cause of injury in the railway accident
is easily traced. Something hit the train; that is to say,
the train was bombarded by a swarm of molecules and
the bombardment spread all the way along it. The
cause is evident—gross, material, absolute—recognised
by everyone, no matter what his frame of reference,
as occurring in the train not the station. Besides injur-
ing the passengers this cause also produced the relative
acceleration of the train and station—an effect which
might equally well have been produced by molecular
bombardment of the station, though in this case it was
not.

The critical reader will probably pursue his objection.
"Are you not being paradoxical when you say that a
molecular bombardment of the train can cause an acceleration of the station—and in fact of the earth and the
rest of the universe? To put it mildly, relative acceleration is a relation with two ends to it, and we may at
first seem to have an option which end we shall grasp
it by; but in this case the causation (molecular bombardment) clearly indicates the right end to take hold
of, and you are merely spinning paradoxes when you
insist on your liberty to take hold of the other."

If there is an absurdity in taking hold of the wrong
end of the relation it has passed into our current
speech and thought. Your suggestion is in fact more

revolutionary than anything Einstein has ventured to advocate. Let us take the problem of a falling stone. There is a relative acceleration of 32 feet per second per second—of the stone relative to ourselves or of ourselves relative to the stone. Which end of the relation must we choose? The one indicated by molecular bombardment? Well, the stone is not bombarded; it is falling freely *in vacuo*. But we are bombarded by the molecules of the ground on which we stand. Therefore it is we who have the acceleration; the stone has zero acceleration, as the man in the lift supposed. Your suggestion makes out the frame of the man in the lift to be the only legitimate one; I only went so far as to admit it to an equality with our own customary frame.

Your suggestion would accept the testimony of the drunken man who explained that "the paving-stone got up and hit him" and dismiss the policeman's account of the incident as "merely spinning paradoxes". What really happened was that the paving-stone had been pursuing the man through space with ever-increasing velocity, shoving the man in front of it so that they kept the same relative position. Then, through an unfortunate wobble of the axis of the man's body, he failed to increase his speed sufficiently, with the result that the paving-stone overtook him and came in contact with his head. That, please understand, is your suggestion; or rather the suggestion which I have taken the liberty of fathering on you because it is the outcome of a very common feeling of objection to the relativity theory. Einstein's position is that whilst this is a perfectly legitimate way of looking at the incident the more usual account given by the policeman is also legitimate; and he endeavours like a good magistrate to reconcile them both.

Time Geometry. Einstein's law of gravitation controls a geometrical quantity *curvature* in contrast to Newton's law which controls a mechanical quantity *force*. To understand the origin of this geometrisation of the world in the relativity theory we must go back a little.

The science which deals with the properties of space is called geometry. Hitherto geometry has not included time in its scope. But now space and time are so interlocked that there must be one science—a somewhat extended geometry—embracing them both. Three-dimensional space is only a section cut through four-dimensional space-time, and moreover sections cut in different directions form the spaces of different observers. We can scarcely maintain that the study of a section cut in one special direction is the proper subject-matter of geometry and that the study of slightly different sections belongs to an altogether different science. Hence the geometry of the world is now considered to include time as well as space. Let us follow up the geometry of time.

You will remember that although space and time are mixed up there is an absolute distinction between a spatial and a temporal relation of two events. Three events will form a space-triangle if the three sides correspond to spatial relations—if the three events are absolutely elsewhere with respect to one another.* Three events will form a time-triangle if the three sides correspond to temporal relations—if the three events are absolutely before or after one another. (It is possible also to have mixed triangles with two sides time-like and one space-like, or *vice versa*.) A well-known law of the space-triangle is that any two sides are together

* This would be an *instantaneous* space-triangle. An enduring triangle is a kind of four-dimensional prism.

greater than the third side. There is an analogous, but significantly different, law for the time-triangle, viz. two of the sides (not *any* two sides) are together less than the third side. It is difficult to picture such a triangle but that is the actual fact.

Let us be quite sure that we grasp the precise meaning of these geometrical propositions. Take first the space-triangle. The proposition refers to the lengths of the sides, and it is well to recall my imaginary discussion with two students as to how lengths are to be measured (p. 23). Happily there is no ambiguity now, because the triangle of three events determines a plane section of the world, and it is only for that mode of section that the triangle is purely spatial. The proposition then expresses that

"If you measure with a scale from A to B and from B to C the sum of your readings will be *greater* than the reading obtained by measuring with a scale from A to C."

For a time-triangle the measurements must be made with an instrument which can measure time, and the proposition then expresses that

"If you measure with a clock from A to B and from B to C the sum of your readings will be *less* than the reading obtained by measuring with a clock from A to C."

In order to measure from an event A to an event B with a clock you must make an adjustment of the clock analogous to orienting a scale along the line AB. What is this analogous adjustment? The purpose in either case is to bring both A and B into the immediate neighbourhood of the scale or clock. For the clock that means that after experiencing the event A it must travel with the appropriate velocity needed to reach the locality of B just at the moment that B happens. Thus the velocity of the clock is prescribed. One further point should be noticed. After measuring with a scale from *A* to *B* you can turn your scale round and measure from *B* to *A,* obtaining the same result. But you cannot turn a clock round, i.e. make it go backwards in time. That is important because it decides *which* two sides are less than the third side. If you choose the wrong pair the enunciation of the time proposition refers to an impossible kind of measurement and becomes meaningless.

You remember the traveller (p. 39) who went off to a distant star and returned absurdly young. He was a clock measuring two sides of a time-triangle. He recorded less time than the stay-at-home observer who was a clock measuring the third side. Need I defend my calling him a clock? We are all of us clocks whose faces tell the passing years. This comparison was simply an example of the geometrical proposition about time-triangles (which in turn is a particular case of Einstein's law of longest track). The result is quite explicable in the ordinary mechanical way. All the particles in the traveller's body increase in mass on account of his high velocity according to the law already discussed and verified by experiment. This renders them more sluggish, and the traveller lives more slowly according to terrestrial time-reckoning. However, the fact that the result is reasonable and explicable does not render it the less true as a proposition of time geometry.

Our extension of geometry to include time as well as space will not be a simple addition of an extra dimension to Euclidean geometry, because the time propositions, though analogous, are not identical with those which Euclid has given us for space alone. Actually the difference between time geometry and space geometry is not very profound, and the mathematician easily glides over it by a discrete use of the symbol $\sqrt{-1}$. We still call (rather loosely) the extended geometry Euclidean; or, if it is necessary to emphasise the distinction, we call it hyperbolic geometry. The term non-Euclidean geometry refers to a more profound change, viz. that involved in the curvature of space and time by which we now represent the phenomenon of gravitation. We start with Euclidean geometry of space, and modify it in a comparatively simple manner when the time-dimension is added; but that still leaves gravitation to be reckoned with, and wherever gravitational effects are observable it is an indication that the extended Euclidean geometry is not quite exact, and the true geometry is a non-Euclidean one—appropriate to a curved region as Euclidean geometry is to a flat region.

Geometry and Mechanics. The point that deserves special attention is that the proposition about time-triangles is a statement as to the behaviour of clocks moving with different velocities. We have usually regarded the behaviour of clocks as coming under the science of mechanics. We found that it was impossible to confine geometry to space alone, and we had to let it expand a little. It has expanded with a vengeance and taken a big slice out of mechanics. There is no stopping it, and bit by bit geometry has now swallowed up the whole of mechanics. It has also made some tentative nibbles at electromagnetism. An ideal shines in front of us, far ahead perhaps but irresistible, that the whole of our knowledge of the physical world may be unified into a single science which will perhaps be expressed in terms of geometrical or quasi-geometrical conceptions. Why not? All the knowledge is derived from measurements made with various instruments. The instruments used in the different fields of inquiry are not fundamentally unlike. There is no reason to regard the partitions of the sciences made in the early stages of human thought as irremovable.

But mechanics in becoming geometry remains none the less mechanics. The partition between mechanics and geometry has broken down and the nature of each of them has diffused through the whole. The apparent supremacy of geometry is really due to the fact that it possesses the richer and more adaptable vocabulary; and since after the amalgamation we do not need the double vocabulary the terms employed are generally taken from geometry. But besides the geometrisation of mechanics there has been a mechanisation of geometry. The proposition about the space-triangle quoted above was seen to have grossly material implications about the behaviour of scales which would not be realised by any-one who thinks of it as if it were a proposition of pure mathematics.

We must rid our minds of the idea that the word space in science has anything to do with *void*. As pre-viously explained it has the other meaning of distance, volume, etc., quantities expressing physical measure-ment just as much as force is a quantity expressing physical measurement. Thus the (rather crude) state-ment that Einstein's theory reduces gravitational force to a property of space ought not to arouse misgiving. In any case the physicist does not conceive of space as void. Where it is empty of all else there is still the aether. Those who for some reason dislike the word aether, scatter mathematical symbols freely through the vacuum, and I presume that they must conceive some kind of characteristic background for these symbols. I do not think any one proposes to build even so relative and elusive a thing as force out of entire nothingness.

Chapter VII

GRAVITATION—THE EXPLANATION

The Law of Curvature. Gravitation can be explained. Einstein's theory is not primarily an explanation of gravitation. When he tells us that the gravitational field corresponds to a curvature of space and time he is giving us a picture. Through a picture we gain the insight necessary to deduce the various observable consequences. There remains, however, a further question whether any reason can be given why the state of things pictured should exist. It is this further inquiry which is meant when we speak of "explaining" gravitation in any far-reaching sense.

At first sight the new picture does not leave very much to explain. It shows us an undulating hummocky world, whereas a gravitationless world would be plane and uniform. But surely a level lawn stands more in need of explanation than an undulating field, and a gravitationless world would be more difficult to account for than a world with gravitation. We are hardly called upon to account for a phenomenon which could only be absent if (in the building of the world) express precautions were taken to exclude it. If the curvature were entirely arbitrary this would be the end of the explanation; but there is a *law* of curvature—Einstein's law of gravitation—and on this law our further inquiry must be focussed. Explanation is needed for regularity, not for diversity; and our curiosity is roused, not by the diverse values of the ten subsidiary coefficients of curvature which differentiate the world from a flat world, but by the vanishing everywhere of the ten principal coefficients.

138

All explanations of gravitation on Newtonian lines have endeavoured to show why something (which I have disrespectfully called a demon) is *present* in the world. An explanation on the lines of Einstein's theory must show why something (which we call principal curvature) is *excluded* from the world.

In the last chapter the law of gravitation was stated in the form—the ten principal coefficients of curvature vanish in empty space. I shall now restate it in a slightly altered form—

The radius of spherical* curvature of every three-dimensional section of the world, cut in any direction at any point of empty space, is always the same constant length.

Besides the alteration of form there is actually a little difference of substance between the two enunciations; the second corresponds to a later and, it is believed, more accurate formula given by Einstein a year or two after his first theory. The modification is made necessary by our realisation that space is finite but unbounded (p. 80). The second enunciation would be exactly equivalent to the first if for "same constant length" we read "infinite length". Apart from very speculative estimates we do not know the constant length referred to, but it must certainly be greater than the distance of the furthest nebula, say 10^{20} miles. A distinction between so great a length and infinite length is unnecessary in most of our arguments and investigations, but it is necessary in the present chapter.

---

* Cylindrical curvature of the world has nothing to do with gravitation, nor so far as we know with any other phenomenon. Anything drawn on the surface of a cylinder can be unrolled into a flat map without distortion, but the curvature introduced in the last chapter was intended to account for the distortion which appears in our customary flat map; it is therefore curvature of the type exemplified by a sphere, not a cylinder.

We must try to reach the vivid significance which lies behind the obscure phraseology of the law. Suppose that you are ordering a concave mirror for a telescope. In order to obtain what you want you will have to specify two lengths (1) the aperture, and (2) the radius of curvature. These lengths both belong to the mirror— both are necessary to describe the kind of mirror you want to purchase—but they belong to it in different ways. You may order a mirror of 100 foot radius of curvature and yet receive it by parcel post. In a certain sense the 100 foot length travels with the mirror, but it does so in a way outside the cognizance of the postal authorities. The 100 foot length belongs especially to the surface of the mirror, a two-dimensional continuum; space-time is a four-dimensional continuum, and you will see from this analogy that there can be lengths belonging in this way to a chunk of space-time—lengths having nothing to do with the largeness or smallness of the chunk, but none the less part of the specification of the particular sample. Owing to the two extra dimensions there are many more such lengths associated with space-time than with the mirror surface. In particular, there is not only one general radius of spherical curvature, but a radius corresponding to any direction you like to take. For brevity I will call this the "directed radius" of the world. Suppose now that you order a chunk of space-time with a directed radius of 500 trillion miles in one direction and 800 trillion miles in another. Nature replies "No. We do not stock that. We keep a wide range of choice as regards other details of specification; but as regards directed radius we have nothing different in different directions, and in fact all our goods have the one standard radius, x trillion miles." I cannot tell you what number to put for x because that is still a secret of the firm.

The fact that this directed radius which, one would think, might so easily differ from point to point and from direction to direction, has only one standard value in the world is Einstein's law of gravitation. From it we can by rigorous mathematical deduction work out the motions of planets and predict, for example, the eclipses of the next thousand years; for, as already explained, the law of gravitation includes also the law of motion. Newton's law of gravitation is an approximate adaptation of it for practical calculation. Building up from the law all is clear; but what lies beneath it? Why is there this unexpected standardisation? That is what we must now inquire into.

Relativity of Length. There is no such thing as absolute length; we can only express the length of one thing in terms of the length of something else.* And so when we speak of the length of the directed radius we mean its length compared with the standard metre scale. Moreover, to make this comparison, the two lengths must lie alongside. Comparison at a distance is as unthinkable as action at a distance; more so, because comparison is a less vague conception than action. We must either convey the standard metre to the site of the length we are measuring, or we must use some device which, we are satisfied, will give the same result as if we actually moved the metre rod.

Now if we transfer the metre rod to another point of space and time, does it necessarily remain a metre long? Yes, of course it does; so long as it is the standard of length it cannot be anything else but a metre. But does it *really* remain the metre that it was? I do not know

---

* This relativity with respect to a standard unit is, of course, additional to and independent of the relativity with respect to the observer's motion treated in chapter II.

what you mean by the question; there is nothing by reference to which we could expose delinquencies of the standard rod, nothing by reference to which we could conceive the nature of the supposed delinquencies. Still the standard rod was chosen with considerable care; its material was selected to fulfil certain conditions—to be affected as little as possible by casual influences such as temperature, strain or corrosion, in order that its extension might depend only on the most essential characteristics of its surroundings, present and past.* We cannot say that it was chosen to keep the same absolute length since there is no such thing known; but it was

---

* In so far as these casual influences are not entirely eliminated by the selection of material and the precautions in using the rod, appropriate corrections must be applied. But the rod must not be corrected for *essential* characteristics of the space it is measuring. We correct the reading of a voltmeter for temperature, but it would be nonsensical to correct it for effects of the applied voltage. The distinction between casual and essential influences—those to be eliminated and those to be left in—depends on the intention of the measurements. The measuring rod is intended for surveying space, and the essential characteristic of space is "metric". It would be absurd to correct the readings of our scale to the values they would have had if the space had some other metric. The region of the world to which the metric refers may also contain an electric field; this will be regarded as a casual characteristic since the measuring rod is not intended for surveying electric fields. I do not mean that from a broader standpoint the electric field is any less essential to the region than its peculiar metric. It would be hard to say in what sense it would remain the same region if any of its qualities were other than they actually are. This point does not trouble us here, because there are vast regions of the world practically empty of all characteristics except metric, and it is to these that the law of gravitation is applied both in theory and in practice. It has seemed, however, desirable to dwell on this distinction between essential and casual characteristics because there are some who, knowing that we cannot avoid in all circumstances corrections for casual influences, regard that as license to adopt any arbitrary system of corrections—a procedure which would merely have the effect of concealing what the measures can teach us about essential characteristics.

chosen so that it might not be prevented by casual influences from keeping the same relative length—relative to what? *Relative to some length inalienably associated with the region in which it is placed.* I can conceive of no other answer. An example of such a length inalienably associated with a region is the directed radius.

The long and short of it is that when the standard metre takes up a new position or direction it measures itself against the directed radius of the world in that region and direction, and takes up an extension which is a definite fraction of the directed radius. I do not see what else it could do. We picture the rod a little bewildered in its new surroundings wondering how large it ought to be—how much of the unfamiliar territory its boundaries ought to take in. It wants to do just what it did before. Recollections of the chunk of space that it formerly filled do not help, because there is nothing of the nature of a landmark. The one thing it can recognise is a directed length belonging to the region where it finds itself; so it makes itself the same fraction of this directed length as it did before.

If the standard metre is always the same fraction of the directed radius, the directed radius is always the same number of metres. Accordingly the directed radius is made out to have the same length for all positions and directions. Hence we have the law of gravitation.

When we felt surprise at finding as a law of Nature that the directed radius of curvature was the same for all positions and directions, we did not realise that our unit of length had already made itself a constant fraction of the directed radius. The whole thing is a vicious circle. The law of gravitation is—a put-up job.

This explanation introduces no new hypothesis. In saying that a material system of standard specification always occupies a constant fraction of the directed radius of the region where it is, we are simply reiterating Einstein's law of gravitation—stating it in the inverse form. Leaving aside for the moment the question whether this behaviour of the rod is to be expected or not, the law of gravitation assures us that that is the behaviour. To see the force of the explanation we must, however, realise the relativity of extension. Extension which is not relative to something in the surroundings has no meaning. Imagine yourself alone in the midst of nothingness, and then try to tell me how large you are. The definiteness of extension of the standard rod can only be a definiteness of its ratio to some other extension. But we are speaking now of the extension of a rod placed in empty space, so that every standard of reference has been removed except extensions belonging to and implied by the metric of the region. It follows that one such extension must appear from our measurements to be constant everywhere (homogeneous and isotropic) on account of its constant relation to what we have accepted as the unit of length.

We approached the problem from the point of view that the actual world with its ten vanishing coefficients of curvature (or its isotropic directed curvature) has a specialisation which requires explanation; we were then comparing it in our minds with a world suggested by the pure mathematician which has entirely arbitrary curvature. But the fact is that a world of arbitrary curvature is a sheer impossibility. If not the directed radius, then some other directed length derivable from the metric, is bound to be homogeneous and isotropic. In applying the ideas of the pure mathematician we overlooked the fact that he was imagining a world surveyed from outside with standards foreign to it. whereas we have to do with a world surveyed from within with standards conformable to it.

The explanation of the law of gravitation thus lies in the fact that we are dealing with a world surveyed from within. From this broader standpoint the foregoing argument can be generalised so that it applies not only to a survey with metre rods but to a survey by optical methods, which in practice are generally substituted as equivalent. When we recollect that surveying apparatus can have no extension in itself but only in relation to the world, so that a survey of space is virtually a self-comparison of space, it is perhaps surprising that such a self-comparison should be able to show up any heterogeneity at all. It can in fact be proved that the metric of a two-dimensional or a three-dimensional world surveyed from within is necessarily uniform. With four or more dimensions heterogeneity becomes possible, but it is a heterogeneity limited by a law which imposes some measure of homogeneity.

I believe that this has a close bearing on the rather heterodox views of Dr. Whitehead on relativity. He breaks away from Einstein because he will not admit the non-uniformity of space-time involved in Einstein's theory. "I deduce that our experience requires and exhibits a basis of uniformity, and that in the case of nature this basis exhibits itself as the uniformity of spatio-temporal relations. This conclusion entirely cuts away the casual heterogeneity of these relations which is the essential of Einstein's later theory."* But we now see that Einstein's theory asserts a casual heterogeneity

* A. N. Whitehead, *The Principle of Relativity*, Preface.

of only one set of ten coefficients and complete uniformity of the other ten. It therefore does not leave us without the basis of uniformity of which Whitehead in his own way perceived the necessity. Moreover, this uniformity is not the result of a law casually imposed on the world; it is inseparable from the conception of survey of the world from within—which is, I think, just the condition that Whitehead would demand. If the world of space-time had been of two or of three dimensions Whitehead would have been entirely right; but then there could have been no Einstein theory of gravitation for him to criticise. Space-time being four-dimensional, we must conclude that Whitehead discovered an important truth about uniformity but misapplied it.

The conclusion that the extension of an object in any direction in the four-dimensional world is determined by comparison with the radius of curvature in that direction has one curious consequence. So long as the direction in the four-dimensional world is space-like, no difficulty arises. But when we pass over to time-like directions (within the cone of absolute past or future) the directed radius is an imaginary length. Unless the object ignores the warning symbol $\sqrt{-1}$ it has no standard of reference for settling its time extension. It has no standard duration. An electron decides how large it ought to be by measuring itself against the radius of the world in its space-directions. It cannot decide how long it ought to exist because there is no real radius of the world in its time-direction. *Therefore it just goes on existing indefinitely.* This is not intended to be a rigorous proof of the immortality of the electron—subject always to the condition imposed throughout these arguments that no agency other than metric interferes with the extension. But it shows that the electron behaves in the simple way which we might at least hope to find.*

Predictions from the Law.   I suppose that it is at first rather staggering to find a law supposed to control the movements of stars and planets turned into a law finicking with the behaviour of measuring rods.   But there is no prediction made by the law of gravitation in which the behaviour of measuring appliances does not play an essential part.   A typical prediction from the law is that on a certain date 384,400,000 metre rods laid end to end would stretch from the earth to the moon. We may use more circumlocutory language, but that is what is meant.   The fact that in testing the prediction we shall trust to indirect evidence, not carrying out the whole operation literally, is not relevant; the prophecy is made in good faith and not with the intention of taking advantage of our remissness in checking it.

We have condemned the law of gravitation as a put-up job.   You will want to know how after such a discreditable exposure it can still claim to predict eclipses and other events which come off.

A famous philosopher has said—

"The stars are not pulled this way and that by mechanical forces; theirs is a free motion.   They go on their way, as the ancients said, like the blessed gods." †

This sounds particularly foolish even for a philosopher; but I believe that there is a sense in which it is true.

* On the other hand a quantum (see chapter IX) has a definite periodicity associated with it, so that it must be able to measure itself against a time-extension.   Anyone who contemplates the mathematical equations of the new quantum theory will see abundant evidence of the battle with the intervening symbol $\sqrt{-1}$.

† Hegel, *Werke* (1842 Ed.), Bd. 7, Abt. 1, p. 97.

We have already had three versions of what the earth is trying to do when it describes its elliptic orbit around the sun.

(1) It is trying to go in a straight line but it is roughly pulled away by a tug emanating from the sun.

(2) It is taking the longest possible route through the curved space-time around the sun.

(3) It is accommodating its track so as to avoid causing any illegal kind of curvature in the empty space around it.

We now add a fourth version.

(4) The earth goes anyhow it likes.

It is not a long step from the third version to the fourth now that we have seen that the mathematical picture of empty space containing "illegal" curvature is a sheer impossibility in a world surveyed from within. For if illegal curvature is a sheer impossibility the earth will not have to take any special precautions to avoid causing it, and can do anything it likes. And yet the non-occurrence of this impossible curvature is the law (of gravitation) by which we calculate the track of the earth!

The key to the paradox is that we ourselves, our conventions, the kind of thing that attracts our interest, are much more concerned than we realise in any account we give of how the objects of the physical world are behaving. And so an object which, viewed through our frame of conventions, may seem to be behaving in a very special and remarkable way may, viewed according to another set of conventions, be doing nothing to excite particular comment. This will be clearer if we consider a practical illustration, and at the same time defend version (4).

You will say that the earth must certainly get into the right position for the eclipse next June (1927); so it cannot be free to go anywhere it pleases. I can put that right. I hold to it that the earth goes anywhere it pleases. The next thing is that *we* must find out where it has been pleased to go. The important question for us is not where the earth has got to in the inscrutable absolute behind the phenomena, but where we shall locate it in our conventional background of space and time. We must take measurements of its position, for

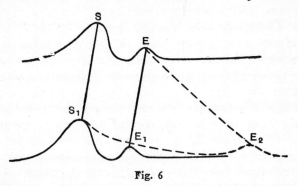

Fig. 6

example, measurements of its distance from the sun. In Fig. 6, SS_1 shows the ridge in the world which we recognise as the sun; I have drawn the earth's ridge in duplicate (EE_1, EE_2) because I imagine it as still undecided which track it will take. If it takes EE_1 we lay our measuring rods end to end down the ridges and across the valley from S_1 to E_1, count up the number, and report the result as the earth's distance from the sun. The measuring rods, you will remember, adjust their lengths proportionately to the radius of curvature of the world. The curvature along this contour is rather large and the radius of curvature small. The rods therefore are small, and there will be more of them in S_1E_1 than the picture would lead you to expect. If the earth chooses to go to E_2 the curvature is less sharp; the greater radius of curvature implies greater length of the rods. The number needed to stretch from S_1 to E_2 will not be so great as the diagram at first suggests; it will not be increased in anything like the proportion of S_1E_2 to S_1E_1 in the figure. We should not be surprised if the number turned out to be the same in both cases. If so, the surveyor will report the same distance of the earth from the sun whether the track is EE_1 or EE_2. And the Superintendent of the Nautical Almanac who published this same distance some years in advance will claim that he correctly predicted where the earth would go.

And so you see that the earth can play truant to any extent but our measurements will still report it in the place assigned to it by the Nautical Almanac. The predictions of that authority pay no attention to the vagaries of the god-like earth; they are based on what will happen when we come to measure up the path that it has chosen. We shall measure it with rods that adjust themselves to the curvature of the world. The mathematical expression of this fact is the law of gravitation used in the predictions.

Perhaps you will object that astronomers do not in practice lay measuring rods end to end through interplanetary space in order to find out where the planets are. Actually the position is deduced from the light rays. But the light as it proceeds has to find out what course to take in order to go "straight", in much the same way as the metre rod has to find out how far to extend. The metric or curvature is a sign-post for the light as it is a gauge for the rod. The light track is in fact controlled by the curvature in such a way that it is incapable of exposing the sham law of curvature. And so wherever the sun, moon and earth may have got to, the light will not give them away. If the law of curvature predicts an eclipse the light will take such a track that there is an eclipse. The law of gravitation is not a stern ruler controlling the heavenly bodies; it is a kind-hearted accomplice who covers up their delinquencies.

I do not recommend you to try to verify from Fig. 6 that the number of rods in S_1E_1 (full line) and S_1E_2 (dotted line) is the same. There are two dimensions of space-time omitted in the picture besides the extra dimensions in which space-time must be supposed to be bent; moreover it is the spherical, not the cylindrical, curvature which is the gauge for the length. It might be an instructive, though very laborious, task to make this direct verification, but we know beforehand that the measured distance of the earth from the sun must be the same for either track. The law of gravitation, expressed mathematically by $G_{\mu\nu} = \lambda g_{\mu\nu}$, means nothing more nor less than that the unit of length everywhere is a constant fraction of the directed radius of the world at that point. And as the astronomer who predicts the future position of the earth does not assume anything more about what the earth will choose to do than is expressed in the law $G_{\mu\nu} = \lambda g_{\mu\nu}$, so we shall find the same position of the earth, if we assume nothing more than that the practical unit of length involved in measurements of the position is a constant fraction of the directed radius. We do not need to decide whether the track is to be represented by EE_1 or EE_2, and it would convey no information as to any observable phenomena if we knew the representation.

I shall have to emphasise elsewhere that the whole of our physical knowledge is based on measures and that the physical world consists, so to speak, of measure-groups resting on a shadowy background that lies outside the scope of physics. Therefore in conceiving a world which had existence apart from the measurements that we make of it, I was trespassing outside the limits of what we call physical reality. I would not dissent from the view that a vagary which by its very nature could not be measurable has no claim to a physical existence. No one knows what is meant by such a vagary. I said that the earth might go anywhere it chose, but did not provide a "where" for it to choose; since our conception of "where" is based on space measurements which were at that stage excluded. But I do not think I have been illogical. I am urging that, do what it will, the earth cannot get out of the track laid down for it by the law of gravitation. In order to show this I must suppose that the earth has made the attempt and stolen nearer to the sun; then I show that our measures conspire quietly to locate it back in its proper orbit. I have to admit in the end that the earth never was out of its proper orbit;* I do not mind that, because meanwhile I have proved my point. The fact that a predictable path through space and time is laid down for the earth is not a genuine restriction on its conduct, but is imposed by the formal scheme in which we draw up our account of its conduct.

* Because I can attach no meaning to an orbit other than an orbit in space and time, i.e. as located by measures. But I could not assume that the alternative orbit would be meaningless (inconsistent with possible measures) until I tried it.

Non-Empty Space. The law that the directed radius is constant does not apply to space which is not completely empty. There is no longer any reason to expect it to hold. The statement that the region is not empty means that it has other characteristics besides metric, and the metre rod can then find other lengths besides curvatures to measure itself against. Referring to the earlier (sufficiently approximate) expression of the law, the ten principal coefficients of curvature are zero in empty space but have non-zero values in non-empty space. It is therefore natural to use these coefficients as *a measure of the fullness of space.*

One of the coefficients corresponds to mass (or energy) and in most practical cases it outweighs the others in importance. The old definition of mass as "quantity of matter" associates it with a fullness of space. Three other coefficients make up the momentum —a directed quantity with three independent components. The remaining six coefficients of principal curvature make up the stress or pressure-system. Mass, momentum and stress accordingly represent the non-emptiness of a region in so far as it is able to disturb the usual surveying apparatus with which we explore space—clocks, scales, light-rays, etc. It should be added, however, that this is a summary description and not a full account of the non-emptiness, because we have other exploring apparatus—magnets, electroscopes, etc.—which provide further details. It is usually considered that when we use these we are exploring not space, but a *field* in space. The distinction thus created is a rather artificial one which is unlikely to be accepted permanently. It would seem that the results of exploring the world with a measuring scale and a magnetic compass respectively ought to be welded together into a unified description, just as we have welded together results of exploration with a scale and a clock. Some progress has been made towards this unification. There is, however, a real reason for admitting a partially separate treatment; the one mode of exploration determines the symmetrical properties and the other the antisymmetrical properties of the underlying world-structure.*

Objection has often been taken, especially by philosophical writers, to the crudeness of Einstein's initial requisitions, viz. a clock and a measuring scale. But the body of experimental knowledge of the world which Einstein's theory seeks to set in order has not come into our minds as a heaven-sent inspiration; it is the result of a survey in which the clock and the scale have actually played the leading part. They may seem very gross instruments to those accustomed to the conceptions of atoms and electrons, but it is correspondingly gross knowledge that we have been discussing in the chapters concerned with Einstein's theory. As the relativity theory develops, it is generally found desirable to replace the clock and scale by the moving particle and light-ray as the primary surveying appliances; these are test bodies of simpler structure. But they are still gross compared with atomic phenomena. The light-ray, for instance, is not applicable to measurements so refined that the diffraction of light must be taken into account. Our knowledge of the external world cannot be divorced from the nature of the appliances with which we have obtained the knowledge. The truth of the law of gravitation cannot be regarded as subsisting apart from the experimental procedure by which we have ascertained its truth.

* See p. 236.

The conception of frames of space and time, and of the non-emptiness of the world described as energy, momentum, etc., is bound up with the survey by gross appliances. When they can no longer be supported by such a survey, the conceptions melt away into meaninglessness. In particular the interior of the atom could not conceivably be explored by a gross survey. We cannot put a clock or a scale into the interior of an atom. It cannot be too strongly insisted that the terms distance, period of time, mass, energy, momentum, etc., cannot be used in a description of an atom with the same meanings that they have in our gross experience. The atomic physicist who uses these terms must find his own meanings for them—must state the appliances which he requisitions when he imagines them to be measured. It is sometimes supposed that (in addition to electrical forces) there is a minute gravitational attraction between an atomic nucleus and the satellite electrons, obeying the same law as the gravitation between the sun and its planets. The supposition seems to me fantastic; but it is impossible to discuss it without any indication as to how the region within the atom is supposed to have been measured up. Apart from such measuring up the electron goes as it pleases "like the blessed gods".

We have reached a point of great scientific and philosophic interest. The ten principal coefficients of curvature of the world are not strangers to us; they are already familiar in scientific discussion under other names (energy, momentum, stress). This is comparable with a famous turning-point in the development of electromagnetic theory. The progress of the subject led to the consideration of waves of electric and magnetic force travelling through the aether; then it flashed upon

Maxwell that these waves were not strangers but were already familiar in our experience under the name of light. The method of identification is the same. It is calculated that electromagnetic waves will have just those properties which light is observed to have; so too it is calculated that the ten coefficients of curvature have just those properties which energy, momentum and stress are observed to have. We refer here to physical properties only. No physical theory is expected to explain why there is a particular kind of image in our minds associated with light, nor why a conception of substance has arisen in our minds in connection with those parts of the world containing mass.

This leads to a considerable simplification, because identity replaces causation. On the Newtonian theory no explanation of gravitation would be considered complete unless it described the mechanism by which a piece of matter gets a grip on the surrounding medium and makes it the carrier of the gravitational influence radiating from the matter. Nothing corresponding to this is required in the present theory. We do not ask how mass gets a grip on space-time and causes the curvature which our theory postulates. That would be as superfluous as to ask how light gets a grip on the electromagnetic medium so as to cause it to oscillate. The light *is* the oscillation; the mass *is* the curvature. There is no causal effect to be attributed to mass; still less is there any to be attributed to matter. The conception of matter, which we associate with these regions of unusual contortion, is a monument erected by the mind to mark the scene of conflict. When you visit the site of a battle, do you ever ask how the monument that commemorates it can have caused so much carnage?

The philosophic outcome of this identification will

occupy us considerably in later chapters. Before leaving the subject of gravitation I wish to say a little about the meaning of space-curvature and non-Euclidean geometry.

Non-Euclidean Geometry. I have been encouraging you to think of space-time as curved; but I have been careful to speak of this as a picture, not as a hypothesis. It is a graphical representation of the things we are talking about which supplies us with insight and guidance. What we glean from the picture can be expressed in a more non-committal way by saying that space-time has non-Euclidean geometry. The terms "curved space" and "non-Euclidean space" are used practically synonymously; but they suggest rather different points of view. When we were trying to conceive finite and unbounded space (p. 81) the difficult step was the getting rid of the inside and the outside of the hypersphere. There is a similar step in the transition from curved space to non-Euclidean space—the dropping of all relations to an external (and imaginary) scaffolding and the holding on to those relations which exist *within* the space itself.

If you ask what is the distance from Glasgow to New York there are two possible replies. One man will tell you the distance measured over the surface of the ocean; another will recollect that there is a still shorter distance by tunnel through the earth. The second man makes use of a dimension which the first had put out of mind. But if two men do not agree as to distances, they will not agree as to geometry; for geometry treats of the laws of distances. To forget or to be ignorant of a dimension lands us into a different geometry. Distances for the second man obey a Euclidean geometry of three dimensions; distances for the first man obey a non-Euclidean geometry of two dimensions. And so if you concentrate your attention on the earth's surface so hard that you forget that there is an inside or an outside to it, you will say that it is a two-dimensional manifold with non-Euclidean geometry; but if you recollect that there is three-dimensional space all round which affords shorter ways of getting from point to point, you can fly back to Euclid after all. You will then "explain away" the non-Euclidean geometry by saying that what you at first took for distances were not the proper distances. This seems to be the easiest way of seeing how a non-Euclidean geometry can arise— through mislaying a dimension—but we must not infer that non-Euclidean geometry is impossible unless it arises from this cause.

In our four-dimensional world pervaded by gravitation the distances obey a non-Euclidean geometry. Is this because we are concentrating attention wholly on its four dimensions and have missed the short cuts through regions beyond? By the aid of six extra dimensions we can return to Euclidean geometry; in that case our usual distances from point to point in the world are not the "true" distances, the latter taking shorter routes through an eighth or ninth dimension. To bend the world in a super-world of ten dimensions so as to provide these short cuts does, I think, help us to form an idea of the properties of its non-Euclidean geometry; at any rate the picture suggests a useful vocabulary for describing those properties. But we are not likely to accept these extra dimensions as a literal fact unless we regard non-Euclidean geometry as a thing which at all costs must be explained away.

Of the two alternatives—a curved manifold in a Euclidean space of ten dimensions or a manifold with non-Euclidean geometry and no extra dimensions—which is right? I would rather not attempt a direct answer, because I fear I should get lost in a fog of metaphysics. But I may say at once that I do not take the ten dimensions seriously; whereas I take the non-Euclidean geometry of the world very seriously, and I do not regard it as a thing which needs explaining away. The view, which some of us were taught at school, that the truth of Euclid's axioms can be seen intuitively, is universally rejected nowadays. We can no more settle the laws of space by intuition than we can settle the laws of heredity. If intuition is ruled out, the appeal must be to experiment—genuine open-minded experiment unfettered by any preconception as to what the verdict ought to be. We must not afterwards go back on the experiments because they make out space to be very slightly non-Euclidean. It is quite true that a way out could be found. By inventing extra dimensions we can make the non-Euclidean geometry of the world depend on a Euclidean geometry of ten dimensions; had the world proved to be Euclidean we could, I believe, have made its geometry depend on a non-Euclidean geometry of ten dimensions. No one would treat the latter suggestion seriously, and no reason can be given for treating the former more seriously.

I do not think that the six extra dimensions have any stalwart defenders; but we often meet with attempts to reimpose Euclidean geometry on the world in another way. The proposal, which is made quite unblushingly, is that since our measured lengths do not obey Euclidean geometry we must apply corrections to them—cook them —till they do. A closely related view often advocated is that space is neither Euclidean nor non-Euclidean; it is all a matter of convention and we are free to adopt any geometry we choose.* Naturally if we hold ourselves free to apply any correction we like to our experimental measures we can make them obey any law; but was it worth while saying this? The assertion that any kind of geometry is permissible could only be made on the assumption that lengths have no fixed value—that the physicist does not (or ought not to) mean anything in particular when he talks of length. I am afraid I shall have a difficulty in making my meaning clear to those who start from the assumption that my words mean nothing in particular; but for those who will accord them some meaning I will try to remove any possible doubt. The physicist is accustomed to state lengths to a great number of significant figures; to ascertain the significance of these lengths we must notice how they are derived; and we find that they are derived from a comparison with the extension of a standard of specified material constitution. (We may pause to notice that the extension of a standard material configuration may rightly be regarded as one of the earliest subjects of inquiry in a physical survey of our environment.) These lengths are a gateway through which knowledge of the world around us is sought. Whether or not they will remain prominent in the final picture of world-structure will transpire as the research proceeds; we do not prejudge that. Actually we soon find that space-lengths or time-lengths taken singly are relative, and only

---

* As a recent illustration of this attitude I may refer to Bertrand Russell's *Analysis of Matter*, p. 78—a book with which I do not often seriously disagree. "Whereas Eddington seems to regard it as necessary to adopt Einstein's variable space, Whitehead regards it as necessary to reject it. For my part, I do not see why we should agree with either view; the matter seems to be one of convenience in the interpretation of formulae." Russell's view is commended in a review by C. D. Broad. See also *footnote*, p. 142.

a combination of them could be expected to appear even in the humblest capacity in the ultimate world-structure. Meanwhile the first step through the gateway takes us to the geometry obeyed by these lengths —very nearly Euclidean, but actually non-Euclidean and, as we have seen, a distinctive type of non-Euclidean geometry in which the ten principal coefficients of curvature vanish. We have shown in this chapter that the limitation is not arbitrary; it is a necessary property of lengths expressed in terms of the extension of a material standard, though it might have been surprising if it had occurred in lengths defined otherwise. Must we stop to notice the interjection that if we had meant something different by length we should have found a different geometry? Certainly we should; and if we had meant something different by electric force we should have found equations different from Maxwell's equations. Not only empirically but also by theoretical reasoning, we reach the geometry which we do because our lengths mean what they do.

I have too long delayed dealing with the criticism of the pure mathematician who is under the impression that geometry is a subject that belongs entirely to him. Each branch of experimental knowledge tends to have associated with it a specialised body of mathematical investigations. The pure mathematician, at first called in as servant, presently likes to assert himself as master; the connexus of mathematical propositions becomes for him the main subject, and he does not ask permission from Nature when he wishes to vary or generalise the original premises. Thus he can arrive at a geometry unhampered by any restriction from actual space measures; a potential theory unhampered by any question as to how gravitational and electrical potentials really behave; a hydrodynamics of perfect fluids doing things which it would be contrary to the nature of any material fluid to do. But it seems to be only in geometry that he has forgotten that there ever was a physical subject of the same name, and even resents the application of the name to anything but his network of abstract mathematics. I do not think it can be disputed that, both etymologically and traditionally, geometry is the science of measurement of the space around us; and however much the mathematical superstructure may now overweigh the observational basis, it is properly speaking an experimental science. This is fully recognised in the "reformed" teaching of geometry in schools; boys are taught to verify by measurement that certain of the geometrical propositions are true or nearly true. No one questions the advantage of an unfettered development of geometry as a pure mathematical subject; but only in so far as this subject is linked to the quantities arising out of observation and measurement, will it find mention in a discussion of the Nature of the Physical World.

Chapter VIII

MAN'S PLACE IN THE UNIVERSE

The Sidereal Universe. The largest telescopes reveal about a thousand million stars. Each increase in telescopic power adds to the number and we can scarcely set a limit to the multitude that must exist. Nevertheless there are signs of exhaustion, and it is clear that the distribution which surrounds us does not extend uniformly through infinite space. At first an increase in light-grasp by one magnitude brings into view three times as many stars; but the factor diminishes so that at the limit of faintness reached by the giant telescopes a gain of one magnitude multiplies the number of stars seen by only 1.8, and the ratio at that stage is rapidly decreasing. It is as though we are approaching a limit at which increase of power will not bring into view very many additional stars.

Attempts have been made to find the whole number of stars by a risky extrapolation of these counts, and totals ranging from 3000 to 30,000 millions are sometimes quoted. But the difficulty is that the part of the stellar universe which we mainly survey is a local condensation or star-cloud forming part of a much greater system. In certain directions in the sky our telescopes penetrate to the limits of the system, but in other directions the extent is too great for us to fathom. The Milky Way, which on a dark night forms a gleaming belt round the sky, shows the direction in which there lie stars behind stars until vision fails. This great flattened distribution is called the Galactic System. It forms a disc of thickness small compared to its areal extent. It is partly broken up into subordinate condensations, which are probably coiled in spiral form like the spiral nebulae which are observed in great numbers in the heavens. The centre of the galactic system lies somewhere in the direction of the constellation Sagittarius; it is hidden from us not only by great distance but also to some extent by tracts of obscuring matter (dark nebulosity) which cuts off the light of the stars behind.

We must distinguish then between our local star-cloud and the great galactic system of which it is a part. Mainly (but not exclusively) the star-counts relate to the local star-cloud, and it is this which the largest telescopes are beginning to exhaust. It too has a flattened form—flattened nearly in the same plane as the galactic system. If the galactic system is compared to a disc, the local star-cloud may be compared to a bun, its thickness being about one-third of its lateral extension. Its size is such that light takes at least 2000 years to cross from one side to the other; this measurement is necessarily rough because it relates to a vague condensation which is probably not sharply separated from other contiguous condensations. The extent of the whole spiral is of the order 100,000 light years. It can scarcely be doubted that the flattened form of the system is due to rapid rotation, and indeed there is direct evidence of strong rotational velocity; but it is one of the unexplained mysteries of evolution that nearly all celestial bodies have come to be endowed with fast rotation.

Amid this great population the sun is a humble unit. It is a very ordinary star about midway in the scale of brilliancy. We know of stars which give at least 10,000 times the light of the sun; we know also of stars which give 1/10,000 of its light. But those of inferior light greatly outnumber those of superior light. In mass, in surface temperature, in bulk, the sun belongs to a very common class of stars; its speed of motion is near the average; it shows none of the more conspicuous phenomena such as variability which excite the attention of astronomers. In the community of stars the sun corresponds to a respectable middle-class citizen. It happens to be quite near the centre of the local star-cloud; but this apparently favoured position is discounted by the fact that the star-cloud itself is placed very eccentrically in relation to the galactic system, being in fact near the confines of it. We cannot claim to be at the hub of the universe.

The contemplation of the galaxy impresses us with the insignificance of our own little world; but we have to go still lower in the valley of humiliation. The galactic system is one among a million or more spiral nebulae. There seems now to be no doubt that, as has long been suspected, the spiral nebulae are "island universes" detached from our own. They too are great systems of stars—or systems in the process of developing into stars—built on the same disc-like plan. We see some of them edgeways and can appreciate the flatness of the disc; others are broadside on and show the arrangement of the condensations in the form of a double spiral. Many show the effects of dark nebulosity breaking into the regularity and blotting out the starlight. In a few of the nearest spirals it is possible to detect the brightest of the stars individually; variable stars and novae (or "new stars") are observed as in our own system. From the apparent magnitudes of the stars of recognisable character (especially the Cepheid variables) it is possible to judge the distance. The nearest spiral nebula is 850,000 light years away.

From the small amount of data yet collected it would seem that our own nebula or galactic system is exceptionally large; it is even suggested that if the spiral nebulae are "islands" the galactic system is a "continent". But we can scarcely venture to claim premier rank without much stronger evidence. At all events these other universes are aggregations of the order of 100 million stars.

Again the question raises itself, How far does this distribution extend? Not the stars this time but universes stretch one behind the other beyond sight. Does this distribution too come to an end? It may be that imagination must take another leap, envisaging supersystems which surpass the spiral nebulae as the spiral nebulae surpass the stars. But there is one feeble gleam of evidence that perhaps this time the summit of the hierarchy has been reached, and that the system of the spirals is actually the whole world. As has already been explained the modern view is that space is finite—finite though unbounded. In such a space light which has travelled an appreciable part of the way "round the world" is slowed down in its vibrations, with the result that all spectral lines are displaced towards the red. Ordinarily we interpret such a red displacement as signifying receding velocity in the line of sight. Now it is a striking fact that a great majority of the spirals which have been measured show large receding velocities often exceeding 1000 kilometres per second. There are only two serious exceptions, and these are the largest spirals which must be nearer to us than most of the others. On ordinary grounds it would be difficult to explain why these other universes should hurry away from us so fast and so unanimously. Why should they shun us like a plague? But the phenomenon is intelligible if what has really been observed is the slowing down of vibrations consequent on the light from these objects having travelled an appreciable part of the way round the world. On that theory the radius of space is of the order twenty times the average distance of the nebulae observed, or say 100 million light years. That leaves room for a few million spirals; but there is nothing beyond. There is no beyond—in spherical space "beyond" brings us back towards the earth from the opposite direction.*

The Scale of Time. The corridor of time stretches back through the past. We can have no conception how it all began. But at some stage we imagine the void to have been filled with matter rarified beyond the most tenuous nebula. The atoms sparsely strewn move hither and thither in formless disorder.

> Behold the throne
> Of Chaos and his dark pavilion spread
> Wide on the wasteful deep.

Then slowly the power of gravitation is felt. Centres of condensation begin to establish themselves and draw in other matter. The first partitions are the star-systems such as our galactic system; sub-condensations separate the star-clouds or clusters; these divide again to give the stars.

Evolution has not reached the same development in

---

* A very much larger radius of space (10^{11} light years) has recently been proposed by Hubble; but the basis of his calculation, though concerned with spiral nebulae, is different and to my mind unacceptable. It rests on an earlier theory of closed space proposed by Einstein which has generally been regarded as superseded. The theory given above (due to W. de Sitter) is, of course, very speculative, but it is the only clue we possess as to the dimensions of space.

all parts. We observe nebulae and clusters in different stages of advance. Some stars are still highly diffuse; others are concentrated like the sun with density greater than water; others, still more advanced, have shrunk to unimaginable density. But no doubt can be entertained that the genesis of the stars is a single process of evolution which has passed and is passing over a primordial distribution. Formerly it was freely speculated that the birth of a star was an individual event like the birth of an animal. From time to time two long extinct stars would collide and be turned into vapour by the energy of the collision; condensation would follow and life as a luminous body would begin all over again. We can scarcely affirm that this will never occur and that the sun is not destined to have a second or third innings; but it is clear from the various relations traced among the stars that the present stage of existence of the sidereal universe is the *first innings*. Groups of stars are found which move across the sky with common proper motion; these must have had a single origin and cannot have been formed by casual collisions. Another abandoned speculation is that lucid stars may be the exception, and that there may exist thousands of dead stars for every one that is seen shining. There are ways of estimating the total mass in interstellar space by its gravitational effect on the average speed of the stars; it is found that the lucid stars account for something approaching the total mass admissible and the amount left over for dark stars is very limited.

Biologists and geologists carry back the history of the earth some thousand million years. Physical evidence based on the rate of transmutation of radioactive substances seems to leave no escape from the conclusion that the older (Archaean) rocks in the earth's crust were laid down 1200 million years ago. The sun must have been burning still longer, living (we now think) on its own matter which dissolves bit by bit into radiation. According to the theoretical time-scale, which seems best supported by astronomical evidence, the beginning of the sun as a luminous star must be dated five billion ($5 \cdot 10^{12}$) years ago. The theory which assigns this date cannot be trusted confidently, but it seems a reasonably safe conclusion that the sun's age does not exceed this limit. The future is not so restricted and the sun may continue as a star of increasing feebleness for 50 or 500 billion years. The theory of sub-atomic energy has prolonged the life of a star from millions to billions of years, and we may speculate on processes of rejuvenescence which might prolong the existence of the sidereal universe from billions to trillions of years. But unless we can circumvent the second law of thermodynamics—which is as much as to say unless we can find cause for time to run backwards—the ultimate decay draws surely nearer and the world will at the last come to a state of uniform changelessness.

Does this prodigality of matter, of space, of time, find its culmination in Man?

Plurality of Worlds. I will here put together the present astronomical evidence as to the habitability of other worlds. The popular idea that an answer to this question is one of the main aims of the study of celestial objects is rather disconcerting to the astronomer. Anything that he has to contribute is of the nature of fragmentary hints picked up in the course of investigations with more practicable and commonplace purposes. Nevertheless, the mind is irresistibly drawn to play with the thought that somewhere in the universe there **may** be other beings "a little lower than the angels" whom Man may regard as his equals—or perhaps his superiors.

It is idle to guess the forms that life might take in conditions differing from those of our planet. If I have rightly understood the view of palaeontologists, mammalian life is the third terrestrial dynasty—Nature's third attempt to evolve an order of life sufficiently flexible to changing conditions and fitted to dominate the earth. Minor details in the balance of circumstances must greatly affect the possibility of life and the type of organism destined to prevail. Some critical branch-point in the course of evolution must be negotiated before life can rise to the level of consciousness. All this is remote from the astronomer's line of study. To avoid endless conjecture I shall assume that the required conditions of habitability are not unlike those on the earth, and that if such conditions obtain life will automatically make its appearance.

We survey first the planets of the solar system; of these only Venus and Mars seem at all eligible. Venus, so far as we know, would be well adapted for life similar to ours. It is about the same size as the earth, nearer the sun but probably not warmer, and it possesses an atmosphere of satisfactory density. Spectroscopic observation has unexpectedly failed to give any indication of oxygen in the upper atmosphere and thus suggests a doubt as to whether free oxygen exists on the planet; but at present we hesitate to draw so definite an inference. If transplanted to Venus we might perhaps continue to live without much derangement of habit—except that I personally would have to find a new profession, since Venus is not a good place for astronomers.

It is completely covered with cloud or mist. For this reason no definite surface markings can be made out, and it is still uncertain how fast it rotates on its axis and in which direction the axis lies. One curious theory may be mentioned though it should perhaps not be taken too seriously. It is thought by some that the great cavity occupied by the Pacific Ocean is a scar left by the moon when it was first disrupted from the earth. Evidently this cavity fulfils an important function in draining away superfluous water, and if it were filled up practically all the continental area would be submerged. Thus indirectly the existence of dry land is bound up with the existence of the moon. But Venus has no moon, and since it seems to be similar to the earth in other respects, it may perhaps be inferred that it is a world which is all ocean—where fishes are supreme. The suggestion at any rate serves to remind us that the destinies of organic life may be determined by what are at first sight irrelevant accidents.

The sun is an ordinary star and the earth is an ordinary planet, but the moon is not an ordinary satellite. No other known satellite is anything like so large in proportion to the planet which it attends. The moon contains about 1/80 part of the mass of the earth which seems a small ratio; but it is abnormally great compared with other satellites. The next highest ratio is found in the system of Saturn whose largest satellite Titan has 1/4000 of the planet's mass. Very special circumstances must have occurred in the history of the earth to have led to the breaking away of so unusual a fraction of the mass. The explanation proposed by Sir George Darwin, which is still regarded as most probable, is that a resonance in period occurred between the solar tides and the natural free period of vibration of the globe of the earth. The tidal deformation of the earth thus grew to large amplitude, ending in a cataclysm which separated the great lump of material that formed the moon. Other planets escaped this dangerous coincidence of period, and their satellites separated by more normal development. If ever I meet a being who has lived in another world, I shall feel very humble in most respects, but I expect to be able to boast a little about the moon.

Mars is the only planet whose solid surface can be seen and studied; and it tempts us to consider the possibility of life in more detail. Its smaller size leads to considerably different conditions; but the two essentials, air and water, are both present though scanty. The Martian atmosphere is thinner than our own but it is perhaps adequate. It has been proved to contain oxygen. There is no ocean; the surface markings represent, not sea and land, but red desert and darker ground which is perhaps moist and fertile. A conspicuous feature is the white cap covering the pole which is clearly a deposit of snow; it must be quite shallow since it melts away completely in the summer. Photographs show from time to time indubitable clouds which blot out temporarily large areas of surface detail; clear weather, however, is more usual. The air, if cloudless, is slightly hazy. W. H. Wright has shown this very convincingly by comparing photographs taken with light of different wave-lengths. Light of short wave-length is much scattered by haze and accordingly the ordinary photographs are disappointingly blurry. Much sharper surface-detail is shown when visual yellow light is employed (a yellow screen being commonly used to adapt visual telescopes for photography); being of longer wave-length the visual rays penetrate the haze more easily.*   Still clearer detail is obtained by photographing with the long infra-red waves.

Great attention has lately been paid to the determination of the temperature of the surface of Mars; it is possible to find this by direct measurement of the heat rediated to us from different parts of the surface. The results, though in many respects informative, are scarcely accurate and accordant enough to give a definite idea of the climatology. Naturally the temperature varies a great deal between day and night and in different latitudes; but on the average the conditions are decidedly chilly. Even at the equator the temperature falls below freezing point at sunset. If we accepted the present determinations as definitive we should have some doubt as to whether life could endure the conditions.

In one of Huxley's Essays there occurs the passage "Until human life is longer and the duties of the present press less heavily I do not think that wise men will occupy themselves with Jovian or Martian natural history." To-day it would seem that Martian natural history is not altogether beyond the limits of serious science. At least the surface of Mars shows a seasonal change such as we might well imagine the forest-clad earth would show to an outside onlooker. This seasonal change of appearance is very conspicuous to the attentive observer. As the spring in one hemisphere advances (I mean, of course, the Martian spring), the darker areas, which are at first few and faint, extend and deepen in contrast. The same regions darken year after

---

* It seems to have been a fortunate circumstance that the pioneers of Martian photography had no suitable photographic telescopes and had to adapt visual telescopes—thus employing visual (yellow) light which, as it turned out, was essential for good results.

year at nearly the same date in the Martian calendar. It may be that there is an inorganic explanation; the spring rains moisten the surface and change its colour. But it is perhaps unlikely that there is enough rain to bring about this change as a direct effect. It is easier to believe that we are witnessing the annual awakening of vegetation so familiar on our own planet.

The existence of oxygen in the Martian atmosphere supplies another argument in support of the existence of vegetable life. Oxygen combines freely with many elements, and the rocks in the earth's crust are thirsty for oxygen. They would in course of time bring about its complete disappearance from the air, were it not that the vegetation extracts it from the soil and sets it free again. If oxygen in the terrestrial atmosphere is maintained in this way, it would seem reasonable to assume that vegetable life is required to play the same part on Mars. Taking this in conjunction with the evidence of the seasonal changes of appearance, a rather strong case for the existence of vegetation seems to have been made out.

If vegetable life must be admitted, can we exclude animal life? I have come to the end of the astronomical data and can take no responsibility for anything further that you may infer. It is true that the late Prof. Lowell argued that certain more or less straight markings on the planet represent an artificial irrigation system and are the signs of an advanced civilisation; but this theory has not, I think, won much support. In justice to the author of this speculation it should be said that his own work and that of his observatory have made a magnificent contribution to our knowledge of Mars; but few would follow him all the way on the more picturesque side of his conclusions.* Finally we may stress one point. Mars has every appearance of being a planet long past its prime; and it is in any case improbable that two planets differing so much as Mars and the Earth would be in the zenith of biological development contemporaneously.

Formation of Planetary Systems. If the planets of the solar system should fail us, there remain some thousands of millions of stars which we have been accustomed to regard as suns ruling attendant systems of planets. It has seemed a presumption, bordering almost on impiety, to deny to them life of the same order of creation as ourselves. It would indeed be rash to assume that nowhere else in the universe has Nature repeated the strange experiment which she has performed on the earth. But there are considerations which must hold us back from populating the universe too liberally.

On examining the stars with a telescope we are surprised to find how many of those which appear single points to the eye are actually two stars close together. When the telescope fails to separate them the spectroscope often reveals two stars in orbital revolution round each other. At least one star in three is double—a pair of self-luminous globes both comparable in dimensions with the sun. The single supreme sun is accordingly not the only product of evolution; not much less frequently the development has taken another turn and resulted in two suns closely associated. We may probably rule out the possibility of planets in double stars.

---

*Mars is not seen under favourable conditions except from low latitudes and high altitudes. Astronomers who have not these advantages are reluctant to form a decided opinion on the many controversial points that have arisen.

Not only is there a difficulty in ascribing to them permanent orbits under the more complicated field of gravitation, but a cause for the formation of planets seems to be lacking. The star has satisfied its impulse to fission in another manner; it has divided into two nearly equal portions instead of throwing off a succession of tiny fragments.

The most obvious cause of division is excessive rotation. As the gaseous globe contracts it spins fast and faster until a time may come when it can no longer hold together, and some kind of relief must be found. According to the nebular hypothesis of Laplace the sun gained relief by throwing off successively rings of matter which have formed the planets. But were it not for this one instance of a planetary system which is known to us, we should have concluded from the thousands of double stars in the sky that the common consequence of excessive rotation is to divide the star into two bodies of equal rank.

It might still be held that the ejection of a planetary system and the fission into a double star are alternative solutions of the problem arising from excessive rotation, the star taking one course or the other according to circumstances. We know of myriads of double stars and of only one planetary system; but in any case it is beyond our power to detect other planetary systems if they exist. We can only appeal to the results of theoretical study of rotating masses of gas; the work presents many complications and the results may not be final; but the researches of Sir J. H. Jeans lead to the conclusion that rotational break-up produces a double star and never a system of planets. The solar system is not the typical product of development of a star; it is not even a common variety of development; it is a freak

By elimination of alternatives it appears that a configuration resembling the solar system would only be formed if at a certain stage of condensation an unusual accident had occurred. According to Jeans the accident was the close approach of another star casually pursuing its way through space. This star must have passed within a distance not far outside the orbit of Neptune; it must not have passed too rapidly, but have slowly overtaken or been overtaken by the sun. By tidal distortion it raised big protuberances on the sun, and caused it to spurt out filaments of matter which have condensed to form the planets. That was more than a thousand million years ago. The intruding star has since gone on its way and mingled with the others; its legacy of a system of planets remains, including a globe habitable by man.

Even in the long life of a star encounters of this kind must be extremely rare. The density of distribution of stars in space has been compared to that of twenty tennis-balls roaming the whole interior of the earth. The accident that gave birth to the solar system may be compared to the casual approach of two of these balls within a few yards of one another. The data are too vague to give any definite estimate of the odds against this occurence, but I should judge that perhaps not one in a hundred millions of stars can have undergone this experience in the right stage and conditions to result in the formation of a system of planets.

However doubtful this conclusion as to the rarity of solar systems may be, it is a useful corrective to the view too facilely adopted which looks upon every star as a likely minister ·to life. We know the prodigality of Nature. How many acorns are scattered for one that grows to an oak? And need she be more careful of her stars than of her acorns? If indeed she has no grander aim than to provide a home for her greatest experiment, Man, it would be just like her methods to scatter a million stars whereof one might haply achieve her purpose.

The number of possible abodes of life severely restricted in this way at the outset may no doubt be winnowed down further. On our house-hunting expedition we shall find it necessary to reject many apparently eligible mansions on points of detail. Trivial circumstances may decide whether organic forms originate at all; further conditions may decide whether life ascends to a complexity like ours or remains in a lower form. I presume, however, that at the end of the weeding out there will be left a few rival earths dotted here and there about the universe.

A further point arises if we have especially in mind contemporaneous life. The time during which man has been on the earth is extremely small compared with the age of the earth or of the sun. There is no obvious physical reason why, having once arrived, man should not continue to populate the earth for another ten billion years or so; but—well, can you contemplate it? Assuming that the stage of highly developed life is a very small fraction of the inorganic history of the star, the rival earths are in general places where conscious life has already vanished or is yet to come. I do not think that the whole purpose of the Creation has been staked on the one planet where we live; and in the long run we cannot deem ourselves the only race that has been or will be gifted with the mystery of consciousness. But I feel inclined to claim that *at the present time* our race is supreme; and not one of the profusion of stars in their myriad clusters looks down on scenes comparable to those which are passing beneath the rays of the sun.

Chapter IX

THE QUANTUM THEORY

The Origin of the Trouble. Nowadays whenever enthusiasts meet together to discuss theoretical physics the talk sooner or later turns in a certain direction. You leave them conversing on their special problems or the latest discoveries; but return after an hour and it is any odds that they will have reached an all-engrossing topic —the desperate state of their ignorance. This is not a pose. It is not even scientific modesty, because the attitude is often one of naïve surprise that Nature should have hidden her fundamental secret successfully from such powerful intellects as ours. It is simply that we have turned a corner in the path of progress and our ignorance stands revealed before us, appalling and insistent. There is something radically wrong with the present fundamental conceptions of physics and we do not see how to set it right.

The cause of all this trouble is a little thing called h which crops up continually in a wide range of experiments. In one sense we know just what h is, because there are a variety of ways of measuring it; h is

.00000000000000000000000000655 erg-seconds.

That will (rightly) suggest to you that h is something very small; but the most important information is contained in the concluding phrase erg-seconds. The erg is the unit of energy and the second is the unit of time; so that we learn that h is of the nature of energy multiplied by time.

Now in practical life it does not often occur to us to

multiply energy by time.   We often *divide* energy by time.   For example, the motorist divides the output of energy of his engine by time and so obtains the horse-power.   Conversely an electric supply company multiplies the horse-power or kilowatts by the number of hours of consumption and sends in its bill accordingly. But to multiply by hours again would seem a very odd sort of thing to do.

But it does not seem quite so strange when we look at it in the absolute four-dimensional world.   Quantities such as energy, which we think of as existing at an instant, belong to three-dimensional space, and they need to be multiplied by a duration to give them a thickness before they can be put into the four-dimensional world. Consider a portion of space, say Great Britain; we should describe the amount of humanity in it as 40 million men.   But consider a portion of space-time, say Great Britain between 1915 and 1925; we must describe the amount of humanity in it as 400 million *man-years*. To describe the human content of the world from a space-time point of view we have to take a unit which is limited not only in space but in time.   Similarly if some other kind of content of space is described as so many ergs, the corresponding content of a region of space-time will be described as so many erg-seconds.

We call this quantity in the four-dimensional world which is the analogue or adaptation of energy in the three-dimensional world by the technical name *action*.   The name does not seem to have any special appropriateness, but we have to accept it.   Erg-seconds or action belongs to Minkowski's world which is common to all observers, and so it is absolute.   It is one of the very few absolute quantities noticed in pre-relativity physics.   Except for action and entropy (which belongs to an entirely different

class of physical conceptions) all the quantities prominent in pre-relativity physics refer to the three-dimensional sections which are different for different observers.

Long before the theory of relativity showed us that
action was likely to have a special importance in the
scheme of Nature on account of its absoluteness, long
before the particular piece of action h began to turn up
in experiments, the investigators of theoretical dynamics
were making great use of action. It was especially the
work of Sir William Hamilton which brought it to the
fore; and since then very extensive theoretical developments of dynamics have been made on this basis.   I
need only refer to the standard treatise on Analytical
Dynamics by your own (Edinburgh) Professor*, which
fairly reeks of it. It was not difficult to appreciate the
fundamental importance and significance of the main
principle; but it must be confessed that to the non-
specialist the interest of the more elaborate developments did not seem very obvious—except as an ingenious
way of making easy things difficult.   In the end the
instinct which led to these researches has justified itself
emphatically.   To follow any of the progress in the
quantum theory of the atom since about 1917, it is
necessary to have plunged rather deeply into the Hamiltonian theory of dynamics.   It is remarkable that just
as Einstein found ready prepared by the mathematicians
the Tensor Calculus which he needed for developing
his great theory of gravitation, so the quantum physicists
found ready for them an extensive action-theory of
dynamics without which they could not have made head-
way.

But neither the absolute importance of action in the
four-dimensional world, nor its earlier prominence in

* Prof. E. T. Whittaker.

Hamiltonian dynamics, prepares us for the discovery that a particular lump of it can have a special importance. And yet a lump of standard size $6.55 \cdot 10^{-27}$ erg-seconds is continually turning up experimentally. It is all very well to say that we must think of action as atomic and regard this lump as the atom of action. We cannot do it. We have been trying hard for the last ten years. Our present picture of the world shows action in a form quite incompatible with this kind of atomic structure, and the picture will have to be redrawn. There must in fact be a radical change in the fundamental conceptions on which our scheme of physics is founded; the problem is to discover the particular change required. Since 1925 new ideas have been brought into the subject which seem to make the deadlock less complete, and give us an inkling of the nature of the revolution that must come; but there has been no general solution of the difficulty. The new ideas will be the subject of the next chapter. Here it seems best to limit ourselves to the standpoint of 1925, except at the very end of the chapter, where we prepare for the transition.

The Atom of Action. Remembering that action has two ingredients, namely, energy and time, we must look about in Nature for a definite quantity of energy with which there is associated some definite period of time. That is the way in which without artificial section a particular lump of action can be separated from the rest of the action which fills the universe. For example, the energy of constitution of an electron is a definite and known quantity; it is an aggregation of energy which occurs naturally in all parts of the universe. But there is no particular duration of time associated with it that we are aware of, and so it does not suggest to us any particular lump of action. We must turn to a form of energy which has a definite and discoverable period of time associated with it, such as a train of light-waves; these carry with them a unit of time, namely, the period of their vibration. The yellow light from sodium consists of aethereal vibrations of period 510 billions to the second. At first sight we seem to be faced with the converse difficulty; we have now our definite period of time; but how are we to cut up into natural units the energy coming from a sodium flame? We should, of course, single out the light proceeding from a single atom, but this will not break up into units unless the atom emits light discontinuously.

It turns out that the atom does emit light discontinuously. It sends out a long train of waves and then stops. It has to be restarted by some kind of stimulation before it emits again. We do not perceive this intermittence in an ordinary beam of light, because there are myriads of atoms engaged in the production.

The amount of energy coming away from the sodium atom during any one of these discontinuous emissions is found to be $3.4 \cdot 10^{-12}$ ergs. This energy is, as we have seen, marked by a distinctive period $1.9 \cdot 10^{-15}$ secs. We have thus the two ingredients necessary for a natural lump of action. Multiply them together, and we obtain $6.55 \cdot 10^{-27}$ erg-seconds. That is the quantity h.

The remarkable law of Nature is that we are continually getting the same numerical results. We may take another source of light—hydrogen, calcium, or any other atom. The energy will be a different number of ergs; the period will be a different number of seconds; but the product will be the same number of erg-seconds. The same applies to X-rays, to gamma rays and to other forms of radiation. It applies to light absorbed by an atom as well as to light emitted, the absorption being discontinuous also. Evidently h is a kind of atom—something which coheres as one unit in the processes of radiation; it is not an atom of matter but an atom or, as we usually call it, a *quantum* of the more elusive entity action. Whereas there are 92 different kinds of material atoms there is only one quantum of action—the same whatever the material it is associated with. I say the *same* without reservation. You might perhaps think that there must be some qualitative difference between the quantum of red light and the quantum of blue light, although both contain the same number of erg-seconds; but the apparent difference is only relative to a frame of space and time and does not concern the absolute lump of action. By approaching the light-source at high speed we change the red light to blue light in accordance with Doppler's principle; the energy of the waves is also changed by being referred to a new frame of reference. A sodium flame and a hydrogen flame are throwing out at us the same lumps of action, only these lumps are rather differently orientated with respect to the Now lines which we have drawn across the four-dimensional world. If we change our motion so as to alter the direction of the Now lines, we can see the lumps of sodium origin under the same orientation in which we formerly saw the lumps of hydrogen origin and recognise that they are actually the same.

We noticed in chapter iv that the shuffling of energy can become complete, so that a definite state is reached known as thermodynamical equilibrium; and we remarked that this is only possible if indivisible units are being shuffled. If the cards can be torn into smaller and smaller pieces without limit there is no end to the process of shuffling. The indivisible units in the shuffling of energy are the quanta. By radiation absorption and scattering energy is shuffled among the different receptacles in matter and aether, but only a whole quantum passes at each step. It was in fact this definiteness of thermodynamical equilibrium which first put Prof. Max Planck on the track of the quantum; and the magnitude of *h* was first calculated by analysis of the observed composition of the radiation in the final state of randomness. Progress of the theory in its adolescent stage was largely due to Einstein so far as concerns the general principles and to Bohr as regards its connection with atomic structure.

The paradoxical nature of the quantum is that although it is indivisible it does not hang together. We examined first a case in which a quantity of energy was obviously cohering together, viz. an electron, but we did not find *h;* then we turned our attention to a case in which the energy was obviously dissolving away through space, viz. light-waves, and immediately *h* appeared. The atom of action seems to have no coherence in space; it has a unity which overleaps space. How can such a unity be made to appear in our picture of a world extended through space and time?

Conflict with the Wave-Theory of Light. The pursuit of the quantum leads to many surprises; but probably none is more outrageous to our preconceptions than the regathering of light and other radiant energy into *h*-units, when all the classical pictures show it to be dispersing more and more. Consider the light-waves which are the result of a single emission by a single atom on the star Sirius. These bear away a certain amount of energy endowed with a certain period, and the product of the two is h. The period is carried by the waves without change, but the energy spreads out in an ever-widening circle. Eight years and nine months after the emission the wave-front is due to reach the earth. A few minutes before the arrival some person takes it into his head to go out and admire the glories of the heavens and—in short—to stick his eye in the way. The light-waves when they started could have had no notion what they were going to hit; for all they knew they were bound on a journey through endless space, as most of their colleagues were. Their energy would seem to be dissipated beyond recovery over a sphere of 50 billion miles' radius. And yet if that energy is ever to enter matter again, if it is to work those chemical changes in the retina which give rise to the sensation of light, it must enter as a single quantum of action h. Just $6.55 \cdot 10^{-27}$ erg-seconds must enter or none at all. Just as the emitting atom regardless of all laws of classical physics is determined that whatever goes out of it shall be just h, so the receiving atom is determined that whatever comes into it shall be just h. Not all the light-waves pass by without entering the eye; for somehow we are able to see Sirius. How is it managed? Do the ripples striking the eye send a message round to the back part of the wave, saying, "We have found an eye. Let's all crowd into it!"

Attempts to account for this phenomenon follow two main devices which we may describe as the "collection-box" theory and the "sweepstake" theory, respectively. Making no effort to translate them into scientific language, they amount to this: In the first the atom holds a collection-box into which each arriving group of waves pays a very small contribution; when the amount in the box reaches a whole quantum, it enters the atom. In the second the atom uses the small fraction of a quantum offered to it to buy a ticket in a sweepstake in which the prizes are whole quanta; some of the atoms will win whole quanta which they can absorb, and it is these winning atoms in our retina which tell us of the existence of Sirius.

The collection-box explanation is not tenable. As Jeans once said, not only does the quantum theory forbid us to kill two birds with one stone; it will not even let us kill one bird with two stones. I cannot go fully into the reasons against this theory, but may illustrate one or two of the difficulties. One serious difficulty would arise from the half-filled collection-boxes. We shall see this more easily if, instead of atoms, we consider molecules which also absorb only full quanta. A molecule might begin to collect the various kinds of light which it can absorb, but before it has collected a quantum of any one kind it takes part in a chemical reaction. New compounds are formed which no longer absorb the old kinds of light; they have entirely different absorption spectra. They would have to start afresh to collect the corresponding kinds of light. What is to be done with the old accumulations now useless, since they can never be completed? One thing is certain; they are not tipped out into the aether when the chemical change occurs.

A phenomenon which seems directly opposed to any kind of collection-box explanation is the photoelectric effect. When light shines on metallic films of sodium, potassium, rubidium, etc., free electrons are discharged from the film. They fly away at high speed, and it is possible to measure experimentally their speed or energy. Undoubtedly it is the incident light which provides the energy of these explosions, but the phenomenon is governed by a remarkable rule. Firstly, the speed of the electrons is not increased by using more powerful light. Concentration of the light produces more explosions but not more powerful explosions. Secondly, the speed is increased by using bluer light, i.e. light of shorter period. For example, the feeble light reaching us from Sirius will cause more powerful ejections of electrons than full sunlight, because Sirius is bluer than the sun; the remoteness of Sirius does not weaken the ejections though it reduces their number.

This is a straightforward quantum phenomenon. Every electron flying out of the metal has picked up just one quantum from the incident light. Since the *h*-rule associates the greater energy with the shorter vibration period, bluer light gives the more intense energy. Experiments show that (after deducting a constant "threshold" energy used up in extricating the electron from the film) each electron comes out with a kinetic energy equal to the energy of the quantum of incident light.

The film can be prepared in the dark; but on exposure to feeble light electrons immediately begin to fly out before any of the collection-boxes could have been filled by fair means. Nor can we appeal to any trigger action of the light releasing an electron already loaded up with energy for its journey; it is the nature of the light which settles the amount of the load. *The light calls the tune, therefore the light must pay the piper.* Only classical theory does not provide light with a pocket to pay from.

It is always difficult to make a fence of objections so thorough as to rule out all progress along a certain line of explanation. But even if it is still possible to wriggle on, there comes a time when one begins to perceive that the evasions are far-fetched.   If we have any instinct that can recognise a fundamental law of Nature when it sees one, that instinct tells us that the interaction of radiation and matter in single quanta is something lying at the root of world-structure and not a casual detail in the mechanism of the atom.   Accordingly we turn to the "sweepstake" theory, which sees in this phenomenon a starting-point for a radical revision of the classical conceptions.

Suppose that the light-waves are of such intensity that, according to the usual reckoning of their energy, one-millionth of a quantum is brought within range of each atom.   The unexpected phenomenon is that instead of each atom absorbing one-millionth of a quantum, one atom out of every million absorbs a whole quantum. That whole quanta are absorbed is shown by the photo-electric experiments already described, since each of the issuing electrons has managed to secure the energy of a whole quantum.

It would seem that what the light-waves were really bearing within reach of each atom was not a millionth of a quantum but a millionth chance of securing a whole quantum.   The wave-theory of light pictures and describes something evenly distributed over the whole wave-front which has usually been identified with energy. Owing to well-established phenomena such as interference and diffraction it seems impossible to deny this uniformity, but we must give it another interpretation; it is a uniform *chance of energy*.   Following the rather old-fashioned definition of energy as "capacity for doing work" the waves carry over their whole front a uniform chance of doing work.   It is the propagation of a chance which the wave-theory studies.

Different views may be held as to how the prize-drawing is conducted on the sweepstake theory. Some hold that the lucky part of the wave-front is already marked before the atom is reached. In addition to the propagation of uniform waves the propagation of a photon or "ray of luck" is involved. This seems to me out of keeping with the general trend of the modern quantum theory; and although most authorities now take this view, which is said to be indicated definitely by certain experiments, I do not place much reliance on the stability of this opinion.

Theory of the Atom. We return now to further experimental knowledge of quanta. The mysterious quantity h crops up inside the atom as well as outside it. Let us take the simplest of all atoms, namely, the hydrogen atom. This consists of a proton and an electron, that is to say a unit charge of positive electricity and a unit charge of negative electricity. The proton carries nearly all the mass of the atom and remains rock-like at the centre, whilst the nimble electron moves round in a circular or elliptic orbit under the inverse square-law of attraction between them. The system is thus very like a sun and a planet. But whereas in the solar system the planet's orbit may be of any size and any eccentricity, the electron's orbit is restricted to a definite series of sizes and shapes. There is nothing in the classical theory of electromagnetism to impose such a restriction; but the restriction exists, and the law imposing it has been discovered. It arises because the atom is arranging to make something in its interior equal to h. The intermediate orbits are excluded because they would involve fractions of h, and h cannot be divided.

But there is one relaxation. When wave-energy is

sent out from or taken into the atom, the amount and period must correspond exactly to h. But as regards its internal arrangements the atom has no objection to $2h$, $3h$, $4h$, etc.; it only insists that fractions shall be excluded. That is why there are many alternative orbits for the electron corresponding to different integral multipliers of h. We call these multipliers *quantum numbers*, and speak of 1-quantum orbits, 2-quantum orbits, etc. I will not enter here into the exact definition of what it is that has to be an exact multiple of h; but it is something which, viewed in the four-dimensional world, is at once seen to be action though this may not be so apparent when we view it in the ordinary way in three-dimensional sections. Also several features of the atom are regulated independently by this rule, and accordingly there are several quantum numbers—one for each feature; but to avoid technical complication I shall refer only to the quantum numbers belonging to one leading feature.

According to this picture of the atom, which is due to Niels Bohr, the only possible change of state is the transfer of an electron from one quantum orbit to another. Such a jump must occur whenever light is absorbed or emitted. Suppose then that an electron which has been travelling in one of the higher orbits jumps down into an orbit of less energy. The atom will then have a certain amount of surplus energy that must be got rid of. The lump of energy is fixed, and it remains to settle the period of vibration that it shall have when it changes into aether-waves. It seems incredible that the atom should get hold of the aether and shake it in any other period than one of those in which it is itself vibrating. Yet it is the experimental fact that, when the atom by radiating sets the aether in vibration, the periods of its electronic circulation are ignored and the period of the aether-waves is settled not by any picturable mechanism but by the seemingly artificial h-rule. It would seem that the atom carelessly throws overboard a lump of energy which, as it glides into the aether, moulds itself into a quantum of action by taking on the period required to make the product of energy and period equal to h. If this unmechanical process of emission seems contrary to our preconceptions, the exactly converse process of absorption is even more so. Here the atom has to look out for a lump of energy of the exact amount required to raise an electron to the higher orbit. It can only extract such a lump from aether-waves of particular period—not a period which has resonance with the structure of the atom, but the period which makes the energy into an exact quantum.

As the adjustment between the energy of the orbit jump and the period of the light carrying away that energy so as to give the constant quantity h is perhaps the most striking evidence of the dominance of the quantum, it will be worth while to explain how the energy of an orbit jump in an atom can be measured. It is possible to impart to a single electron a known amount of energy by making it travel along an electric field with a measured drop of potential. If this projectile hits an atom it may cause one of the electrons circulating in the atom to jump to an upper orbit, but, of course, only if its energy is sufficient to supply that required for the jump; if the electron has too little energy it can do nothing and must pass on with its energy intact. Let us fire a stream of electrons all endowed with the same known energy into the midst of a group of atoms. If the energy is below that corresponding to an orbit jump, the stream will pass through without interference other than ordinary scattering. Now gradually increase the energy of the electrons; quite suddenly we find that the electrons are leaving a great deal of their energy behind. That means that the critical energy has been reached and orbit jumps are being excited. Thus we have a means of measuring the critical energy which is just that of the jump—the difference of energy of the two states of the atom. This method of measurement has the advantage that it does not involve any knowledge of the constant *h*, so that there is no fear of a vicious circle when we use the measured energies to test the *h* rule.* Incidentally this experiment provides another argument against the collection-box theory. Small contributions of energy are not thankfully received, and electrons which offer anything less than the full contribution for a jump are not allowed to make any payment at all.

Relation of Classical Laws to Quantum Laws. To follow up the verification and successful application of the quantum laws would lead to a detailed survey of the greater part of modern physics—specific heats, magnetism, X-rays, radioactivity, and so on. We must leave this and return to a general consideration of the relation between classical laws and quantum laws. For at least fifteen years we have used classical laws and quantum laws alongside one another notwithstanding the irreconcilability of their conceptions. In the model atom the electrons are supposed to traverse their orbits under the classical laws of electrodynamics; but they jump from one orbit to another in a way entirely inconsistent with those laws. The energies of the orbits

---

* Since the *h* rule is now well established the energies of different states of the atoms are usually calculated by its aid; to use these to test the rule would be a vicious circle.

in hydrogen are calculated by classical laws; but one of the purposes of the calculation is to verify the association of energy and period in the unit h, which is contrary to classical laws of radiation. The whole procedure is glaringly contradictory but conspicuously successful.

In my observatory there is a telescope which condenses the light of a star on a film of sodium in a photoelectric cell. I rely on the classical theory to conduct the light through the lenses and focus it in the cell; then I switch on to the quantum theory to make the light fetch out electrons from the sodium film to be collected in an electrometer. If I happen to transpose the two theories, the quantum theory convinces me that the light will never get concentrated in the cell and the classical theory shows that it is powerless to extract the electrons if it does get in. I have no logical reason for not using the theories this way round; only experience teaches me that I must not. Sir William Bragg was not overstating the case when he said that we use the classical theory on Mondays, Wednesday and Fridays, and the quantum theory on Tuesdays, Thursdays and Saturdays. Perhaps that ought to make us feel a little sympathetic towards the man whose philosophy of the universe takes one form on weekdays and another form on Sundays.

In the last century—and I think also in this—there must have been many scientific men who kept their science and religion in watertight compartments. One set of beliefs held good in the laboratory and another set of beliefs in church, and no serious effort was made to harmonise them. The attitude is defensible. To discuss the compatibility of the beliefs would lead the scientist into regions of thought in which he was inexpert; and any answer he might reach would be undeserving of strong confidence. Better admit that there was some truth both in science and religion; and if they must fight, let it be elsewhere than in the brain of a hard-working scientist. If we have ever scorned this attitude, Nemesis has overtaken us. For ten years we have had to divide modern science into two compartments; we have one set of beliefs in the classical compartment and another set of beliefs in the quantum compartment. Unfortunately *our* compartments are not watertight.

We must, of course, look forward to an ultimate reconstruction of our conceptions of the physical world which will embrace both the classical laws and the quantum laws in harmonious association. There are still some who think that the reconciliation will be effected by a development of classical conceptions. But the physicists of what I may call "the Copenhagen school" believe that the reconstruction has to start at the other end, and that in the quantum phenomena we are getting down to a more intimate contact with Nature's way of working than in the coarse-grained experience which has furnished the classical laws. The classical school having become convinced of the existence of these uniform lumps of action, speculates on the manufacture of the chopper necessary to carve off uniform lumps; the Copenhagen school on the other hand sees in these phenomena the insubstantial pageant of space, time and matter crumbling into grains of action. I do not think that the Copenhagen school has been mainly influenced by the immense difficulty of constructing a satisfactory chopper out of classical material; its view arises especially from a study of the meeting point of quantum and classical laws.

The classical laws are the limit to which the quantum laws tend when states of very high quantum number are concerned.

This is the famous Correspondence Principle enunciated by Bohr. It was at first a conjecture based on rather slight hints; but as our knowledge of quantum laws has grown, it has been found that when we apply them to states of very high quantum number they converge to the classical laws, and predict just what the classical laws would predict.

For an example, take a hydrogen atom with its electron in a circular orbit of very high quantum number, that is to say far away from the proton. On Monday, Wednesday and Friday it is governed by classical laws. These say that it must emit a feeble radiation continuously, of strength determined by the acceleration it is undergoing and of period agreeing with its own period of revolution. Owing to the gradual loss of energy it will spiral down towards the proton. On Tuesday, Thursday and Saturday it is governed by quantum laws and jumps from one orbit to another. There is a quantum law that I have not mentioned which prescribes that (for circular orbits only) the jump must always be to the circular orbit next lower, so that the electron comes steadily down the series of steps without skipping any. Another law prescribes the average time between each jump and therefore the average time between the successive emissions of light. The small lumps of energy cast away at each step form light-waves of period determined by the h rule.

"Preposterous! You cannot seriously mean that the electron does different things on different days of the week!"

But did I say that it does different things? I used different words to describe its doings. I run down the stairs on Tuesday and slide down the banisters on Wednesday; but if the staircase consists of innumerable infinitesimal steps, there is no essential difference in my mode of progress on the two days. And so it makes no difference whether the electron steps from one orbit to the next lower or comes down in a spiral when the number of steps is innumerably great. The succession of lumps of energy cast overboard merges into a continuous outflow. If you had the formulae before you, you would find that the period of the light and the strength of radiation are the same whether calculated by the Monday or the Tuesday method—*but only when the quantum number is infinitely great*. The disagreement is not very serious when the number is moderately large; but for small quantum numbers the atom cannot sit on the fence. It has to decide between Monday (classical) and Tuesday (quantum) rules. It chooses Tuesday rules.

If, as we believe, this example is typical, it indicates one direction which the reconstruction of ideas must take. We must not try to build up from classical conceptions, because the classical laws only become true and the conceptions concerned in them only become defined in the limiting case when the quantum numbers of the system are very large. We must start from new conceptions appropriate to low as well as to high numbered states; out of these the classical conceptions should emerge, first indistinctly, then definitely, as the number of the state increases, and the classical laws become more and more nearly true. I cannot foretell the result of this remodelling, but presumably room must be found for a conception of "states", the unity of a state replacing the kind of tie expressed by classical forces. For low numbered states the current vocabulary of physics is inappropriate; at the moment we can scarcely avoid using it, but the present contradictoriness of our theories arises from this misuse. For such states space and time do not exist—at least I can see no reason to believe that they do. But it must be supposed that when high numbered states are considered there will be found in the new scheme approximate counterparts of the space and time of current conception—something ready to merge into space and time when the state numbers are infinite. And simultaneously the interactions described by transitions of states will merge into classical forces exerted across space and time. So that in the limit the classical description becomes an available alternative. Now in practical experience we have generally had to deal with systems whose ties are comparatively loose and correspond to very high quantum numbers; consequently our first survey of the world has stumbled across the classical laws and our present conceptions of the world consist of those entities which only take definite shape for high quantum numbers. But in the interior of the atom and molecule, in the phenomena of radiation, and probably also in the constitution of very dense stars such as the Companion of Sirius, the state numbers are not high enough to admit this treatment. These phenomena are now forcing us back to the more fundamental conceptions out of which the classical conceptions (sufficient for the other types of phenomena) ought to emerge as one extreme limit.

For an example I will borrow a quantum conception from the next chapter. It may not be destined to survive in the present rapid evolution of ideas, but at any rate it will illustrate my point. In Bohr's semi-classical model of the hydrogen atom there is an electron describing a circular or elliptic orbit. This is only a model; the real atom contains nothing of the sort. The real atom contains something which it has not entered into the mind of man to conceive, which has, however, been described symbolically by Schrödinger. This "something" is spread about in a manner by no means comparable to an electron describing an orbit. Now excite the atom into successively higher and higher quantum states. In the Bohr model the electron leaps into higher and higher orbits. In the real atom Schrödinger's "something" begins to draw itself more and more together until it begins sketchily to outline the Bohr orbit and even imitates a condensation running round. Go on to still higher quantum numbers, and Schrödinger's symbol now represents a compact body moving round in the same orbit and the same period as the electron in Bohr's model, and moreover radiating according to the classical laws of an electron. And so when the quantum number reaches infinity, and the atom bursts, a genuine classical electron flies out. The electron, as it leaves the atom, crystallises out of Schrödinger's mist like a genie emerging from his bottle.

Chapter X

THE NEW QUANTUM THEORY

The conflict between quantum theory and classical theory becomes especially acute in the problem of the propagation of light. Here in effect it becomes a conflict between the corpuscular theory of light and the wave theory.

In the early days it was often asked, How large is a quantum of light? One answer is obtained by examining a star image formed with the great 100-inch reflector at Mt. Wilson. The diffraction pattern shows that each emission from each atom must be filling the whole mirror. For if one atom illuminates one part only and another atom another part only, we ought to get the same effect by illuminating different parts of the mirror by different stars (since there is no particular virtue in using atoms from the same star); actually the diffraction pattern then obtained is not the same. *The quantum must be large enough to cover a* 100-*inch mirror.*

But if this same star-light without any artificial concentration falls on a film of potassium, electrons will fly out each with the whole energy of a quantum. This is not a trigger action releasing energy already stored in the atom, because the amount of energy is fixed by the nature of the light, not by the nature of the atom. A whole quantum of light energy must have gone into the atom and blasted away the electron. *The quantum must be small enough to enter an atom.*

I do not think there is much doubt as to the ultimate origin of this contradiction. We must not think about space and time in connection with an individual quantum; and the extension of a quantum in space has no real meaning. To apply these conceptions to a single quantum is like reading the Riot Act to one man. A single quantum has not travelled 50 billion miles from Sirius; it has not been 8 years on the way. But when enough quanta are gathered to form a quorum there will be found among them *statistical properties* which are the genesis of the 50 billion miles' distance of Sirius and the 8 years' journey of the light.

Wave-Theory of Matter. It is comparatively easy to realise what we have got to do. It is much more difficult to start to do it. Before we review the attempts in the last year or two to grapple with this problem we shall briefly consider a less drastic method of progress initiated by De Broglie. For the moment we shall be content to accept the mystery as a mystery. Light, we will say, is an entity with the wave property of spreading out to fill the largest object glass and with all the well-known properties of diffraction and interference; simultaneously it is an entity with the corpuscular or bullet property of expending its whole energy on one very small target. We can scarcely describe such an entity as a wave or as a particle; perhaps as a compromise we had better call it a "wavicle".

There is nothing new under the sun, and this latest *volte-face* almost brings us back to Newton's theory of light—a curious mixture of corpuscular and wave-theory. There is perhaps a pleasing sentiment in this "return to Newton". But to suppose that Newton's scientific reputation is especially vindicated by De Broglie's theory of light, is as absurd as to suppose that it is shattered by Einstein's theory of gravitation. There was no phenomenon known to Newton which could not be amply covered by the wave-theory; and the clearing away of false evidence for a partly corpuscular theory, which influenced Newton, is as much a part of scientific progress as the bringing forward of the (possibly) true evidence, which influences us to-day. To imagine that Newton's great scientific reputation is tossing up and down in these latter-day revolutions is to confuse science with omniscience.

To return to the wavicle.—If that which we have commonly regarded as a wave partakes also of the nature of a particle, may not that which we have commonly regarded as a particle partake also of the nature of a wave? It was not until the present century that experiments were tried of a kind suitable to bring out the corpuscular aspect of the nature of light; perhaps experiments may still be possible which will bring out a wave aspect of the nature of an electron.

So, as a first step, instead of trying to clear up the mystery we try to extend it. Instead of explaining how anything can possess simultaneously the incongruous properties of wave and particle we seek to show experimentally that these properties are universally associated. There are no pure waves and no pure particles.

The characteristic of a wave-theory is the spreading of a ray of light after passing through a narrow aperture—a well-known phenomenon called diffraction. The scale of the phenomenon is proportional to the wavelength of the light. De Broglie has shown us how to calculate the lengths of the waves (if any) associated with an electron, i.e. considering it to be no longer a pure particle but a wavicle. It appears that in some circumstances the scale of the corresponding diffraction effects will not be too small for experimental detection. There are now a number of experimental results quoted as verifying this prediction. I scarcely know whether they are yet to be considered conclusive, but there does seem to be serious evidence that in the scattering of electrons by atoms phenomena occur which would not be produced according to the usual theory that electrons are purely corpuscular. These effects analogous to the diffraction and interference of light carry us into the stronghold of the wave-theory. Long ago such phenomena ruled out all purely corpuscular theories of light; perhaps to-day we are finding similar phenomena which will rule out all purely corpuscular theories of matter.*

A similar idea was entertained in a "new statistical mechanics" developed by Einstein and Bose—at least that seems to be the physical interpretation of the highly abstract mathematics of their theory. As so often happens the change from the classical mechanics, though far-reaching in principle, gave only insignificant corrections when applied to ordinary practical problems. Significant differences could only be expected in matter much denser than anything yet discovered or imagined. Strange to say, just about the time when it was realised that very dense matter might have strange properties different from those expected according to classical conceptions, very dense matter was found in the universe. Astronomical evidence seems to leave practically no doubt that in the so-called *white dwarf* stars the density of matter far transcends anything of which we have terrestrial experience; in the Companion of Sirius, for example, the density is about a ton to the cubic inch. This condition is explained by the fact that the high temperature and correspondingly intense agitation of

---

* The evidence is much stronger now than when the lectures were delivered.

the material breaks up (ionises) the outer electron systems of the atoms, so that the fragments can be packed
much more closely together. At ordinary temperatures
the minute nucleus of the atom is guarded by outposts
of sentinel electrons which ward off other atoms from
close approach even under the highest pressures; but at
stellar temperatures the agitation is so great that the
electrons leave their posts and run all over the place.
Exceedingly tight packing then becomes possible under
high enough pressure. R. H. Fowler has found that in
the white dwarf stars the density is so great that classical methods are inadequate and the new statistical
mechanics must be used. In particular he has in this
way relieved an anxiety which had been felt as to their
ultimate fate; under classical laws they seemed to be
heading towards an intolerable situation—the star could
not stop losing heat, but it would have insufficient energy
to be able to cool down!*

Transition to a New Theory. By 1925 the machinery
of current theory had developed another flaw and was
urgently calling for reconstruction; Bohr's model of the
atom had quite definitely broken down. This is the
model, now very familiar, which pictures the atom as
a kind of solar system with a central positively charged
nucleus and a number of elecrons describing orbits about
it like planets, the important feature being that the
possible orbits are limited by the rules referred to on
p. 190. Since each line in the spectrum of the atom is
emitted by the jump of an electron between two par-

---

* The energy is required because on cooling down the matter must
regain a more normal density and this involves a great expansion of
volume of the star. In the expansion work has to be done against the
force of gravity.

ticular orbits, the classification of the spectral lines must run parallel with the classification of the orbits by their quantum numbers in the model. When the spectroscopists started to unravel the various series of lines in the spectra they found it possible to assign an orbit jump for every line—they could say what each line meant in terms of the model. But now questions of finer detail have arisen for which this correspondence ceases to hold. One must not expect too much from a model, and it would have been no surprise if the model had failed to exhibit minor phenomena or if its accuracy had proved imperfect. But the kind of trouble now arising was that only two orbit jumps were provided in the model to represent three obviously associated spectral lines; and so on. The model which had been so helpful in the interpretation of spectra up to a point, suddenly became altogether misleading; and spectroscopists were forced to turn away from the model and complete their classification of lines in a way which ignored it. They continued to speak of orbits and orbit jumps but there was no longer a complete one-to-one correspondence with the orbits shown in the model.*

The time was evidently ripe for the birth of a new theory. The situation then prevailing may be summarised as follows:

(1) The general working rule was to employ the classical laws with the supplementary proviso that whenever anything of the nature of action appears it

---

*Each orbit or state of the atom requires three (or, for later refinements, four) quantum numbers to define it. The first two quantum numbers are correctly represented in the Bohr model; but the third number which discriminates the different lines forming a doublet or multiplet spectrum is represented wrongly—a much more serious failure than if it were not represented at all.

must be made equal to h, or sometimes to an integral multiple of h.

(2) The proviso often led to a self-contradictory use of the classical theory. Thus in the Bohr atom the acceleration of the electron in its orbit would be governed by classical electrodynamics whilst its radiation would be governed by the h rule. But in classical electrodynamics the acceleration and the radiation are indissolubly connected.

(3) The proper sphere of classical laws was known. They are a form taken by the more general laws in a limiting case, viz. when the number of quanta concerned is very large. Progress in the investigation of the complete system of more general laws must not be hampered by classical conceptions which contemplate only the limiting case.

(4) The present compromise involved the recognition that light has both corpuscular and wave properties. The same idea seems to have been successfully extended to matter and confirmed by experiment. But this success only renders the more urgent some less contradictory way of conceiving these properties.

(5) Although the above working rule had generally been successful in its predictions, it was found to give a distribution of electron orbits in the atom differing in some essential respects from that deduced spectroscopically. Thus a reconstruction was required not only to remove logical objections but to meet the urgent demands of practical physics.

Development of the New Quantum Theory. The "New Quantum Theory" originated in a remarkable paper by Heisenberg in the autumn of 1925. I am writing the first draft of this lecture just twelve months after the appearance of the paper. That does not give long for development; nevertheless the theory has already gone through three distinct phases associated with the names of Born and Jordan, Dirac, Schrödinger. My chief anxiety at the moment is lest another phase of reinterpretation should be reached before the lecture can be delivered. In an ordinary way we should describe the three phases as three distinct theories. The pioneer work of Heisenberg governs the whole, but the three theories show wide differences of thought. The first entered on the new road in a rather matter-of-fact way; the second was highly transcendental, almost mystical; the third seemed at first to contain a reaction towards classical ideas, but that was probably a false impression. You will realise the anarchy of this branch of physics when three successive pretenders seize the throne in twelve months; but you will not realise the steady progress made in that time unless you turn to the mathematics of the subject. As regards philosophical ideas the three theories are poles apart; as regards mathematical content they are one and the same. Unfortunately the mathematical content is just what I am forbidden to treat of in these lectures.

I am, however, going to transgress to the extent of writing down one mathematical formula for you to contemplate; I shall not be so unreasonable as to expect you to understand it. All authorities seem to be agreed that at, or nearly at, the root of everything in the physical world lies the mystic formula

$$qp - pq = ih/2\pi$$

We do not yet understand that; probably if we could understand it we should not think it so fundamental.

Where the trained mathematician has the advantage is that he can use it, and in the past year or two it has been used in physics with very great advantage indeed. It leads not only to those phenomena described by the older quantum laws such as the h rule, but to many related phenomena which the older formulation could not treat.

On the right-hand side, besides h (the atom of action) and the merely numerical factor 2π, there appears i (the square root of -1) which may seem rather mystical. But this is only a well-known subterfuge; and far back in the last century physicists and engineers were well aware that $\sqrt{-1}$ in their formulae was a kind of signal to look out for waves or oscillations. The right-hand side contains nothing unusual, but the left-hand side baffles imagination. We call q and p co-ordinates and momenta, borrowing our vocabulary from the world of space and time and other coarse-grained experience; but that gives no real light on their nature, nor does it explain why qp is so ill-behaved as to be unequal to pq.

It is here that the three theories differ most essentially. Obviously q and p cannot represent simple numerical measures, for then $qp-pq$ would be zero. For Schrödinger p is an *operator*. His "momentum" is not a quantity but a signal to us to perform a certain mathematical operation on any quantities which may follow. For Born and Jordan p is a *matrix*—not one quantity, nor several quantities, but an infinite number of quantities arranged in systematic array. For Dirac p is a symbol without any kind of numerical interpretation; he calls it a *q*-number, which is a way of saying that it is not a number at all.

I venture to think that there is an idea implied in

Dirac's treatment which may have great philosophical significance, independently of any question of success in this particular application. The idea is that in digging deeper and deeper into that which lies at the base of physical phenomena we must be prepared to come to entities which, like many things in our conscious experience, are not measurable by numbers in any way; and further it suggests how exact science, that is to say the science of phenomena correlated to measure-numbers, can be founded on such a basis.

One of the greatest changes in physics between the nineteenth century and the present day has been the change in our ideal of scientific explanation. It was the boast of the Victorian physicist that he would not claim to understand a thing until he could make a model of it; and by a model he meant something constructed of levers, geared wheels, squirts, or other appliances familiar to an engineer. Nature in building the universe was supposed to be dependent on just the same kind of resources as any human mechanic; and when the physicist sought an explanation of phenomena his ear was straining to catch the hum of machinery. The man who could make gravitation out of cog-wheels would have been a hero in the Victorian age.

Nowadays we do not encourage the engineer to build the world for us out of his material, but we turn to the mathematician to build it out of his material. Doubtless the mathematician is a loftier being than the engineer, but perhaps even he ought not to be entrusted with the Creation unreservedly. We are dealing in physics with a symbolic world, and we can scarcely avoid employing the mathematician who is the professional wielder of symbols; but he must rise to the full opportunities of the responsible task entrusted to him and not indulge too freely his own bias for symbols with an arithmetical interpretation. If we are to discern controlling laws of Nature not dictated by the mind it would seem necessary to escape as far as possible from the cut-and-dried framework into which the mind is so ready to force everything that it experiences.

I think that in principle Dirac's method asserts this kind of emancipation. He starts with basal entities inexpressible by numbers or number-systems and his basal laws are symbolic expressions unconnected with arithmetical operations. The fascinating point is that as the development proceeds actual numbers are *exuded* from the symbols. Thus although p and q individually have no arithmetical interpretation, the combination $qp-pq$ has the arithmetical interpretation expressed by the formula above quoted. By furnishing numbers, though itself non-numerical, such a theory can well be the basis for the measure-numbers studied in exact science. The measure-numbers, which are all that we glean from a physical survey of the world, cannot be the whole world; they may not even be so much of it as to constitute a self-governing unit. This seems the natural interpretation of Dirac's procedure in seeking the governing laws of exact science in a non-arithmetical calculus.

I am afraid it is a long shot to predict anything like this emerging from Dirac's beginning; and for the moment Schrödinger has rent much of the mystery from the p's and q's by showing that a less transcendental interpretation is adequate for present applications. But I like to think that we may have not yet heard the last of the idea.

Schrödinger's theory is now enjoying the full tide of popularity, partly because of intrinsic merit, but also,

I suspect, partly because it is the only one of the three
that is simple enough to be misunderstood. Rather
against my better judgment I will try to give a rough
impression of the theory. It would probably be wiser
to nail up over the door of the new quantum theory a
notice, "Structural alterations in progress—No admit-
tance except on business", and particularly to warn the
doorkeeper to keep out prying philosophers. I will,
however, content myself with the protest that, whilst
Schrödinger's theory is guiding us to sound and rapid
progress in many of the mathematical problems confronting us and is indispensable in its practical utility,
I do not see the least likelihood that his ideas will survive long in their present form.

Outline of Schrödinger's Theory. Imagine a sub-aether
whose surface is covered with ripples. The oscillations
of the ripples are a million times faster than those of
visible light—too fast to come within the scope of our
gross experience. Individual ripples are beyond our
ken; what we can appreciate is a combined effect—when
by convergence and coalescence the waves conspire to
create a disturbed area of extent large compared with
individual ripples but small from our own Brobding-
nagian point of view. Such a disturbed area is recognised as a material particle; in particular it can be an
electron.

The sub-aether is a dispersive medium, that is to say
the ripples do not all travel with the same velocity; like
water-ripples their speed depends on their wave-length
or period. Those of shorter period travel faster. Moreover the speed may be modified by local conditions.
This modification is the counterpart in Schrödinger's
theory of a field of force in classical physics. It will

readily be understood that if we are to reduce all phenomena to a propagation of waves, then the influence
of a body on phenomena in its neighbourhood (commonly described as the field of force caused by its
presence) must consist in a modification of the propagation of waves in the region surrounding it.

We have to connect these phenomena in the sub-
aether with phenomena in the plane of our gross experience. As already stated, a local stormy region is
detected by us as a particle; to this we now add that the
frequency (number of oscillations per second) of the
waves constituting the disturbance is recognised by us
as the energy of the particle. We shall presently try to
explain how the period manages to manifest itself to us
in this curiously camouflaged way; but however it comes
about, the recognition of a frequency in the sub-aether
as an energy in gross experience gives at once the constant relation between period and energy which we have
called the h rule.

Generally the oscillations in the sub-aether are too
rapid for us to detect directly; their frequency reaches
the plane of ordinary experience by affecting the speed
of propagation, because the speed depends (as already
stated) on the wave-length or frequency. Calling the
frequency ν, the equation expressing the law of propagation of the ripples will contain a term in ν. There will
be another term expressing the modification caused by
the "field of force" emanating from the bodies present
in the neighbourhood. This can be treated as a kind of
spurious ν, since it emerges into our gross experience
by the same method that ν does. If ν produces those
phenomena which make us recognise it as energy, the
spurious ν will produce similar phenomena corresponding to a spurious kind of energy. Clearly the latter will

be what we call potential energy, since it originates from influences attributable to the presence of surrounding objects.

Assuming that we know both the real ν and the spurious or potential ν for our ripples, the equation of wave-propagation is settled, and we can proceed to solve any problem concerning wave-propagation. In particular we can solve the problem as to how the stormy areas move about. This gives a remarkable result which provides the first check on our theory. The stormy areas (if small enough) move under precisely the same laws that govern the motions of particles in classical mechanics. *The equations for the motion of a wave-group with given frequency and potential frequency are the same as the classical equations of motion of a particle with the corresponding energy and potential energy.*

It has to be noticed that the velocity of a stormy area or group of waves is not the same as the velocity of an individual wave. This is well known in the study of water-waves as the distinction between group-velocity and wave-velocity. It is the group-velocity that is observed by us as the motion of the material particle.

We should have gained very little if our theory did no more than re-establish the results of classical mechanics on this rather fantastic basis. Its distinctive merits begin to be apparent when we deal with phenomena not covered by classical mechanics. We have considered a stormy area of so small extent that its position is as definite as that of a classical particle, but we may also consider an area of wider extent. No precise delimitation can be drawn between a large area and a small area, so that we shall continue to associate the idea of a particle with it; but whereas a small concentrated storm fixes the position of the particle

closely, a more extended storm leaves it very vague.   If
we try to interpret an extended wave-group in classical
language we say that it is a particle which is not at any
definite point of space, but is loosely associated with a
wide region.

Perhaps you may think that an extended stormy area
ought to represent *diffused* matter in contrast to a concentrated particle.   That is not Schrödinger's theory.
The spreading is not a spreading of density; it is an
indeterminacy of position, or a wider distribution of the
probability that the particle lies within particular limits
of position.   Thus if we come across Schrödinger waves
uniformly filling a vessel, the interpretation is not that
the vessel is filled with matter of uniform density, but
that it contains one particle which is equally likely to be
anywhere.

The first great success of this theory was in representing the emission of light from a hydrogen atom—
a problem far outside the scope of classical theory.   The
hydrogen atom consists of a proton and electron which
must be translated into their counterparts in the sub-
aether.   We are not interested in what the proton is
doing, so we do not trouble about its representation by
waves; what we want from it is its field of force, that is
to say, the spurious ν which it provides in the equation
of wave-propagation for the electron.   The waves
travelling in accordance with this equation constitute
Schrödinger's equivalent for the electron; and any solution of the equation will correspond to some possible
state of the hydrogen atom.   Now it turns out that
(paying attention to the obvious physical limitation that
the waves must not anywhere be of infinite amplitude)
solutions of this wave-equation only exist for waves with
particular frequencies.   Thus in a hydrogen atom the

sub-aethereal waves are limited to a particular discrete series of frequencies. Remembering that a frequency in the sub-aether means an energy in gross experience, the atom will accordingly have a discrete series of possible energies. It is found that this series of energies is precisely the same as that assigned by Bohr from his rules of quantisation (p. 191). It is a considerable advance to have determined these energies by a wave-theory instead of by an inexplicable mathematical rule. Further, when applied to more complex atoms Schrödinger's theory succeeds on those points where the Bohr model breaks down; it always gives the right number of energies or "orbits" to provide one orbit jump for each observed spectral line.

It is, however, an advantage not to pass from wave-frequency to classical energy at this stage, but to follow the course of events in the sub-aether a little farther. It would be difficult to think of the electron as having two energies (i.e. being in two Bohr orbits) simultaneously; but there is nothing to prevent waves of two different frequencies being simultaneously present in the sub-aether. Thus the wave-theory allows us easily to picture a condition which the classical theory could only describe in paradoxical terms. Suppose that two sets of waves are present. If the difference of frequency is not very great the two systems of waves will produce "beats". If two broadcasting stations are transmitting on wave-lengths near together we hear a musical note or shriek resulting from the beats of the two carrier waves; the individual oscillations are too rapid to affect the ear, but they combine to give beats which are slow enough to affect the ear. In the same way the individual wave-systems in the sub-aether are composed of oscillations too rapid to affect our gross senses; but their beats are sometimes slow enough to come within the octave covered by the eye. These beats are the source of the light coming from the hydrogen atom, and mathematical calculation shows that their frequencies are precisely those of the observed light from hydrogen. Heterodyning of the radio carrier waves produces sound; heterodyning of the sub-aethereal waves produces light. Not only does this theory give the periods of the different lines in the spectra, but it also predicts their intensities—a problem which the older quantum theory had no means of tackling. It should, however, be understood that the beats are not themselves to be identified with light-waves; they are in the sub-aether, whereas light-waves are in the aether. They provide the oscillating source which in some way not yet traced sends out light-waves of its own period.

What precisely is the entity which we suppose to be oscillating when we speak of the waves in the sub-aether? It is denoted by ψ, and properly speaking we should regard it as an elementary indefinable of the wave-theory. But can we give it a classical interpretation of any kind? It seems possible to interpret it as a probability. The probability of the particle or electron being within a given region is proportional to the amount of ψ in that region. So that if ψ is mainly concentrated in one small stormy area, it is practically certain that the electron is there; we are then able to localise it definitely and conceive of it as a classical particle. But the ψ-waves of the hydrogen atom are spread about all over the atom; and there is no definite localisation of the electron, though some places are more probable than others.*

---

* The probability is often stated to be proportional to ψ^2, instead of ψ, as assumed above. The whole interpretation is very obscure, but it

Attention must be called to one highly important consequence of this theory. A small enough stormy area corresponds very nearly to a particle moving about under the classical laws of motion; it would seem therefore that a particle definitely localised as a moving point is strictly the limit when the stormy area is reduced to a point. But curiously enough by continually reducing the area of the storm we never quite reach the ideal classical particle; we approach it and then recede from it again. We have seen that the wave-group moves like a particle (localised somewhere within the area of the storm) having an energy corresponding to the frequency of the waves; therefore to imitate a particle exactly, not only must the area be reduced to a point but the group must consist of waves of only one frequency. The two conditions are irreconcilable. With one frequency we can only have an infinite succession of waves not terminated by any boundary. A boundary to the group is provided by interference of waves of slightly different length, so that while reinforcing one another at the centre they cancel one another at the boundary. Roughly speaking, if the group has a diameter of 1000 wavelengths there must be a range of wave-length of 0·1 per cent., so that 1000 of the longest waves and 1001 of the shortest occupy the same distance. If we take a more concentrated stormy area of diameter 10 wave-

---

seems to depend on whether you are considering the probability *after you know what has happened* or the probability for the purposes of prediction. The ψ^2 is obtained by introducing two symmetrical systems of ψ-waves travelling in opposite directions in time; one of these must presumably correspond to probable inference from what is known (or is stated) to have been the condition at a later time. Probability necessarily means "probability in the light of certain given information", so that the probability cannot possibly be represented by the same function in different classes of problems with different initial data.

lengths the range is increased to 10 per cent.; 10 of the longest and 11 of the shortest waves must extend the same distance. In seeking to make the position of the particle more definite by reducing the area we make its energy more vague by dispersing the frequencies of the waves. So our particle can never have simultaneously a perfectly definite position and a perfectly definite energy; it always has a vagueness of one kind or the other unbefitting a classical particle. Hence in delicate experiments we must not under any circumstances expect to find particles behaving exactly as a classical particle was supposed to do—a conclusion which seems to be in accordance with the modern experiments on diffraction of electrons already mentioned.

We remarked that Schrödinger's picture of the hydrogen atom enabled it to possess something that would be impossible on Bohr's theory, viz. two energies at once. For a particle or electron this is not merely permissive, but compulsory—otherwise we can put no limits to the region where it may be. You are not asked to imagine the state of a particle with several energies; what is meant is that our current picture of an electron as a particle with single energy has broken down, and we must dive below into the sub-aether if we wish to follow the course of events. The picture of a particle may, however, be retained when we are not seeking high accuracy; if we do not need to know the energy more closely than 1 per cent., a series of energies ranging over 1 per cent. can be treated as one definite energy.

Hitherto I have only considered the waves corresponding to one electron; now suppose that we have a problem involving two electrons. How shall they be represented? "Surely, that is simple enough! We have only to take two stormy areas instead of one." I am afraid not.   Two stormy areas would correspond to a single electron uncertain as to which area it was located in. So long as there is the faintest probability of the first electron being in any region, we cannot make the Schrödinger waves there represent a probability belonging to a second electron.   Each electron wants the whole of three-dimensional space for its waves; so Schrödinger generously allows three dimensions for each of them. For two electrons he requires a six-dimensional sub-aether.   He then successfully applies his method on the same lines as before.   I think you will see now that Schrödinger has given us what seemed to be a comprehensible physical picture only to snatch it away again. His sub-aether does not exist in physical space; it is in a "configuration space" imagined by the mathematician for the purpose of solving his problems, and imagined afresh with different numbers of dimensions according to the problem proposed.   It was only an accident that in the earliest problems considered the configuration space had a close correspondence with physical space, suggesting some degree of objective reality of the waves.   Schrödinger's wave-mechanics is not a physical theory but a dodge—and a very good dodge too.

The fact is that the almost universal applicability of this wave-mechanics spoils all chance of our taking it seriously as a physical theory.   A delightful illustration of this occurs incidentally in the work of Dirac.   In one of the problems, which he solves by Schrödinger waves, the frequency of the waves represents the number of systems of a given kind.   The wave-equation is formulated and solved, and (just as in the problem of the hydrogen atom) it is found that solutions only exist for a series of special values of the frequency.   Consequently the number of systems of the kind considered must have one of a discrete series of values. In Dirac's problem the series turns out to be the series of integers. Accordingly we infer that the number of systems must be either 1, 2, 3, 4, . . ., but can never be 2¾ for example. It is satisfactory that the theory should give a result so well in accordance with our experience! But we are not likely to be persuaded that the true explanation of why we count in integers is afforded by a system of waves.

Principle of Indeterminacy. My apprehension lest a fourth version of the new quantum theory should appear before the lectures were delivered was not fulfilled; but a few months later the theory definitely entered on a new phase. It was Heisenberg again who set in motion the new development in the summer of 1927, and the consequences were further elucidated by Bohr. The outcome of it is a fundamental general principle which seems to rank in importance with the principle of relativity. I shall here call it the "principle of indeterminacy".

The gist of it can be stated as follows: *a particle may have position or it may have velocity but it cannot in any exact sense have both.*

If we are content with a certain margin of inaccuracy and if we are content with statements that claim no certainty but only high probability, then it is possible to ascribe both position and velocity to a particle. But if we strive after a more accurate specification of position a very remarkable thing happens; the greater accuracy can be attained, but it is compensated by a greater inaccuracy in the specification of the velocity. Similarly if the specification of the velocity is made more accurate the position becomes less determinate.

Suppose for example that we wish to know the position and velocity of an electron at a given moment. Theoretically it would be possible to fix the position with a probable error of about 1/1000 of a millimetre and the velocity with a probable error of 1 kilometre per second. But an error of 1/1000 of a millimetre is large compared with that of some of our space measurements; is there no conceivable way of fixing the position to 1/10,000 of a millimetre? Certainly; but in that case it will only be possible to fix the velocity with an error of 10 kilometres per second.

The conditions of our exploration of the secrets of Nature are such that the more we bring to light the secret of position the more the secret of velocity is hidden. They are like the old man and woman in the weather-glass; as one comes out of one door, the other retires behind the other door. When we encounter unexpected obstacles in finding out something which we wish to know, there are two possible courses to take. It may be that the right course is to treat the obstacle as a spur to further efforts; but there is a second possibility—that we have been trying to find something which does not exist. You will remember that that was how the relativity theory accounted for the apparent concealment of our velocity through the aether.

When the concealment is found to be perfectly systematic, then we must banish the corresponding entity from the physical world. There is really no option. The link with our consciousness is completely broken. When we cannot point to any causal effect on anything that comes into our experience, the entity merely becomes part of the unknown—undifferentiated from the rest of the vast unknown. From time to time physical discoveries are made; and new entities, coming out of the unknown, become connected to our experience and are duly named. But to leave a lot of unattached labels floating in the as yet undifferentiated unknown in the hope that they may come in useful later on, is no particular sign of prescience and is not helpful to science. From this point of view we assert that the description of the position and velocity of an electron beyond a limited number of places of decimals is an attempt to describe something that does not exist; although curiously enough the description of position or of velocity if it had stood alone might have been allowable.

Ever since Einstein's theory showed the importance of securing that the physical quantities which we talk about are actually connected to our experience, we have been on our guard to some extent against meaningless terms. Thus distance is defined by certain operations of measurement and not with reference to nonsensical conceptions such as the "amount of emptiness" between two points. The minute distances referred to in atomic physics naturally aroused some suspicion, since it is not always easy to say how the postulated measurements could be imagined to be carried out. I would not like to assert that this point has been cleared up; but at any rate it did not seem possible to make a clean sweep of all minute distances, because cases could be cited in which there seemed no natural limit to the accuracy of determination of position. Similarly there are ways of determining momentum apparently unlimited in accuracy. What escaped notice was that the two measurements interfere with one another in a systematic way, so that the combination of position with momentum, legitimate on the large scale, becomes indefinable on the small scale. The principle of indeterminacy is scientifically stated as follows: if q is a co-ordinate and p the corresponding momentum, the necessary uncertainty of our knowledge of q multiplied by the uncertainty of p is of the order of magnitude of the quantum constant h.

A general kind of reason for this can be seen without much difficulty. Suppose it is a question of knowing the position and momentum of an electron. So long as the electron is not interacting with the rest of the universe we cannot be aware of it. We must take our chance of obtaining knowledge of it at moments when it is interacting with something and thereby producing effects that can be observed. But in any such interaction a complete quantum is involved; and the passage of this quantum, altering to an important extent the conditions at the moment of our observation, makes the information out of date even as we obtain it.

Suppose that (ideally) an electron is observed under a powerful microscope in order to determine its position with great accuracy. For it to be seen at all it must be illuminated and scatter light to reach the eye. The least it can scatter is one quantum. In scattering this it receives from the light a kick of unpredictable amount; we can only state the respective probabilities of kicks of different amounts. Thus the condition of our ascertaining the position is that we disturb the electron in an incalculable way which will prevent our subsequently ascertaining how much momentum it had. However, we shall be able to ascertain the momentum with an uncertainty represented by the kick, and if the probable kick is small the probable error will be small. To keep the kick small we must use a quantum of small energy, that is to say, light of long wave-length. But to use long wave-length reduces the accuracy of our microscope. The longer the waves, the larger the diffraction images. And it must be remembered that it takes a great many quanta to outline the diffraction image; our one scattered quantum can only stimulate one atom in the retina of the eye, at some haphazard point within the theoretical diffraction image. Thus there will be an uncertainty in our determination of position of the electron proportional to the size of the diffraction image. We are in a dilemma. We can improve the determination of the position with the microscope by using light of shorter wave-length, but that gives the electron a greater kick and spoils the subsequent determination of momentum.

A picturesque illustration of the same dilemma is afforded if we imagine ourselves trying to see one of the electrons in an atom. For such finicking work it is no use employing ordinary light to see with; it is far too gross, its wave-length being greater than the whole atom. We must use fine-grained illumination and train our eyes to see with radiation of short wave-length— with X-rays in fact. It is well to remember that X-rays have a rather disastrous effect on atoms, so we had better use them sparingly. The least amount we can use is one quantum. Now, if we are ready, will you watch, whilst I flash one quantum of X-rays on to the atom? I may not hit the electron the first time; in that case, of course, you will not see it. Try again; this time my quantum has hit the electron. Look sharp, and notice where it is. Isn't it there? Bother! I must have blown the electron out of the atom.

This is not a casual difficulty; it is a cunningly arranged plot—a plot to prevent you from seeing something that does not exist, viz. the locality of the electron within the atom. If I use longer waves which do no harm, they will not define the electron sharply enough for you to see where it is. In shortening the wave-length, just as the light becomes fine enough its quantum becomes too rough and knocks the electron out of the atom.

Other examples of the reciprocal uncertainty have been given, and there seems to be no doubt that it is entirely general. The suggestion is that an association of exact position with exact momentum can never be discovered by us *because there is no such thing in Nature*. This is not inconceivable. Schrödinger's model of the particle as a wave-group gives a good illustration of how it can happen. We have seen (p. 217) that as the position of a wave-group becomes more defined the energy (frequency) becomes more indeterminate, and *vice versa*. I think that that is the essential value of Schrödinger's theory; it refrains from attributing to a particle a kind of determinacy which does not correspond to anything in Nature. But I would not regard the principle of indeterminacy as a result to be deduced from Schrödinger's theory; it is the other way about. The principle of indeterminacy, like the principle of relativity, represents the abandonment of a mistaken assumption which we never had sufficient reason for making. Just as we were misled into untenable ideas of the aether through trusting to an analogy with the material ocean, so we have been misled into untenable ideas of the attributes of the microscopic elements of world-structure through trusting to analogy with gross particles.

A New Epistemology. The principle of indeterminacy is epistemological. It reminds us once again that the world of physics is a world contemplated from within surveyed by appliances which are part of it and subject to its laws. What the world might be deemed like if probed in some supernatural manner by appliances not furnished by itself we do not profess to know.

There is a doctrine well known to philosophers that the moon ceases to exist when no one is looking at it. I will not discuss the doctrine since I have not the least idea what is the meaning of the word existence when used in this connection. At any rate the science of astronomy has not been based on this spasmodic kind of moon. In the scientific world (which has to fulfil functions less vague than merely existing) there is a moon which appeared on the scene before the astronomer; it reflects sunlight when no one sees it; it has mass when no one is measuring the mass; it is distant 240,000 miles from the earth when no one is surveying the distance; and it will eclipse the sun in 1999 even if the human race has succeeding in killing itself off before that date. The moon—the scientific moon—has to play the part of a continuous causal element in a world conceived to be all causally interlocked.

What should we regard as a *complete* description of this scientific world? We must not introduce anything like velocity through aether, which is meaningless since it is not assigned any causal connection with our experience. On the other hand we cannot limit the description to the immediate data of our own spasmodic observations. The description should include nothing that is unobservable but a great deal that is actually unobserved. Virtually we postulate an infinite army of watchers and measurers. From moment to moment they survey everything that can be surveyed and measure everything that can be measured by methods which we ourselves might conceivably employ. Everything they measure goes down as part of the complete description of the scientific world. We can, of course, introduce derivative descriptions, words expressing mathematical combinations of the immediate measures which may give greater point to the description—so that we may not miss seeing the wood for the trees.

By employing the known physical laws expressing the uniformities of Nature we can to a large extent dispense with this army of watchers. We can afford to let the moon out of sight for an hour or two and deduce where it has been in the meantime. But when I assert that the moon (which I last saw in the west an hour ago) is now setting, I assert this not as my deduction but as a true fact of the scientific world. I am still postulating the imaginary watcher; I do not consult him, but I retain him to corroborate my statement if it is challenged. Similarly, when we say that the distance of Sirius is 50 billion miles we are not giving a merely conventional interpretation to its measured parallax; we intend to give it the same status in knowledge as if someone had actually gone through the operation of laying measuring rods end to end and counted how many were needed to reach to Sirius; and we should listen patiently to anyone who produced reasons for thinking that our deductions did not correspond to the "real facts", i.e. the facts as known to our army of measurers. If we happen to make a deduction which could not conceivably be corroborated or disproved by these diligent measurers, there is no criterion of its truth or falsehood and it is thereby a meaningless deduction.

This theory of knowledge is primarily intended to apply to our macroscopic or large-scale survey of the physical world, but it has usually been taken for granted that it is equally applicable to a microscopic study. We have at last realised the disconcerting fact that though it applies to the moon it does not apply to the electron.

It does not hurt the moon to look at it. There is no

inconsistency in supposing it to have been under the surveillance of relays of watchers whilst we were asleep. But it is otherwise with an electron.   At certain times, viz. when it is interacting with a quantum, it might be detected by one of our watchers; but between whiles it virtually disappears from the physical world, having no interaction with it.   We might arm our observers with flash-lamps to keep a more continuous watch on its doings; but the trouble is that under the flashlight it will not go on doing what it was doing in the dark. There is a fundamental inconsistency in conceiving the microscopic structure of the physical world to be under continuous survey because the surveillance would itself wreck the whole machine.

I expect that at first this will sound to you like a merely dialectical difficulty.   But there is much more in it than that.   The deliberate frustration of our efforts to bring knowledge of the microscopic world into orderly plan, is a strong hint to alter the plan.

It means that we have been aiming at a false ideal of a complete description of the world.   There has not yet been time to make serious search for a new epistemology adapted to these conditions.   It has become doubtful whether it will ever be possible to construct a physical world solely out of the knowable—the guiding principle in our macroscopic theories.   If it is possible, it involves a great upheaval of the present foundations.   It seems more likely that we must be content to admit a mixture of the knowable and unknowable.   This means a denial of determinism, because the data required for a pre- diction of the future will include the unknowable ele- ments of the past.   I think it was Heisenberg who said, "The question whether from a complete knowledge of the past we can predict the future, does not arise because

a complete knowledge of the past involves a self-con-
tradiction."

It is only through a quantum action that the outside
world can interact with ourselves and knowledge of it
can reach our minds.   A quantum action may be the
means of revealing to us some fact about Nature, but
simultaneously a fresh unknown is implanted in the womb
of Time.   An addition to knowledge is won at the expense of an addition to ignorance.   It is hard to empty
the well of Truth with a leaky bucket.

Chapter XI

WORLD BUILDING

We have an intricate task before us. We are going to build a World—a physical world which will give a shadow performance of the drama enacted in the world of experience. We are not very expert builders as yet; and you must not expect the performance to go off without a hitch or to have the richness of detail which a critical audience might require. But the method about to be described seems to give the bold outlines; doubtless we have yet to learn other secrets of the craft of world building before we can complete the design.

The first problem is the building material. I remember that as an impecunious schoolboy I used to read attractive articles on how to construct wonderful contrivances out of mere odds and ends. Unfortunately these generally included the works of an old clock, a few superfluous telephones, the quicksilver from a broken barometer, and other oddments which happened not to be forthcoming in my lumber room. I will try not to let you down like that. I cannot make the world out of nothing, but I will demand as little specialised material as possible. Success in the game of World Building consists in the greatness of the contrast between the specialised properties of the completed structure and the unspecialised nature of the basal material.

Relation Structure. We take as building material *relations* and *relata*. The relations unite the relata; the relata are the meeting points of the relations. The one is unthinkable apart from the other. I do not think that a more general starting-point of structure could be conceived.

To distinguish the relata from one another we assign to them *monomarks*. The monomark consists of four numbers ultimately to be called "co-ordinates". But co-ordinates suggest space and geometry and as yet there is no such thing in our scheme; hence for the present we shall regard the four identification numbers as no more than an arbitrary monomark. Why *four* numbers? We use four because it turns out that ultimately the structure can be brought into better order that way; but we do not know why this should be so. We have got so far as to understand that if the relations insisted on a threefold or a fivefold ordering it would be much more difficult to build anything interesting out of them; but that is perhaps an insufficient excuse for the special assumption of fourfold order in the primitive material.

The relation between two human individuals in its broadest sense comprises every kind of connection or comparison between them—consanguinity, business transactions, comparative stature, skill at golf—any kind of description in which both are involved. For generality we shall suppose that the relations in our world-material are likewise composite and in no way expressible in numerical measure. Nevertheless there must be some kind of comparability or likeness of relations, as there is in the relations of human individuals; otherwise there would be nothing more to be said about the world than that everything in it was utterly unlike everything else. To put it another way, we must postulate not only relations between the relata but some kind of relation of likeness between some of the relations. The slightest concession in this direction will enable us to link the whole into a structure.

We assume then that, considering a relation between two relata, it will in general be possible to pick out two other relata close at hand which stand to one another in a "like" relation. By "like" I do not mean "like in every respect", but like in respect to one of the aspects of the composite relation. How is the particular aspect selected? If our relata were human individuals different judgments of likeness would be made by the genealogist, the economist, the psychologist, the sportsman, etc.; and the building of structure would here diverge along a number of different lines. Each could build his own world-structure from the common basal material of humanity. There is no reason to deny that a similar diversity of worlds could be built out of our postulated material. But all except one of these worlds will be stillborn. Our labour will be thrown away unless the world we have built is the one which the mind chooses to vivify into a world of experience. The only definition we can give of the aspect of the relations chosen for the criterion of likeness, is that it is the aspect which will ultimately be concerned in the getting into touch of mind with the physical world. But that is beyond the province of physics.

This one-to-one correspondence of "likeness" is only supposed to be definite in the limit when the relations are very close together in the structure. Thus we avoid any kind of comparison at a distance which is as objectionable as action at a distance. Let me confess at once that I do not know what I mean here by "very close together". As yet space and time have not been built. Perhaps we might say that only a few of the relata possess relations whose comparability to the first is definite, and take the definiteness of the comparability as the criterion of contiguity. I hardly know. The building at this point shows some cracks, but I think it should not be beyond the resources of the mathematical logician to cement them up. We should also arrange at this stage that the monomarks are so assigned as to give an indication of contiguity.

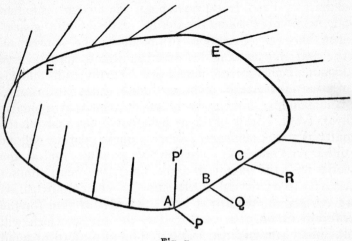

Fig. 7

Let us start with a relatum A and a relation AP radiating from it. Now step to a contiguous relatum B and pick out the "like" relation BQ. Go on to another contiguous relatum C and pick out the relation CR which is like BQ. (Note that since C is farther from A than from B, the relation at C which is like AP is not so definite as the relation which is like BQ.) Step by step we may make the comparison round a route $AEFA$ which returns to the starting-point. There is nothing to ensure that the final relation AP' which has, so to speak, been carried round the circuit will be the relation AP with which we originally started.

We have now two relations AP, AP' radiating from the first relatum, their difference being connected with a certain circuit in the world $AEFA$. The loose ends of the relations P and P' have their monomarks, and we can take the difference of the monomarks (i.e. the difference of the identification numbers comprised in them) as the code expression for the change introduced by carrying AP round the circuit. As we vary the circuit and the original relation, so the change PP' varies; and the next step is to find a mathematical formula expressing this dependence. There are virtually four things to connect, the circuit counting double since, for example, a rectangular circuit would be described by specifying two sides. Each of them has to be specified by four identification numbers (either monomarks or derived from monomarks); consequently, to allow for all combinations, the required mathematical formula contains 4^4 or 256 numerical coefficients. *These coefficients give a numerical measure of the structure surrounding the initial relatum.*

This completes the first part of our task to introduce numerical measure of structure into the basal material. The method is not so artificial as it appears at first sight. Unless we shirk the problem by putting the desired physical properties of the world directly into the original relations and relata, we must derive them from the structural interlocking of the relations; and such interlocking is naturally traced by following circuits among the relations. The axiom of comparability of contiguous relations only discriminates between like and unlike, and does not initially afford any means of classifying various degrees and kinds of unlikeness:

but we have found a means of specifying the kind of unlikeness of AP and AP' by reference to a circuit which "transforms" one into the other. Thus we have built a quantitative study of diversity on a definition of similarity.

The numerical measures of structure will be dependent on, and vary according to, the arbitrary code of monomarks used for the identification of relata. This, however, renders them especially suitable for building the ordinary quantities of physics. When the monomarks become co-ordinates of space and time the arbitrary choice of the code will be equivalent to the arbitrary choice of a frame of space and time; and it is in accordance with the theory of relativity that the measures of structure and the physical quantities to be built from them should vary with the frame of space and time. Physical quantities in general have no absolute value, but values relative to chosen frames of reference or codes of monomarks.

We have now fashioned our bricks from the primitive clay and the next job is to build with them. The 256 measures of structure varying from point to point of the world are somewhat reduced in number when duplicates are omitted; but even so they include a great deal of useless lumber which we do not require for the building. That seems to have worried a number of the most eminent physicists; but I do not quite see why. Ultimately it is the mind that decides what is lumber— which part of our building will shadow the things of common experience, and which has no such counterpart. It is no part of our function as purveyors of building material to anticipate what will be chosen for the palace of the mind. The lumber will now be dropped as irrelevant in the further operations, but I do not agree with those who think it a blemish on the theory that the lumber should ever have appeared in it.

By adding together certain of the measures of structure in a symmetrical manner and by ignoring others we reduce the really important measures to 16.* These can be divided into 10 forming a symmetrical scheme and 6 forming an antisymmetrical scheme. This is the great point of bifurcation of the world.

Symmetrical coefficients (10). Out of these we find it possible to construct Geometry and Mechanics. They are the ten potentials of Einstein $(g_{\mu\nu})$. We derive from them space, time, and the world-curvatures representing the mechanical properties of matter, viz. momentum, energy, stress, etc.

Antisymmetrical coefficients (6). Out of these we construct Electromagnetism. They are the three components of electric intensity and three components of magnetic force. We derive electric and magnetic potential, electric charge and current, light and other electric waves.

We do not derive the laws and phenomena of atomicity. Our building operation has somehow been too coarse to furnish the microscopic structure of the world, so that atoms, electrons and quanta are at present beyond our skill.

But in regard to what is called *field-physics* the construction is reasonably complete. The metrical, gravitational and electromagnetic fields are all included. We build the quantities enumerated above; and they obey the great laws of field-physics *in virtue of the way in which they have been built*. That is the special feature; the field laws—conservation of energy, mass, mo-

---

* Mathematically we contract the original tensor of the fourth rank to one of the second rank.

mentum and of electric charge, the law of gravitation, Maxwell's equations—are not controlling laws.* They are truisms. Not truisms when approached in the way the mind looks out on the world, but truisms when we encounter them in a building up of the world from a basal structure. I must try to make clear our new attitude to these laws.

Identical Laws. Energy momentum and stress, which we have identified with the ten principal curvatures of the world, are the subject of the famous laws of conservation of energy and momentum. Granting that the identification is correct, *these laws are mathematical identities*. Violation of them is unthinkable. Perhaps I can best indicate their nature by an analogy.

An aged college Bursar once dwelt secluded in his rooms devoting himself entirely to accounts. He realised the intellectual and other activities of the college only as they presented themselves in the bills. He vaguely conjectured an objective reality at the back of it all— some sort of parallel to the real college—though he could only picture it in terms of the pounds, shillings and pence which made up what he would call "the commonsense college of everyday experience". The method of account-keeping had become inveterate habit handed down from generations of hermit-like bursars; he accepted the form of accounts as being part of the nature of things. But he was of a scientific turn and he wanted to learn more about the college. One day in looking over his books he discovered a remarkable law.

* One law commonly grouped with these, viz. the law of ponderomotive force of the electric field, is not included. It seems to be impossible to get at the origin of this law without tackling electron structure which is beyond the scope of our present exercise in world-building.

For every item on the credit side an equal item appeared somewhere else on the debit side. "Ha!" said the Bursar, "I have discovered one of the great laws controlling the college. It is a perfect and exact law of the real world. Credit must be called plus and debit minus; and so we have the law of conservation of £ s. d. This is the true way to find out things, and there is no limit to what may ultimately be discovered by this scientific method. I will pay no more heed to the superstitions held by some of the Fellows as to a beneficent spirit called the King or evil spirits called the University Commissioners. I have only to go on in this way and I shall succeed in understanding why prices are always going up."

I have no quarrel with the Bursar for believing that scientific investigation of the accounts is a road to exact (though necessarily partial) knowledge of the reality behind them. Things may be discovered by this method which go deeper than the mere truism revealed by his first effort. In any case his life is especially concerned with accounts and it is proper that he should discover the laws of accounts whatever their nature. But I would point out to him that a discovery of the overlapping of the different aspects in which the realities of the college present themselves in the world of accounts, is not a discovery of the laws controlling the college; that he has not even begun to find the controlling laws. The college may totter but the Bursar's accounts still balance.

The law of conservation of momentum and energy results from the overlapping of the different aspects in which the "non-emptiness of space" presents itself to our practical experience. Once again we find that a fundamental law of physics is no controlling law but a "put-up job" as soon as we have ascertained the nature of that which is obeying it. We can measure certain forms of energy with a thermometer, momentum with a ballistic pendulum, stress with a manometer. Commonly we picture these as separate physical entities whose behaviour towards each other is controlled by a law. But now the theory is that the three instruments measure different but slightly overlapping aspects of a single physical condition, and a law connecting their measurements is of the same tautological type as a "law" connecting measurements with a metre-rule and a foot-rule.

I have said that violation of these laws of conservation is unthinkable. Have we then found physical laws which will endure for all time unshaken by any future revolution? But the proviso must be remembered, "granting that the identification [of their subject matter] is correct". The law itself will endure as long as two and two make four; but its practical importance depends on our knowing that which obeys it. We think we have this knowledge, but do not claim infallibility in this respect. From a practical point of view the law would be upset, if it turned out that the thing conserved was not that which we are accustomed to measure with the above-mentioned instruments but something slightly different.

Selective Influence of the Mind. This brings us very near to the problem of bridging the gulf between the scientific world and the world of everyday experience. The simpler elements of the scientific world have no immediate counterparts in everyday experience; we use them to build things which have counterparts. Energy, momentum and stress in the scientific world shadow well-known features of the familiar world.

I feel *stress* in my muscles; one form of *energy* gives me the sensation of warmth; the ratio of *momentum* to mass is velocity, which generally enters into my experience as change of position of objects. When I say that I feel these things I must not forget that the feeling, in so far as it is located in the physical world at all, is not in the things themselves but in a certain corner of my brain. In fact, the mind has also invented a craft of world-building; its familiar world is built not from the distribution of relata and relations but by its own peculiar interpretation of the code messages transmitted along the nerves into its sanctum.

Accordingly we must not lose sight of the fact that the world which physics attempts to describe arises from the convergence of two schemes of world-building. If we look at it only from the physical side there is inevitably an arbitrariness about the building. Given the bricks—the 16 measures of world-structure—there are all sorts of things we might build. Or we might take up again some of the rejected lumber and build a still wider variety of things. But we do not build arbitrarily; we build to order. The things we build have certain remarkable properties; they have these properties in virtue of the way they are built, but they also have them because such properties were *ordered*. There is a general description which covers at any rate most of the building operations needed in the construction of the physical world; in mathematical language the operation consists in Hamiltonian differentiation of an invariant function of the 16 measures of structure. I do not think that there is anything in the basal relation-structure that cries out for this special kind of combination; the significance of this process is not in inorganic nature. Its significance is that it corresponds to an outlook adopted by the mind for its own reasons; and any other building process would not converge to the mental scheme of world-building. The Hamiltonian derivative has just that kind of quality which makes it stand out in our minds as an active agent against a passive extension of space and time; and Hamiltonian differentiation is virtually the symbol for creation of an active world out of the formless background. Not once in the dim past, but continuously by conscious mind is the miracle of the Creation wrought.

By following this particular plan of building we construct things which satisfy the law of conservation, that is to say things which are permanent. The law of conservation is a truism for the things which satisfy it; but its prominence in the scheme of law of the physical world is due to the mind having demanded permanence. We might have built things which do not satisfy this law. In fact we do build one very important thing "action" which is not permanent; in respect to "action" physics has taken the bit in her teeth, and has insisted on recognising this as the most fundamental thing of all, although the mind has not thought it worthy of a place in the familiar world and has not vivified it by any mental image or conception. You will understand that the building to which I refer is not a shifting about of material; it is like building constellations out of stars. The things which we might have built but did not, are there just as much as those we did build. What we have called building is rather a selection from the patterns that weave themselves.

The element of permanence in the physical world, which is familiarly represented by the conception of substance, is essentially a contribution of the mind to the plan of building or selection. We can see this selective tendency at work in a comparatively simple problem, viz. the hydrodynamical theory of the ocean. At first sight the problem of what happens when the water is given some initial disturbance depends solely on inorganic laws; nothing could be more remote from the intervention of conscious mind. In a sense this is true; the laws of matter enable us to work out the motion and progress of the different portions of the water; and there, so far as the inorganic world is concerned, the problem might be deemed to end. But actually in hydrodynamical textbooks the investigation is diverted in a different direction, viz. to the study of the motions of waves and wave-groups. The progress of a wave is not progress of any material mass of water, but of a form which travels over the surface as the water heaves up and down; again the progress of a wave-group is not the progress of a wave. These forms have a certain degree of permanence amid the shifting particles of water. Anything permanent tends to become dignified with an attribute of substantiality. An ocean traveller has even more vividly the impression that the ocean is made of waves than that it is made of water.* Ultimately it is this innate hunger for permanence in our minds which directs the course of development of hydrodynamics, and likewise directs the world-building out of the sixteen measures of structure.

Perhaps it will be objected that other things besides mind can appreciate a permanent entity such as mass; a weighing machine can appreciate it and move a pointer to indicate how much mass there is. I do not think that is a valid objection. In building the physical world we must of course build the measuring appliances

---

* This was not intended to allude to certain consequential effects of the waves; it is true, I think, of the happier impressions of the voyage.

which are part of it; and the measuring appliances result from the plan of building in the same way as the entities which they measure. If, for example, we had used some of the "lumber" to build an entity *x,* we could presumably construct from the same lumber an appliance for measuring *x.* The difference is this—if the pointer of the weighing machine is reading 5 lbs. a human consciousness is in a mysterious way (not yet completely traced) aware of the fact, whereas if the measuring appliance for *x* reads 5 units no human mind is aware of it. Neither *x* nor the appliance for measuring *x* have any interaction with consciousness. Thus the responsibility for the fact that the scheme of the scientific world includes mass but excludes *x* rests ultimately with the phenomena of consciousness.

Perhaps a better way of expressing this selective influence of mind on the laws of Nature is to say that *values* are created by the mind. All the "light and shade" in our conception of the world of physics comes in this way from the mind, and cannot be explained without reference to the characteristics of consciousness.

The world which we have built from the relation-structure is no doubt doomed to be pulled about a good deal as our knowledge progresses. The quantum theory shows that some radical change is impending. But I think that our building exercise has at any rate widened our minds to the possibilities and has given us a different orientation towards the idea of physical law. The points which I stress are:

Firstly, a strictly quantitative science can arise from a basis which is purely qualitative. The comparability that has to be assumed axiomatically is a merely qualitative discrimination of likeness and unlikeness.

Secondly, the laws which we have hitherto regarded

as the most typical natural laws are of the nature of truisms, and the ultimate controlling laws of the basal structure (if there are any) are likely to be of a different type from any yet conceived.

Thirdly, the mind has by its selective power fitted the processes of Nature into a frame of law of a pattern largely of its own choosing; and in the discovery of this system of law the mind may be regarded as regaining from Nature that which the mind has put into Nature.

Three Types of Law. So far as we are able to judge, the laws of Nature divide themselves into three classes: (1) identical laws, (2) statistical laws, (3) transcendental laws. We have just been considering the identical laws, i.e. the laws obeyed as mathematical identities in virtue of the way in which the quantities obeying them are built. They cannot be regarded as genuine laws of control of the basal material of the world. Statistical laws relate to the behaviour of crowds, and depend on the fact that although the behaviour of each individual may be extremely uncertain average results can be predicted with confidence. Much of the apparent uniformity of Nature is a uniformity of averages. Our gross senses only take cognisance of the average effect of vast numbers of individual particles and processes; and the regularity of the average might well be compatible with a great degree of lawlessness of the individual. I do not think it is possible to dismiss statistical laws (such as the second law of thermodynamics) as merely mathematical adaptations of the other classes of law to certain practical problems. They involve a peculiar element of their own connected with the notion of *a priori* probability; but we do not yet seem able to find a place for this in any of the current conceptions of the world substratum.

If there are any genuine laws of control of the physical world they must be sought in the third group—the transcendental laws. The transcendental laws comprise all those which have not become obvious identities implied in the scheme of world-building. They are concerned with the particular behaviour of atoms, electrons and quanta—that is to say, the laws of atomicity of matter, electricity and action. We seem to be making some progress towards formulating them, but it is clear that the mind is having a much harder struggle to gain a rational conception of them than it had with the classical field-laws. We have seen that the field-laws, especially the laws of conservation, are indirectly imposed by the mind which has, so to speak, commanded a plan of world-building to satisfy them. It is a natural suggestion that the greater difficulty in elucidating the transcendental laws is due to the fact that we are no longer engaged in recovering from Nature what we have ourselves put into Nature, but are at last confronted with its own intrinsic system of government. But I scarcely know what to think. We must not assume that the possible developments of the new attitude towards natural law have been exhausted in a few short years. It may be that the laws of atomicity, like the laws of conservation, arise only in the presentation of the world to us and can be recognised as identities by some extension of the argument we have followed. But it is perhaps as likely that after we have cleared away all the superadded laws which arise solely in our mode of apprehension of the world about us, there will be left an external world developing under genuine laws of control.

At present we can notice the contrast that the laws

which we now recognise as man-made are characterised by continuity, whereas the laws to which the mind as yet lays no claim are characterised by atomicity. The quantum theory with its avoidance of fractions and insistence on integral units seems foreign to any scheme which we should be likely subconsciously to have imposed as a frame for natural phenomena. Perhaps our final conclusion as to the world of physics will resemble Kronecker's view of pure mathematics.

"God made the integers, all else is the work of man."*

* Die ganzen Zahlen hat Gott gemacht; alles anderes ist Menschenwerk.

Chapter XII

POINTER READINGS

Familiar Conceptions and Scientific Symbols. We have said in the Introduction that the raw material of the scientific world is not borrowed from the familiar world. It is only recently that the physicist has deliberately cut himself adrift from familiar conceptions. He did not set out to discover a new world but to tinker with the old. Like everyone else he started with the idea that things *are* more or less what they seem, and that our vivid impression of our environment may be taken as a basis to work from. Gradually it has been found that some of its most obvious features must be rejected. We learn that instead of standing on a firm immovable earth proudly rearing our heads towards the vault of heaven, we are hanging by our feet from a globe careering through space at a great many miles a second. But this new knowledge can still be grasped by a rearrangement of familiar conceptions. I can picture to myself quite vividly the state of affairs just described; if there is any strain, it is on my credulity, not on my powers of conception. Other advances of knowledge can be accommodated by that very useful aid to comprehension—"like this only more so". For example, if you think of something like a speck of dust *only more so* you have the atom as it was conceived up to a fairly recent date.

In addition to the familiar entities the physicist had to reckon with mysterious agencies such as gravitation or electric force; but this did not disturb his general outlook. We cannot say what electricity is "like"; but

247

at first its aloofness was not accepted as final. It was taken to be one of the main aims of research to discover how to reduce these agencies to something describable in terms of familiar conceptions—in short to "explain" them. For example, the true nature of electric force might be some kind of displacement of the aether. (Aether was at that time a familiar conception—like some extreme kind of matter *only more so.*) Thus there grew up a waiting-list of entities which should one day take on their rightful relation to conceptions of the familiar world. Meanwhile physics had to treat them as best it could without knowledge of their nature.

It managed surprisingly well. Ignorance of the nature of these entities was no bar to successful prediction of behaviour. We gradually awoke to the fact that the scheme of treatment of quantities on the waiting-list was becoming more precise and more satisfying than our knowledge of familiar things. Familiar conceptions did not absorb the waiting-list, but the waiting-list began to absorb familiar conceptions. Aether, after being in turn an elastic solid, a jelly, a froth, a conglomeration of gyrostats, was denied a material and substantial nature and put back on the waiting-list. It was found that science could accomplish so much with entities whose nature was left in suspense that it began to be questioned whether there was any advantage in removing the suspense. The crisis came when we began to construct familiar entities such as matter and light out of things on the waiting-list. Then at last it was seen that the linkage to familiar concepts should be through the advanced constructs of physics and not at the beginning of the alphabet. We have suffered, and we still suffer, from expectations that electrons and quanta must be in some fundamental respects like materials or forces familiar in the workshop—that all we have got to do is to imagine the usual kind of thing on an infinitely smaller scale. It must be our aim to avoid such prejudgments, which are surely illogical; and since we must cease to employ familiar concepts, symbols have become the only possible alternative.

The synthetic method by which we build up from its own symbolic elements a world which will imitate the actual behaviour of the world of familiar experience is adopted almost universally in scientific theories. Any ordinary theoretical paper in the scientific journals tacitly assumes that this approach is adopted. It has proved to be the most successful procedure; and it is the actual procedure underlying the advances set forth in the scientific part of this book. But I would not claim that no other way of working is admissible. We agree that at the end of the synthesis there must be a linkage to the familiar world of consciousness, and we are not necessarily opposed to attempts to reach the physical world from that end. From the point of view of philosophy it is desirable that this entrance should be explored, and it is conceivable that it may be fruitful scientifically. If I have rightly understood Dr. Whitehead's philosophy, that is the course which he takes. It involves a certain amount of working backwards (as we should ordinarily describe it); but his method of "extensive abstraction" is intended to overcome some of the difficulties of such a procedure. I am not qualified to form a critical judgment of this work, but in principle it appears highly interesting. Although this book may in most respects seem diametrically opposed to Dr. Whitehead's widely read philosophy of Nature, I think it would be truer to regard him as an ally who from the opposite side of the mountain is tunnelling to meet his less philosophically minded colleagues. The important thing is not to confuse the two entrances.

Nature of Exact Science. One of the characteristics of physics is that it is an exact science, and I have generally identified the domain of physics with the domain of exact science. Strictly speaking the two are not synonymous. We can imagine a science arising which has no contact with the usual phenomena and laws of physics, which yet admits of the same kind of exact treatment. It is conceivable that the Mendelian theory of heredity may grow into an independent science of this kind, for it would seem to occupy in biology the same position that the atomic theory occupied in chemistry a hundred years ago. The trend of the theory is to analyse complex individuals into "unit characters". These are like indivisible atoms with affinities and repulsions; their matings are governed by the same laws of chance which play so large a part in chemical thermodynamics; and numerical statistics of the characters of a population are predictable in the same way as the results of a chemical reaction.

Now the effect of such a theory on our philosophical views of the significance of life does not depend on whether the Mendelian atom admits of a strictly physical explanation or not. The unit character may be contained in some configuration of the physical molecules of the carrier, and perhaps even literally correspond to a chemical compound; or it may be something superadded which is peculiar to living matter and is not yet comprised in the schedule of physical entities. That is a side-issue. We are drawing near to the great question whether there is any domain of activity—of life, of consciousness, of deity—which will not be engulfed by the advance of exact science; and our apprehension is not directed against the particular entities of physics but against all entities of the category to which exact science can apply. For exact science invokes, or has seemed to invoke, a type of law inevitable and soulless against which the human spirit rebels. If science finally declares that man is no more than a fortuitous concourse of atoms, the blow will not be softened by the explanation that the atoms in question are the Mendelian unit characters and not the material atoms of the chemist.

Let us then examine the kind of knowledge which is handled by exact science. If we search the examination papers in physics and natural philosophy for the more intelligible questions we may come across one beginning something like this: "An elephant slides down a grassy hillside. . . ." The experienced candidate knows that he need not pay much attention to this; it is only put in to give an impression of realism. He reads on: "The mass of the elephant is two tons." Now we are getting down to business; the elephant fades out of the problem and a mass of two tons takes its place. What exactly is this two tons, the real subject-matter of the problem? It refers to some property or condition which we vaguely describe as "ponderosity" occurring in a particular region of the external world. But we shall not get much further that way; the nature of the external world is inscrutable, and we shall only plunge into a quagmire of indescribables. Never mind what two tons *refers* to; what *is* it? How has it actually entered in so definite a way into our experience? Two tons *is* the reading of the pointer when the elephant was placed on a weighing-machine. Let us pass on. "The slope of the hill is 60°." Now the hillside fades out of the problem and an angle of 60° takes its place. What is 60°? There is no need to struggle with mystical conceptions of direction; 60° *is* the reading of a plumb-line against the divisions of a protractor. Similarly for the other data of the problem. The softly yielding turf on which the elephant slid is replaced by a coefficient of friction, which though perhaps not directly a pointer reading is of kindred nature. No doubt there are more roundabout ways used in practice for determining the weights of elephants and the slopes of hills, but these are justified because it is known that they give the same results as direct pointer readings.

And so we see that the poetry fades out of the problem, and by the time the serious application of exact science begins we are left with only pointer readings. If then only pointer readings or their equivalents are put into the machine of scientific calculation, how can we grind out anything but pointer readings? But that is just what we do grind out. The question presumably was to find the time of descent of the elephant, and the answer is a pointer reading on the seconds' dial of our watch.

The triumph of exact science in the foregoing problem consisted in establishing a numerical connection between the pointer reading of the weighing-machine in one experiment on the elephant and the pointer reading of the watch in another experiment. And when we examine critically other problems of physics we find that this is typical. The whole subject-matter of exact science consists of pointer readings and similar indications. We cannot enter here into the definition of what are to be classed as similar indications. The observation of approximate coincidence of the pointer with a scale-division can generally be extended to include the observation of any kind of coincidence—or, as it is usually expressed in the language of the general relativity theory, an intersection of world-lines.   The essential point is that, although we seem to have very definite conceptions of objects in the external world, those conceptions do not enter into exact science and are not in any way confirmed by it. Before exact science can begin to handle the problem they must be replaced by quantities representing the results of physical measurement.

Perhaps you will object that although only the pointer readings enter into the actual calculation it would make nonsense of the problem to leave out all reference to anything else.   The problem necessarily involves some kind of connecting background.   It was not the pointer reading of the weighing-machine that slid down the hill! And yet from the point of view of exact science the thing that really did descend the hill can only be described as a bundle of pointer readings. (It should be remembered that the hill also has been replaced by pointer readings, and the sliding down is no longer an active adventure but a functional relation of space and time measures.)   The word elephant calls up a certain association of mental impressions, but it is clear that mental impressions as such cannot be the subject handled in the physical problem. We have, for example, an impression of bulkiness. To this there is presumably some direct counterpart in the external world, but that counterpart must be of a nature beyond our apprehension, and science can make nothing of it. Bulkiness enters into exact science by yet another substitution; we replace it by a series of readings of a pair of calipers. Similarly the greyish black appearance in our mental impression is replaced in exact science by the readings of a photometer for various wave-lengths of light. And so on until all the characteristics of the elephant are exhausted and it has become reduced to a schedule of measures. There is always the triple correspondence—

(*a*) a mental image, which is in our minds and not in the external world;

(*b*) some kind of counterpart in the external world, which is of inscrutable nature;

(*c*) a set of pointer readings, which exact science can study and connect with other pointer readings.

And so we have our schedule of pointer readings ready to make the descent. And if you still think that this substitution has taken away all reality from the problem, I am not sorry that you should have a foretaste of the difficulty in store for those who hold that exact science is all-sufficient for the description of the universe and that there is nothing in our experience which cannot be brought within its scope.

I should like to make it clear that the limitation of the scope of physics to pointer readings and the like is not a philosophical craze of my own but is essentially the current scientific doctrine. It is the outcome of a tendency discernible far back in the last century but only formulated comprehensively with the advent of the relativity theory. The vocabulary of the physicist comprises a number of words such as length, angle, velocity, force, potential, current, etc., which we call "physical quantities". It is now recognised as essential that these should be *defined* according to the way in which we actually recognise them when confronted with them, and not according to the metaphysical significance which we may have anticipated for them. In the old textbooks mass was defined as "quantity of matter";

but when it came to an actual determination of mass, an experimental method was prescribed which had no bearing on this definition. The belief that the quantity determined by the accepted method of measurement represented the quantity of matter in the object was merely a pious opinion. At the present day there is no sense in which the quantity of matter in a pound of lead can be said to be equal to the quantity in a pound of sugar. Einstein's theory makes a clean sweep of these pious opinions, and insists that each physical quantity should be defined as the result of certain operations of measurement and calculation. You may if you like think of mass as something of inscrutable nature to which the pointer reading has a kind of relevance. But in physics at least there is nothing much to be gained by this mystification, because it is the pointer reading itself which is handled in exact science; and if you embed it in something of a more transcendental nature, you have only the extra trouble of digging it out again.

It is quite true that when we say the mass is two tons we have not specially in mind the reading of the particular machine on which the weighing was carried out. That is because we do not start to tackle the problem of the elephant's escapade *ab initio* as though it were the first inquiry we had ever made into the phenomena of the external world. The examiner would have had to be much more explicit if he had not presumed a general acquaintance with the elementary laws of physics, i.e. laws which permit us to deduce the readings of other indicators from the reading of one. *It is this connectivity of pointer readings, expressed by physical laws, which supplies the continuous background that any realistic problem demands.*

It is obviously one of the conditions of the problem that the same elephant should be concerned in the weighing experiment and in the tobogganing experiment. How can this identity be expressed in a description of the world by pointer readings only? Two readings may be *equal,* but it is meaningless to inquire if they are *identical*; if then the elephant is a bundle of pointer readings, how can we ask whether it is continually the *identical* bundle? The examiner does not confide to us how the identity of the elephant was ensured; we have only his personal guarantee that there was no substitution. Perhaps the creature answered to its name on both occasions; if so the test of identity is clearly outside the present domain of physics. The only test lying purely in the domain of physics is that of continuity; the elephant must be watched all the way from the scales to the hillside. The elephant, we must remember, is a tube in the four-dimensional world demarcated from the rest of space-time by a more or less abrupt boundary. Using the retina of his eye as an indicator and making frequent readings of the outline of the image, the observer satisfied himself that he was following one continuous and isolated world-tube from beginning to end. If his vigilance was intermittent he took a risk of substitution, and consequently a risk of the observed time of descent failing to agree with the time calculated.* Note that we do not infer that there is any identity of the contents of the isolated world-tube throughout its length; such identity would be meaning-

* A good illustration of such substitution is afforded by astronomical observations of a certain double star with two components of equal brightness. After an intermission of observation the two components were inadvertently interchanged, and the substitution was not detected until the increasing discrepancy between the actual and predicted orbits was inquired into.

less in physics. We use instead the law of conservation of mass (either as an empirical law or deduced from the law of gravitation) which assures us that, provided the tube is isolated, the pointer reading on the schedule derived from the weighing-machine type of experiment has a constant value along the tube. For the purpose of exact science "the same object" becomes replaced by "isolated world-tube". The constancy of certain properties of the elephant is not assumed as self-evident from its *sameness*, but is an inference from experimental and theoretical laws relating to world-tubes which are accepted as well established.

Limitations of Physical Knowledge. Whenever we state the properties of a body in terms of physical quantities we are imparting knowledge as to the response of various metrical indicators to its presence, *and nothing more*. After all, knowledge of this kind is fairly comprehensive. A knowledge of the response of all kinds of objects—weighing-machines and other indicators—would determine completely its relation to its environment, leaving only its inner un-get-atable nature undetermined. In the relativity theory we accept this as full knowledge, the nature of an object in so far as it is ascertainable by scientific inquiry being the abstraction of its relations to all surrounding objects. The progress of the relativity theory has been largely due to the development of a powerful mathematical calculus for dealing compendiously with an infinite scheme of pointer readings, and the technical term *tensor* used so largely in treatises on Einstein's theory may be translated *schedule of pointer readings*. It is part of the aesthetic appeal of the mathematical theory of relativity that the mathematics is so closely adapted to the physical conceptions. It is not so in all subjects. For example, we may admire the triumph of patience of the mathematician in predicting so closely the positions of the moon, but aesthetically the lunar theory is atrocious; it is obvious that the moon and the mathematician use different methods of finding the lunar orbit. But by the use of tensors the mathematical physicist precisely describes the nature of his subject-matter as a schedule of indicator readings; and those accretions of images and conceptions which have no place in physical science are automatically dismissed.

The recognition that our knowledge of the objects treated in physics consists solely of readings of pointers and other indicators transforms our view of the status of physical knowledge in a fundamental way. Until recently it was taken for granted that we had knowledge of a much more intimate kind of the entities of the external world. Let me give an illustration which takes us to the root of the great problem of the relations of matter and spirit. Take the living human brain endowed with mind and thought. Thought is one of the indisputable facts of the world. I know that I think, with a certainty which I cannot attribute to any of my physical knowledge of the world. More hypothetically, but on fairly plausible evidence, I am convinced that you have minds which think. Here then is a world fact to be investigated. The physicist brings his tools and commences systematic exploration. All that he discovers is a collection of atoms and electrons and fields of force arranged in space and time, apparently similar to those found in inorganic objects. He may trace other physical characteristics, energy, temperature, entropy. None of these is identical with thought. He might set down thought as an illusion—some perverse interpretation of the interplay of the physical entities that he has found. Or if he sees the folly of calling the most undoubted element of our experience an illusion, he will have to face the tremendous question, How can this collection of ordinary atoms be a thinking machine? But what knowledge have we of the nature of atoms which renders it at all incongruous that they should constitute a thinking object? The Victorian physicist felt that he knew just what he was talking about when he used such terms as *matter* and *atoms*. Atoms were tiny billiard balls, a crisp statement that was supposed to tell you all about their nature in a way which could never be achieved for transcendental things like consciousness, beauty or humour. But now we realise that science has nothing to say as to the intrinsic nature of the atom. The physical atom is, like everything else in physics, a schedule of pointer readings. The schedule is, we agree, attached to some unknown background. Why not then attach it to something of spiritual nature of which a prominent characteristic is *thought*. It seems rather silly to prefer to attach it to something of a so-called "concrete" nature inconsistent with thought, and then to wonder where the thought comes from. We have dismissed all preconception as to the background of our pointer readings, and for the most part we can discover nothing as to its nature. But in one case—namely, for the pointer readings of my own brain—I have an insight which is not limited to the evidence of the pointer readings. That insight shows that they are attached to a background of consciousness. Although I may expect that the background of other pointer readings in physics is of a nature continuous with that revealed to me in this particular case, I do not suppose that it always has the more specialised attributes of consciousness.* But in regard to my one piece of insight into the background no problem of irreconcilability arises; I have no other knowledge of the background with which to reconcile it.

In science we study the linkage of pointer readings with pointer readings. The terms link together in endless cycle with the same inscrutable nature running through the whole. *There is nothing to prevent the assemblage of atoms constituting a brain from being of itself a thinking object in virtue of that nature which physics leaves undetermined and undeterminable.* If we must embed our schedule of indicator readings in some kind of background, at least let us accept the only hint we have received as to the significance of the background—namely that it has a nature capable of manifesting itself as mental activity.

Cyclic Method of Physics. I must explain this reference to an endless cycle of physical terms. I will refer again to Einstein's law of gravitation. I have already expounded it to you more than once and I hope you gained some idea of it from the explanation. This time I am going to expound it in a way so complete that there is not much likelihood that anyone will understand it. Never mind. We are not now seeking further light on the cause of gravitation; we are interested in seeing

---

* For example, we should most of us assume (hypothetically) that the dynamical quality of the world referred to in chapter v is characteristic of the *whole* background. Apparently it is not to be found in the pointer readings, and our only insight into it is in the feeling of "becoming" in our consciousness. "Becoming" like "reasoning" is known to us only through its occurrence in our own minds; but whereas it would be absurd to suppose that the latter extends to inorganic aggregations of atoms, the former may be (and commonly is) extended to the inorganic world, so that it is not a matter of indifference whether the progress of the inorganic world is viewed from past to future or from future to past.

what would really be involved in a *complete* explanation of anything physical.

Einstein's law in its analytical form is a statement that in empty space certain quantities called *potentials* obey certain lengthy differential equations. We make a memorandum of the word "potential" to remind us that we must later on explain what it means. We might conceive a world in which the potentials at every moment and every place had quite arbitrary values. The actual world is not so unlimited, the potentials being restricted to those values which conform to Einstein's equations. The next question is, What are potentials? They can be defined as quantities derived by quite simple mathematical calculations from certain fundamental quantities called *intervals*. (MEM. Explain "interval".) If we know the values of the various intervals throughout the world definite rules can be given for deriving the values of the potentials. What are intervals? They are relations between pairs of events which can be measured with a *scale* or a *clock* or with both. (MEM. Explain "scale" and "clock".) Instructions can be given for the correct use of the scale and clock so that the interval is given by a prescribed combination of their readings. What are scales and clocks? A scale is a graduated strip of *matter* which. . . . (MEM. Explain "matter".) On second thoughts I will leave the rest of the description as "an exercise to the reader" since it would take rather a long time to enumerate all the properties and niceties of behaviour of the material standard which a physicist would accept as a perfect scale or a perfect clock. We pass on to the next question, What is matter? We have dismissed the metaphysical conception of substance. We might perhaps here describe the atomic and electrical structure of matter, but that leads to the microscopic aspects of the world, whereas we are here taking the macroscopic outlook. Confining ourselves to mechanics, which is the subject in which the law of gravitation arises, matter may be defined as the embodiment of three related physical quantities, *mass* (or energy), *momentum* and *stress*. What are "mass", "momentum" and "stress"? It is one of the most far-reaching achievements of Einstein's theory that it has given an exact answer to this question. They are rather formidable looking expressions containing the *potentials* and their first and second derivatives with respect to the co-ordinates. What are the potentials? Why, that is just what I have been explaining to you!

The definitions of physics proceed according to the method immortalised in "The House that Jack built": This is the potential, that was derived from the interval, that was measured by the scale, that was made from the matter, that embodied the stress, that. . . . But instead of finishing with Jack, whom of course every youngster must know without need for an introduction, we make a circuit back to the beginning of the rhyme: . . . that worried the cat, that killed the rat, that ate the malt, that lay in the house, that was built by the priest all shaven and shorn, that married the man. . . . Now we can go round and round for ever.

But perhaps you have already cut short my explanation of gravitation. When we reached *matter* you had had enough of it. "Please do not explain any more, I happen to know what matter is." Very well; matter is something that Mr. X knows. Let us see how it goes: This is the potential that was derived from the interval that was measured by the scale that was made from the matter that Mr. X knows. Next question, What is Mr. X?

Well, it happens that physics is not at all anxious to

pursue the question, What is Mr. X? It is not disposed to admit that its elaborate structure of a physical universe is "The House that Mr. X built". It looks upon Mr. X—and more particularly the part of Mr. X that *knows*—as a rather troublesome tenant who at a late stage of the world's history has come to inhabit a

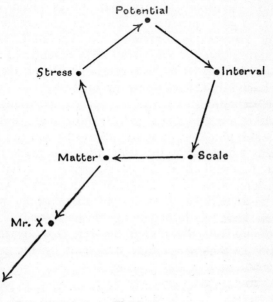

Fig. 8

structure which inorganic Nature has by slow evolutionary progress contrived to build. And so it turns aside from the avenue leading to Mr. X—and beyond—and closes up its cycle leaving him out in the cold.

From its own point of view physics is entirely justified. That matter in some indirect way comes within the purview of Mr. X's mind is not a fact of any utility for a theoretical scheme of physics. We cannot embody it in a differential equation. It is ignored; and the physical properties of matter and other entities are expressed by their linkages in the cycle. And you can see how by the ingenious device of the cycle physics secures for itself a self-contained domain for study with no loose ends projecting into the unknown. All other physical definitions have the same kind of interlocking. Electric force is defined as something which causes motion of an electric charge; an electric charge is something which exerts electric force. So that an electric charge is something that exerts something that produces motion of something that exerts something that produces . . *ad infinitum.*

But I am not now writing of pure physics, and from a broader standpoint I do not see how we can leave out Mr. X. The fact that matter is "knowable to Mr. X" must be set down as one of the fundamental attributes of matter. I do not say that it is very distinctive, since other entities of physics are also knowable to him; but the potentiality of the whole physical world for awaking impressions in consciousness is an attribute not to be ignored when we compare the actual world with worlds which, we fancy, *might* have been created. There seems to be a prevalent disposition to minimise the importance of this. The attitude is that "knowableness to Mr. X" is a negligible attribute, because Mr. X is so clever that he could know pretty much anything that there was to know. I have already urged the contrary view—that there is a definitely selective action of the mind; and since physics treats of what is knowable to mind * its

* This is obviously true of all experimental physics, and must be true of theoretical physics if it is (as it professes to be) based on experiment.

subject-matter has undergone, and indeed retains evidences of, this process of selection.

Actuality. "Knowableness to mind" is moreover a property which differentiates the actual world of our experience from imaginary worlds in which the same general laws of Nature are supposed to hold true. Consider a world—Utopia, let us say—governed by all the laws of Nature known and unknown which govern our own world, but containing better stars, planets, cities, animals, etc.—a world which might exist, but it just happens that it doesn't. How can the physicist test that Utopia is not the actual world? We refer to a piece of matter in it; it is not real matter but it attracts any other piece of (unreal) matter in Utopia according to the law of gravitation. Scales and clocks constructed of this unreal matter will measure wrong intervals, but the physicist cannot detect that they are wrong unless he has first shown the unreality of the matter. As soon as any element in it has been shown to be unreal Utopia collapses; but so long as we keep to the cycles of physics we can never find the vulnerable point, for each element is correctly linked to the rest of the cycle, all our laws of Nature expressed by the cycle being obeyed in Utopia by hypothesis. The unreal stars emit unreal light which falls on unreal retinas and ultimately reaches unreal brains. The next step takes it outside the cycle and gives the opportunity of exposing the whole deception. Is the brain disturbance translated into consciousness? That will test whether the brain is real or unreal. There is no question about consciousness being real or not; consciousness is self-knowing and the epithet real adds nothing to that. Of the infinite number of worlds which are examples of what might be possible under the laws of Nature, there is one which does something more than fulfil those laws of Nature. This property, which is evidently not definable with respect to any of the laws of Nature, we describe as "actuality"—generally using the word as a kind of halo of indefinite import. We have seen that the trend of modern physics is to reject these indefinite attributions and to define its terms according to the way in which we recognise the properties when confronted by them. We recognise the actuality of a particular world because it is that world alone with which consciousness interacts. However much the theoretical physicist may dislike a reference to consciousness, the experimental physicist uses freely this touchstone of actuality. He would perhaps prefer to believe that his instruments and observations are certified as actual by his material sense organs; but the final guarantor is the mind that comes to know the indications of the material organs. Each of us is armed with this touchstone of actuality; by applying it we decide that this sorry world of ours is actual and Utopia is a dream. As our individual consciousnesses are different, so our touchstones are different; but fortunately they all agree in their indication of actuality—or at any rate those which agree are in sufficient majority to shut the others up in lunatic asylums.

It is natural that theoretical physics in its formulation of a general scheme of law should leave out of account actuality and the guarantor of actuality. For it is just this omission which makes the difference between a law of Nature and a particular sequence of events. That which is possible (or not "too improbable") is the domain of natural science; that which is actual is the domain of natural history. We need scarcely add that the contemplation in natural science of a wider domain than the actual leads to a far better understanding of the actual.

From a broader point of view than that of elaborating the physical scheme of law we cannot treat the connection with mind as merely an incident in a self-existent inorganic world. In saying that the differentiation of the actual from the non-actual is only expressible by reference to mind I do not mean to imply that a universe without conscious mind would have no more status than Utopia. But its property of actuality would be indefinable since the one approach to a definition is cut off. The actuality of Nature is like the beauty of Nature. We can scarcely describe the beauty of a landscape as non-existent when there is no conscious being to witness it; but it is through consciousness that we can attribute a meaning to it. And so it is with the actuality of the world. If actuality means "known to mind" then it is a purely subjective character of the world; to make it objective we must substitute "knowable to mind". The less stress we lay on the accident of parts of the world being known at the present era to particular minds, the more stress we must lay on the *potentiality* of being known to mind as a fundamental objective property of matter, giving it the status of actuality whether individual consciousness is taking note of it or not.

In the diagram Mr. X has been linked to the cycle at a particular point in deference to his supposed claim that he knows matter; but a little reflection will show that the point of contact of mind with the physical universe is not very definite. Mr. X knows a table; but the point of contact with his mind is not in the material of the table. Light waves are propagated from the table to the eye; chemical changes occur in the retina; propagation of some kind occurs in the optic nerves;

atomic changes follow in the brain. Just where the final leap into consciousness occurs is not clear. We do not know the last stage of the message in the physical world before it became a sensation in consciousness. This makes no difference. The physical entities have a cyclic connection, and whatever intrinsic nature we attribute to one of them runs as a background through the whole cycle. It is not a question whether matter or electricity or potential is the direct stimulus to the mind; in their physical aspects these are equally represented as pointer readings or schedules of pointer readings. According to our discussion of world building they are the measures of structure arising from the comparability of certain aspects of the basal relations—measures which by no means exhaust the significance of those relations. I do not believe that the activity of matter at a certain point of the brain stimulates an activity of mind; my view is that in the activity of matter there is a metrical description of certain aspects of the activity of mind. The activity of the matter is our way of recognising a combination of the measures of structure; the activity of the mind is our insight into the complex of relations whose comparability gives the foundation of those measures.

"What is Mr. X?" In the light of these considerations let us now see what we can make of the question, What is Mr. X? I must undertake the inquiry single-handed; I cannot avail myself of your collaboration without first answering or assuming an answer to the equally difficult question, What are you? Accordingly the whole inquiry must take place in the domain of my own consciousness. I find there certain data purporting to relate to this unknown X; and I can (by using powers

which respond to my volition) extend the data, i.e. I can perform experiments on X. For example I can make a chemical analysis. The immediate result of these experiments is the occurrence of certain visual or olfactory sensations in my consciousness. Clearly it is a long stride from these sensations to any rational inference about Mr. X. For example, I learn that Mr. X has carbon in his brain, but the *immediate* knowledge was of something (not carbon) in my own mind. The reason why I, on becoming aware of something in my mind, can proceed to assert knowledge of something elsewhere, is because there is a systematic scheme of inference which can be traced from the one item of knowledge to the other. Leaving aside instinctive or commonsense inference—the crude precursor of scientific inference—the inference follows a linkage, which can only be described symbolically, extending from the point in the symbolic world where I locate myself to the point where I locate Mr. X.

One feature of this inference is that I never discover what carbon really is. It remains a symbol. There is carbon in my own brain-mind; but the self-knowledge of my mind does not reveal this to me. I can only know that the symbol for carbon must be placed there by following a route of inference through the external world similar to that used in discovering it in Mr. X; and however closely associated this carbon may be with my thinking powers, it is as a symbol divorced from any thinking capacity that I learn of its existence. Carbon is a symbol definable only in terms of the other symbols belonging to the cyclic scheme of physics. What I have discovered is that, in order that the symbols describing the physical world may conform to the mathematical formulae which they are designed to obey, it is necessary to place the symbol for carbon (amongst others) in the locality of Mr. X. By similar means I can make an exhaustive physical examination of Mr. X and discover the whole array of symbols to be assigned to his locality.

Will this array of symbols give me the whole of Mr. X? There is not the least reason to think so. The voice that comes to us over the telephone wire is not the whole of what is at the end of the wire. The scientific linkage is like the telephone wire; it can transmit just what it is constructed to transmit and no more.

It will be seen that the line of communication has two aspects. It is a chain of inference stretching from the symbols immediately associated with the sensations in my mind to the symbols descriptive of Mr. X; and it is a chain of stimuli in the external world starting from Mr. X and reaching my brain. Ideally the steps of the inference exactly reverse the steps of the physical transmission which brought the information. (Naturally we make many short cuts in inference by applying accumulated experience and knowledge.) Commonly we think of it only in its second aspect as a physical transmission; but because it is also a line of inference it is subject to limitations which we should not necessarily expect a physical transmission to conform to.

The system of inference employed in physical investigation reduces to mathematical equations governing the symbols, and so long as we adhere to this procedure we are limited to symbols of arithmetical character appropriate to such mathematical equations.* Thus there is no opportunity for acquiring by any physical

---

* The solitary exception is, I believe, Dirac's generalisation which introduces q-numbers (p. 210). There is as yet no approach to a general system of inference on a non-numerical basis.

investigation a knowledge of Mr. X other than that which can be expressed in numerical form so as to be passed through a succession of mathematical equations.

Mathematics is the model of exact inference; and in physics we have endeavoured to replace all cruder inference by this rigorous type. Where we cannot complete the mathematical chain we confess that we are wandering in the dark and are unable to assert real knowledge. Small wonder then that physical science should have evolved a conception of the world consisting of entities rigorously bound to one another by mathematical equations forming a deterministic scheme. This knowledge has all been inferred and it was bound therefore to conform to the system of inference that was used. The determinism of the physical laws simply reflects the determinism of the method of inference. This soulless nature of the scientific world need not worry those who are persuaded that the main significances of our environment are of a more spiritual character. Anyone who studied the method of inference employed by the physicist could predict the general characteristics of the world that he must necessarily find. What he could not have predicted is the great success of the method— the submission of so large a proportion of natural phenomena to be brought into the prejudged scheme. But making all allowance for future progress in developing the scheme, it seems to be flying in the face of obvious facts to pretend that it is all comprehensive. Mr. X is one of the recalcitrants. When sound-waves impinge on his ear he moves, not in accordance with a mathematical equation involving the physical measure numbers of the waves, but in accordance with the *meaning* that those sound-waves are used to convey. To know what there is about Mr. X which makes him behave in this strange way, we must look not to a physical system of inference, but to that insight beneath the symbols which in our own minds we possess.   It is by this insight that we can finally reach an answer to our question, What is Mr. X?

Chapter XIII

REALITY

The Real and the Concrete. One of our ancestors, taking arboreal exercise in the forest, failed to reach the bough intended and his hand closed on nothingness. The accident might well occasion philosophical reflections on the distinctions of substance and void—to say nothing of the phenomenon of gravity. However that may be, his descendants down to this day have come to be endowed with an immense respect for substance arising we know not how or why. So far as familiar experience is concerned, substance occupies the centre of the stage, rigged out with the attributes of form, colour, hardness, etc., which appeal to our several senses. Behind it is a subordinate background of space and time permeated by forces and unconcrete agencies to minister to the star performer.

Our conception of substance is only vivid so long as we do not face it. It begins to fade when we analyse it. We may dismiss many of its supposed attributes which are evidently projections of our sense-impressions outwards into the external world. Thus the colour which is so vivid to us is in our minds and cannot be embodied in a legitimate conception of the substantial object itself. But in any case colour is no part of the essential nature of substance. Its supposed nature is that which we try to call to mind by the word "concrete", which is perhaps an outward projection of our sense of touch.

273

When I try to abstract from the bough everything but its substance or concreteness and concentrate on an effort to apprehend this, all ideas elude me; but the effort brings with it an instinctive tightening of the fingers—from which perhaps I might infer that my conception of substance is not very different from my arboreal ancestor's.

So strongly has substance held the place of leading actor on the stage of experience that in common usage *concrete* and *real* are almost synonymous. Ask any man who is not a philosopher or a mystic to name something typically real; he is almost sure to choose a concrete thing. Put the question to him whether Time is real; he will probably decide with some hesitation that it must be classed as real, but he has an inner feeling that the question is in some way inappropriate and that he is being cross-examined unfairly.

In the scientific world the conception of substance is wholly lacking, and that which most nearly replaces it, viz. electric charge, is not exalted as star-performer above the other entities of physics. For this reason the scientific world often shocks us by its appearance of unreality. It offers nothing to satisfy our demand for the concrete. How should it, when we cannot formulate that demand? I tried to formulate it; but nothing resulted save a tightening of the fingers. Science does not overlook the provision for tactual and muscular sensation. In leading us away from the concrete, science is reminding us that our contact with the real is more varied than was apparent to the ape-mind, to whom the bough which supported him typified the beginning and end of reality.

It is not solely the scientific world that will now occupy our attention. In accordance with the last chapter we are taking a larger view in which the cyclical schemes of physics are embraced with much besides. But before venturing on this more risky ground I have to emphasise one conclusion which is definitely scientific. The modern scientific theories have broken away from the common standpoint which identifies the real with the concrete. I think we might go so far as to say that time is more typical of physical reality than matter, because it is freer from those metaphysical associations which physics disallows. It would not be fair, being given an inch, to take an ell, and say that having gone so far physics may as well admit at once that reality is spiritual. We must go more warily. But in approaching such questions we are no longer tempted to take up the attitude that everything which lacks concreteness is thereby self-condemned.

The cleavage between the scientific and the extra-scientific domain of experience is, I believe, not a cleavage between the concrete and the transcendental but between the metrical and the non-metrical. I am at one with the materialist in feeling a repugnance towards any kind of pseudo-science of the extra-scientific territory. Science is not to be condemned as narrow because it refuses to deal with elements of experience which are unadapted to its own highly organised method; nor can it be blamed for looking superciliously on the comparative disorganisation of our knowledge and methods of reasoning about the non-metrical part of experience. But I think we have not been guilty of pseudo-science in our attempt to show in the last two chapters how it comes about that within the whole domain of experience a selected portion is capable of that exact metrical representation which is requisite for development by the scientific method.

Mind-Stuff. I will try to be as definite as I can as to the glimpse of reality which we seem to have reached. Only I am well aware that in committing myself to details I shall probably blunder. Even if the right view has here been taken of the philosophical trend of modern science, it is premature to suggest a cut-and-dried scheme of the nature of things. If the criticism is made that certain aspects are touched on which come more within the province of the expert psychologist, I must admit its pertinence. The recent tendencies of science do, I believe, take us to an eminence from which we can look down into the deep waters of philosophy; and if I rashly plunge into them,, it is not because I have confidence in my powers of swimming, but to try to show that the water is really deep.

To put the conclusion crudely—the stuff of the world is mind-stuff. As is often the way with crude statements, I shall have to explain that by "mind" I do not here exactly mean mind and by "stuff" I do not at all mean stuff. Still this is about as near as we can get to the idea in a simple phrase. The mind-stuff of the world is, of course, something more general than our individual conscious minds; but we may think of its nature as not altogether foreign to the feelings in our consciousness. The realistic matter and fields of force of former physical theory are altogether irrelevant—except in so far as the mind-stuff has itself spun these imaginings. The symbolic matter and fields of force of present-day theory are more relevant, but they bear to it the same relation that the bursar's accounts bear to the activity of the college. Having granted this, the mental activity of the part of the world constituting ourselves occasions no surprise; it is known to us by direct self-knowledge, and we do not explain it away as something other than we know it to be—or, rather, it knows itself to be. It is the physical aspects of the world that we have to explain, presumably by some such method as that set forth in our discussion on world-building. Our bodies are more mysterious than our minds—at least they would be, only that we can set the mystery on one side by the device of the cyclic scheme of physics, which enables us to study their phenomenal behaviour without ever coming to grips with the underlying mystery.

The mind-stuff is not spread in space and time; these are part of the cyclic scheme ultimately derived out of it. But we must presume that in some other way or aspect it can be differentiated into parts. Only here and there does it rise to the level of consciousness, but from such islands proceeds all knowledge. Besides the direct knowledge contained in each self-knowing unit, there is inferential knowledge. The latter includes our knowledge of the physical world. It is necessary to keep reminding ourselves that all knowledge of our environment from which the world of physics is constructed, has entered in the form of messages transmitted along the nerves to the seat of consciousness. Obviously the messages travel in code. When messages relating to a table are travelling in the nerves, the nerve-disturbance does not in the least resemble either the external table that originates the mental impression or the conception of the table that arises in consciousness.* In the central clearing station the incoming messages are sorted and decoded, partly by instinctive image-building inherited

* I mean, resemble in intrinsic nature. It is true (as Bertrand Russell has emphasised) that the symbolic description of structure will be identical for the table in the external world and for the conception of the table in consciousness if the conception is scientifically correct. If the physicist does not attempt to penetrate beneath the structure he is indifferent as to which of the two we imagine ourselves to be discussing.

from the experience of our ancestors, partly by scientific comparison and reasoning. By this very indirect and hypothetical inference all our supposed acquaintance with and our theories of a world outside us have been built up. We are acquainted with an external world because its fibres run into our consciousness; it is only our own ends of the fibres that we actually know; from those ends we more or less successfully reconstruct the rest, as a palaeontologist reconstructs an extinct monster from its footprint.

The mind-stuff is the aggregation of relations and relata which form the building material for the physical world. Our account of the building process shows, however, that much that is implied in the relations is dropped as unserviceable for the required building. Our view is practically that urged in 1875 by W. K. Clifford—

"The succession of feelings which constitutes a man's consciousness is the reality which produces in our minds the perception of the motions of his brain."

That is to say, that which the man himself knows as a succession of feelings is the reality which when probed by the appliances of an outside investigator affects their readings in such a way that it is identified as a configuration of brain-matter. Again Bertrand Russell writes—*

What the physiologist sees when he examines a brain is in the physiologist, not in the brain he is examining. What is in the brain by the time the physiologist examines it if it is dead, I do not profess to know; but while its owner was alive, part, at least, of the contents of his brain consisted of his percepts, thoughts, and feelings. Since his brain also consisted of electrons, we are compelled to conclude that an electron is a grouping of events,

* *Analysis of Matter*, p. 320.

and that if the electron is in a human brain, some of the events composing it are likely to be some of the "mental states" of the man to whom the brain belongs. Or, at any rate, they are likely to be parts of such "mental states"—for it must not be assumed that part of a mental state must be a mental state. I do not wish to discuss what is meant by a "mental state"; the main point for us is that the term must include percepts. Thus a percept is an event or a group of events, each of which belongs to one or more of the groups constituting the electrons in the brain. This, I think, is the most concrete statement that can be made about electrons; everything else that can be said is more or less abstract and mathematical.

I quote this partly for the sake of the remark that it must not be assumed that part of a mental state must necessarily be a mental state. We can no doubt analyse the content of consciousness during a short interval of time into more or less elementary constituent feelings; but it is not suggested that this psychological analysis will reveal the elements out of whose measure-numbers the atoms or electrons are built. The brain-matter is a partial aspect of the whole mental state; but the analysis of the brain-matter by physical investigation does not run at all parallel with the analysis of the mental state by psychological investigation. I assume that Russell meant to warn us that, in speaking of part of a mental state, he was not limiting himself to parts that would be recognised as such psychologically, and he was admitting a more abstract kind of dissection.

This might give rise to some difficulty if we were postulating complete identity of mind-stuff with consciousness. But we know that in the mind there are memories not in consciousness at the moment but capable of being summoned into consciousness. We are vaguely aware that things we cannot recall are lying somewhere about and may come into the mind at any moment. Consciousness is not sharply defined, but fades into subconsciousness; and beyond that we must postulate something indefinite but yet continuous with our mental nature. This I take to be the world-stuff. We liken it to our conscious feelings because, now that we are convinced of the formal and symbolic character of the entities of physics, there is nothing else to liken it to.

It is sometimes urged that the basal stuff of the world should be called "neutral stuff" rather than "mind-stuff", since it is to be such that both mind and matter originate from it. If this is intended to emphasise that only limited islands of it constitute actual minds, and that even in these islands that which is known mentally is not equivalent to a complete inventory of all that may be there, I agree. In fact I should suppose that the self-knowledge of consciousness is mainly or wholly a knowledge which eludes the inventory method of description. The term "mind-stuff" might well be amended; but neutral stuff seems to be the wrong kind of amendment. It implies that we have two avenues of approach to an understanding of its nature. We have only one approach, namely, through our direct knowledge of mind. The supposed approach through the physical world leads only into the cycle of physics, where we run round and round like a kitten chasing its tail and never reach the world-stuff at all.

I assume that we have left the illusion of substance so far behind that the word "stuff" will not cause any misapprehension. I certainly do not intend to materialise or substantialise mind. Mind is—but you know what mind is like, so why should I say more about its nature? The word "stuff" has reference to the function it has to perform as a basis of world-building and does not imply any modified view of its nature.

It is difficult for the matter-of-fact physicist to accept the view that the substratum of everything is of mental character. But no one can deny that mind is the first and most direct thing in our experience, and all else is remote inference—inference either intuitive or deliberate. Probably it would never have occurred to us (as a serious hypothesis) that the world could be based on anything else, had we not been under the impression that there was a rival stuff with a more comfortable kind of "concrete" reality—something too inert and stupid to be capable of forging an illusion. The rival turns out to be a schedule of pointer readings; and though a world of symbolic character can well be constructed from it, this is a mere shelving of the inquiry into the nature of the world of experience.

This view of the relation of the material to the spiritual world perhaps relieves to some extent a tension between science and religion. Physical science has seemed to occupy a domain of reality which is self-sufficient, pursuing its course independently of and indifferent to that which a voice within us asserts to be a higher reality. We are jealous of such independence. We are uneasy that there should be an apparently self-contained world in which God becomes an unnecessary hypothesis. We acknowledge that the ways of God are inscrutable; but is there not still in the religious mind something of that feeling of the prophets of old, who called on God to assert his kingship and by sign or miracle proclaim that the forces of Nature are subject to his command? And yet if the scientist were to repent and admit that it was necessary to include among the agents controlling the stars and the electrons an omnipresent spirit to whom we trace the sacred things of consciousness, would there not be even graver apprehension?

We should suspect an intention to reduce God to a system of differential equations, like the other agents which at various times have been introduced to restore order in the physical scheme. That fiasco at any rate is avoided. For the sphere of the differential equations of physics is the metrical cyclic scheme extracted out of the broader reality. However much the ramifications of the cycles may be extended by further scientific discovery, they cannot from their very nature trench on the background in which they have their being—their actuality. It is in this background that our own mental consciousness lies; and here, if anywhere, we may find a Power greater than but akin to consciousness. It is not possible for the controlling laws of the spiritual substratum, which in so far as it is known to us in consciousness is essentially nonmetrical, to be analogous to the differential and other mathematical equations of physics which are meaningless unless they are fed with metrical quantities. So that the crudest anthropomorphic image of a spiritual deity can scarcely be so wide of the truth as one conceived in terms of metrical equations.

The Definition of Reality. It is time we came to grips with the loose terms Reality and Existence, which we have been using without any inquiry into what they are meant to convey. I am afraid of this word Reality, not connoting an ordinarily definable characteristic of the things it is applied to but used as though it were some kind of celestial halo. I very much doubt if any one of us has the faintest idea of what is meant by the reality or existence of anything but our own Egos. That is a bold statement, which I must guard against misinterpretation. It is, of course, possible to obtain consistent use of the word "reality" by adopting a conventional definition. My own practice would probably be covered by the definition that a thing may be said to be real if it is the goal of a type of inquiry to which I personally attach importance. But if I insist on no more than this I am whittling down the significance that is generally assumed. In physics we can give a cold scientific definition of reality which is free from all sentimental mystification. But this is not quite fair play, because the word "reality" is generally used *with the intention of evoking sentiment*. It is a grand word for a peroration. "The right honourable speaker went on to declare that the concord and amity for which he had unceasingly striven had now become a reality (loud cheers)." The conception which it is so troublesome to apprehend is not "reality" but "reality (loud cheers)".

Let us first examine the definition according to the purely scientific usage of the word, although it will not take us far enough. The only subject presented to me for study is the content of my consciousness. You are able to communicate to me part of the content of your consciousness which thereby becomes accessible in my own. For reasons which are generally admitted, though I should not like to have to prove that they are conclusive, I grant your consciousness equal status with my own; and I use this second-hand part of my consciousness to "put myself in your place". Accordingly my subject of study becomes differentiated into the contents of many consciousnesses, each content constituting a *view-point*. There then arises the problem of combining the view-points, and it is through this that the external world of physics arises. Much that is in any one consciousness is individual, much is apparently alterable by volition; but there is a stable element which is common to other consciousnesses. That common element we desire to study, to describe as fully and accurately as possible, and to discover the laws by which it combines now with one view-point, now with another. This common element cannot be placed in one man's consciousness rather than in another's; it must be in neutral ground—an external world.

It is true that I have a strong impression of an external world apart from any communication with other conscious beings. But apart from such communication I should have no reason to trust the impression. Most of our common impressions of substance, world-wide instants, and so on, have turned out to be illusory, and the externality of the world might be equally untrustworthy. The impression of externality is equally strong in the world that comes to me in dreams; the dream-world is less rational, but that might be used as an argument in favour of its externality as showing its dissociation from the internal faculty of reason. So long as we have to deal with one consciousness alone, the hypothesis that there is an external world responsible for part of what appears in it is an idle one. All that can be asserted of this external world is a mere duplication of the knowledge that can be much more confidently asserted of the world appearing in the consciousness. The hypothesis only becomes useful when it is the means of bringing together the worlds of many consciousnesses occupying different view-points.

The external world of physics is thus a symposium of the worlds presented to different view-points. There is general agreement as to the principles on which the symposium should be formed. Statements made about this external world, if they are unambiguous, must be either true or false. This has often been denied by philosophers. It is quite commonly said that scientific theories about the world are neither true nor false but merely convenient or inconvenient. A favourite phrase is that the gauge of value of a scientific theory is that it economises thought. Certainly a simple statement is preferable to a circumlocutory one; and as regards any current scientific theory, it is much easier to show that it is convenient or that it economises thought than that it is true. But whatever lower standards we may apply in practice we need not give up our ideals; and so long as there is a distinction between true and false theories our aim must be to eliminate the false. For my part I hold that the continual advance of science is not a mere utilitarian progress; it is progress towards ever purer truth. Only let it be understood that the truth we seek in science is the truth about an external world propounded as the theme of study, and is not bound up with any opinion as to the status of that world—whether or not it wears the halo of reality, whether or not it is deserving of "loud cheers".

Assuming that the symposium has been correctly carried out, the external world and all that appears in it are called real without further ado. When we (scientists) assert of anything in the external world that it is real and that it exists, we are expressing our belief that the rules of the symposium have been correctly applied— that it is not a false concept introduced by an error in the process of synthesis, or a hallucination belonging to only one individual consciousness, or an incomplete representation which embraces certain view-points but conflicts with others. We refuse to contemplate the awful contingency that the external world, after all our care in arriving at it, might be disqualified by failing to exist; because we have no idea what the supposed qualification would consist in, nor in what way the prestige of the world would be enhanced if it passed the implied test. The external world is the world that confronts that experience which we have in common, and for us no other world could fill the same rôle, no matter how high honours it might take in the qualifying examination.

This domestic definition of existence for scientific purposes follows the principle now adopted for all other definitions in science, namely, that a thing must be defined according to the way in which it is in practice recognised and not according to some ulterior significance that we imagine it to possess. Just as matter must shed its conception of substantiality, so existence must shed its halo, before we can admit it into physical science. But clearly if we are to assert or to question the existence of anything not comprised in the external world of physics, we must look beyond the physical definition. The mere questioning of the reality of the physical world implies some higher censorship than the scientific method itself can supply.

The external world of physics has been formulated as an answer to a particular problem encountered in human experience. Officially the scientist regards it as a problem which he just happened across, as he might take up a cross-word problem encountered in a newspaper. His sole business is to see that the problem is correctly solved. But questions may be raised about a problem which play no part and need not be considered in connection with the solving of the problem. The extraneous question naturally raised about the problem of the external world is whether there is some higher justification for embarking on this world-solving competition rather than on other problems which our experience might suggest to us. Just what kind of justification the scientist would claim for his quest is not very clear, because it is not within the province of science to formulate such a claim.   But certainly he makes claims which do not rest on the aesthetic perfection of the solution or on material benefits derived from scientific research.   He would not allow his subject to be shoved aside in a symposium on truth.   We can scarcely say anything more definite than that science claims a "halo" for its world.

If we are to find for the atoms and electrons of the external world not merely a conventional reality but "reality (loud cheers)" we must look not to the end but to the beginning of the quest.   It is at the beginning that we must find that sanction which raises these entities above the mere products of an arbitrary mental exercise. This involves some kind of assessment of the impulse which sets us forth on the voyage of discovery.   How can we make such assessment?   Not by any reasoning that I know of.   Reasoning would only tell us that the impulse might be judged by the success of the adventure —whether it leads in the end to things which really exist and wear the halo in their own right; it takes us to and fro like a shuttle along the chain of inference in vain search for the elusive halo.   But, legitimately or not, the mind is confident that it can distinguish certain quests as sanctioned by indisputable authority.   We may put it in different ways; the impulse to this quest is part of our very nature; it is the expression of a purpose which has possession of us.   Is this precisely what we meant when we sought to affirm the reality of the external world?   It goes some way towards giving it a meaning but is scarcely the full equivalent.   I doubt if we really satisfy the conceptions behind that demand unless we make the bolder hypothesis that the quest and all that is reached by it are of worth in the eyes of an Absolute Valuer.

Whatever justification at the source we accept to vindicate the reality of the external world, it can scarcely fail to admit on the same footing much that is outside physical science. Although no long chains of regularised inference depend from them we recognise that other fibres of our being extend in directions away from sense-impressions. I am not greatly concerned to borrow words like "existence" and "reality" to crown these other departments of the soul's interest. I would rather put it that any raising of the question of reality in its transcendental sense (whether the question emanates from the world of physics or not) leads us to a perspective from which we see man not as a bundle of sensory impressions, but conscious of purpose and responsibilities to which the external world is subordinate.

From this perspective we recognise a spiritual world alongside the physical world. Experience—that is to say, the self *cum* environment—comprises more than can be embraced in the physical world, restricted as it is to a complex of metrical symbols. The physical world is, we have seen, the answer to one definite and urgent problem arising in a survey of experience; and no other problem has been followed up with anything like the same precision and elaboration. Progress towards an understanding of the non-sensory constituents of our nature is not likely to follow similar lines, and indeed is not animated by the same aims. If it is felt that this difference is so wide that the phrase spiritual *world* is a misleading analogy, I will not insist on the term. All I would claim is that those who in the search for truth start from consciousness as a seat of self-knowledge with interests and responsibilities not confined to the material plane, are just as much facing the hard facts of experience as those who start from consciousness as a device for reading the indications of spectroscopes and micrometers.

Physical Illustrations. If the reader is unconvinced that there can be anything indefinite in the question whether a thing exists or not, let him glance at the following problem. Consider a distribution of matter in Einstein's spherical "finite but unbounded" space. Suppose that the matter is so arranged that every particle has an exactly similar particle at its antipodes. (There is some reason to believe that the matter would *necessarily* have this arrangement in consequence of the law of gravitation; but this is not certain.) Each group of particles will therefore be exactly like the antipodal group not only in its structure and configuration but in its entire surroundings; the two groups will in fact be indistinguishable by any possible experimental test. Starting on a journey round the spherical world we come across a group A, and then after going half round we come to an exactly similar group A' indistinguishable by any test; another half circle again brings us to an exactly similar group, which, however, we decide is the original group A. Now let us ponder a little. We realise that in any case by going on far enough we come back to the same group. Why do we not accept the obvious conclusion that this happened when we reached A'; everything was exactly as though we had reached the starting-point again? We have encountered a succession of precisely similar phenomena but for some arbitrary reason have decided that only the alternate ones are *really* the same. There is no difficulty in identifying all of them; in that case the space is "elliptical" instead of "spherical". But which is the real truth? Disregard the fact that I introduced A and A' to you as though they were not the same particles, because that begs the question; imagine that you have actually had this adventure in a world you had not been told about. You cannot find out the answer. Can you conceive what the question means? I cannot. All that turns on the answer is whether we shall provide two separate haloes for A and A' or whether one will suffice.

Descriptions of the phenomena of atomic physics have an extraordinary vividness. We see the atoms with their girdles of circulating electrons darting hither and thither, colliding and rebounding. Free electrons torn from the girdles hurry away a hundred times faster, curving sharply round the atoms with side slips and hairbreadth escapes. The truants are caught and attached to the girdles and the escaping energy shakes the aether into vibration. X-rays impinge on the atoms and toss the electrons into higher orbits. We see these electrons falling back again, sometimes by steps, some-times with a rush, caught in a cul-de-sac of metasta-bility, hesitating before "forbidden passages". Behind it all the quantum h regulates each change with mathe-matical precision. This is the sort of picture that appeals to our understanding—no insubstantial pageant to fade like a dream.

The spectacle is so fascinating that we have perhaps forgotten that there was a time when we wanted to be told what an electron is. The question was never answered. No familiar conceptions can be woven round the electron; it belongs to the waiting list. Similarly the description of the processes must be taken with a grain of salt. The tossing up of the electron is a con-ventional way of depicting a particular change of state of the atom which cannot really be associated with movements in space as macroscopically conceived. *Something unknown is doing we don't know what*—that is what our theory amounts to. It does not sound a particularly illuminating theory. I have read something like it elsewhere—

> The slithy toves
> Did gyre and gimble in the wabe.

There is the same suggestion of activity. There is the same indefiniteness as to the nature of the activity and of what it is that is acting. And yet from so unpromising a beginning we really do get somewhere. We bring into order a host of apparently unrelated phenomena; we make predictions, and our predictions come off. The reason—the sole reason—for this progress is that our description is not limited to unknown agents executing unknown activities, but *numbers* are scattered freely in the description. To contemplate electrons circulating in the atom carries us no further; but by contemplating eight circulating electrons in one atom and seven circulating electrons in another we begin to realise the difference between oxygen and nitrogen. Eight slithy toves gyre and gimble in the oxygen wabe; seven in nitrogen. By admitting a few numbers even "Jabberwocky" may become scientific. We can now venture on a prediction; if one of its toves escapes, oxygen will be masquerading in a garb properly belonging to nitrogen. In the stars and nebulae we do find such wolves in sheep's clothing which might otherwise have startled us. It would not be a bad reminder of the essential unknownness of the fundamental entities of physics to translate it into "Jabberwocky"; provided all numbers—all metrical attributes

—are unchanged, it does not suffer in the least. Out of the numbers proceeds that harmony of natural law which it is the aim of science to disclose. We can grasp the tune but not the player. Trinculo might have been referring to modern physics in the words, "This is the tune of our catch, played by the picture of Nobody".

Chapter XIV

CAUSATION

In the old conflict between freewill and predestination it has seemed hitherto that physics comes down heavily on the side of predestination. Without making extravagant claims for the scope of natural law, its moral sympathy has been with the view that whatever the future may bring forth is already foretold in the configurations of the past—

> Yea, the first Morning of Creation wrote
> What the Last Dawn of Reckoning shall read.

I am not so rash as to invade Scotland with a solution of a problem which has rent her from the synod to the cottage. Like most other people, I suppose, I think it incredible that the wider scheme of Nature which includes life and consciousness can be completely predetermined; yet I have not been able to form a satisfactory conception of any kind of law or causal sequence which shall be other than deterministic. It seems contrary to our feeling of the dignity of the mind to suppose that it merely registers a dictated sequence of thoughts and emotions; but it seems equally contrary to its dignity to put it at the mercy of impulses with no causal antecedents. I shall not deal with this dilemma. Here I have to set forth the position of physical science on this matter so far as it comes into her territory. It does come into her territory, because that which we call human will cannot be entirely dissociated from the consequent motions of the muscles and disturbance of the material world. On the scientific side a new situation has arisen. It is a consequence of the advent of the quantum theory that *physics is no longer pledged to a scheme of deterministic law*. Determinism has dropped out altogether in the latest formulations of theoretical physics and it is at least open to doubt whether it will ever be brought back.

The foregoing paragraph is from the manuscript of the original lecture delivered in Edinburgh. The attitude of physics at that time was one of indifference to determinism. If there existed a scheme of strictly causal law at the base of phenomena the search for it was not at present practical politics, and meanwhile another ideal was being pursued. The fact that a causal basis had been lost sight of in the new theories was fairly well known; many regretted it, and held that its restoration was imperative.*

In rewriting this chapter a year later I have had to mingle with this attitude of indifference an attitude more definitely hostile to determinism which has arisen from the acceptance of the Principle of Indeterminacy (p. 220). There has been no time for more than a hurried examination of the far-reaching consequences of this principle; and I should have been reluctant to include "stop-press" ideas were it not that they appear to clinch the conception towards which the earlier developments were leading. The future is a combination of the causal influences of the past together with unpredictable elements—unpredictable not merely because it is im-

---

* A few days after the course of lectures was completed, Einstein wrote in his message on the Newton Centenary, "It is only in the quantum theory that Newton's differential method becomes inadequate, and indeed strict causality fails us. But the last word has not yet been said. May the spirit of Newton's method give us the power to restore unison between physical reality and the profoundest characteristic of Newton's teaching—strict causality." (*Nature*, 1927, March 26, p. 467.)

practicable to obtain the data of prediction, but because no data connected causally with our experience exist. It will be necessary to defend so remarkable a change of opinion at some length. Meanwhile we may note that science thereby withdraws its moral opposition to free-will. Those who maintain a deterministic theory of mental activity must do so as the outcome of their study of the mind itself and not with the idea that they are thereby making it more conformable with our experimental knowledge of the laws of inorganic nature.

Causation and Time's Arrow. Cause and effect are closely bound up with time's arrow; the cause must precede the effect. The relativity of time has not obliterated this order. An event Here-Now can only cause events in the cone of absolute future; it can be caused by events in the cone of absolute past; it can neither cause nor be caused by events in the neutral wedge, since the necessary influence would in that case have to be transmitted with a speed faster than light. But curiously enough this elementary notion of cause and effect is quite inconsistent with a strictly causal scheme. How can I cause an event in the absolute future, if the future was predetermined before I was born? The notion evidently implies that something may be born into the world at the instant Here-Now, which has an influence extending throughout the future cone but no corresponding linkage to the cone of absolute past. The primary laws of physics do not provide for any such one-way linkage; any alteration in a prescribed state of the world implies alterations in its past state symmetrical with the alterations in its future state. Thus in primary physics, which knows nothing of time's arrow, there is no discrimination of cause and effect; but events are connected by a *symmetrical* causal relation which is the same viewed from either end.

Primary physics postulates a strictly causal scheme, but the causality is a symmetrical relation and not the one-way relation of cause and effect. Secondary physics can distinguish cause and effect but its foundation does not rest on a causal scheme and it is indifferent as to whether or not strict causality prevails.

The lever in a signal box is moved and the signal drops. We can point out the relation of constraint which associates the positions of lever and signal; we can also find that the movements are not synchronous, and calculate the time-difference. But the laws of mechanics do not ascribe an absolute sign to this time-difference; so far as they are concerned we may quite well suppose that the drop of the signal causes the motion of the lever. To settle which is the cause, we have two options. We can appeal to the signalman who is confident that *he* made the mental decision to pull the lever; but this criterion will only be valid if we agree that there was a genuine decision between two possible courses and not a mere mental registration of what was already predetermined. Or we can appeal to secondary law which takes note of the fact that there was more of the random element in the world when the signal dropped than when the lever moved. But the feature of secondary law is that it ignores strict causation; it concerns itself not with what must happen but with what is likely to happen. Thus distinction of cause and effect has no meaning in the closed system of primary laws of physics; to get at it we have to break into the scheme, introducing considerations of volition or of probability which are foreign to it. This is rather analogous to the ten vanishing coefficients of curvature which could only be recognised if the closed system of the world were broken into by standards foreign to it.

For convenience I shall call the relation of effect to cause *causation,* and the symmetrical relation which does not distinguish between cause and effect *causality.* In primary physics causality has completely replaced causation. Ideally the whole world past and future is connected into a deterministic scheme by relations of causality. Up till very recently it was universally held that such a determinate scheme must exist (possibly subject to suspension by supernatural agencies outside the scope of physics); we may therefore call this the "orthodox" view. It was, of course, recognised that we were only acquainted with part of the structure of this causal scheme, but it was the settled aim of theoretical physics to discover the whole.

This replacement in orthodox science of causation by causality is important in one respect. We must not let causality borrow an intuitive sanction which really belongs only to causation. We may think we have an intuition that the same cause cannot have two alternative effects; but we do not claim any intuition that the same effect may not spring from two alternative causes. For this reason the assumption of a rigid determinateness enforced by relations of causality cannot be said to be insisted on by intuition.

What is the ground for so much ardent faith in the orthodox hypothesis that physical phenomena rest ultimately on a scheme of completely deterministic laws? I think there are two reasons—

(1) The principal laws of Nature which have been discovered are apparently of this deterministic type, and these have furnished the great triumphs of physical prediction. It is natural to trust to a line of progress

which has served us well in the past. Indeed it is a healthy attitude to assume that nothing is beyond the scope of scientific prediction until the limits of prediction actually declare themselves.

(2) The current epistemology of science presupposes a deterministic scheme of this type. To modify it involves a much deeper change in our attitude to natural knowledge than the mere abandonment of an untenable hypothesis.

In explanation of the second point we must recall that knowledge of the physical world has to be inferred from the nerve-messages which reach our brains, and the current epistemology assumes that there exists a determinate scheme of inference (lying before us as an ideal and gradually being unravelled). But, as has already been pointed out, the chains of inference are simply the converse of the chains of physical causality by which distant events are connected to the nerve-messages. If the scheme of transmission of these messages through the external world is not deterministic then the scheme of inference as to their source cannot be deterministic, and our epistemology has been based on an impossible ideal. In that case our attitude to the whole scheme of natural knowledge must be profoundly modified.

These reasons will be considered at length, but it is convenient to state here our answers to them in equally summary form.

(1) In recent times some of the greatest triumphs of physical prediction have been furnished by admittedly statistical laws which do not rest on a basis of causality. Moreover the great laws hitherto accepted as causal appear on minuter examination to be of statistical character.

(2) Whether or not there is a causal scheme at the base of atomic phenomena, modern atomic theory is not now attempting to find it; and it is making rapid progress because it no longer sets this up as a practical aim. We are in the position of holding an epistemological theory of natural knowledge which does not correspond to actual aim of current scientific investigation.

Predictability of Events. Let us examine a typical case of successful scientific prediction. A total eclipse of the sun visible in Cornwall is prophesied for 11 August 1999. It is generally supposed that this eclipse is already predetermined by the present configuration of the sun, earth and moon. I do not wish to arouse unnecessary misgiving as to whether the eclipse will come off. I expect it will; but let us examine the grounds of expectation. It is predicted as a consequence of the law of gravitation—a law which we found in chapter VII to be a mere truism. That does not diminish the value of the prediction; but it does suggest that we may not be able to pose as such marvellous prophets when we come up against laws which are not mere truisms. I might venture to predict that 2 + 2 will be equal to 4 even in 1999; but if this should prove correct it will not help to convince anyone that the universe (or, if you like, the human mind) is governed by laws of deterministic type. I suppose that in the most erratically governed world *something* can be predicted if truisms are not excluded.

But we have to look deeper than this. The law of gravitation is only a truism when regarded from a macroscopic point of view. It presupposes space, and measurement with gross material or optical arrangements. It cannot be refined to an accuracy beyond the

limits of these gross appliances; so that it is a truism
with a probable error—small, but not infinitely small.
The classical laws hold good in the limit when exceedingly large quantum numbers are involved. The system
comprising the sun, earth and moon has exceedingly
high state-number (p. 198); and the predictability of
its configurations is not characteristic of natural phenomena in general but of those involving great numbers
of atoms of action—such that we are concerned not
with individual but with average behaviour.

Human life is proverbially uncertain; few things are
more certain than the solvency of a life-insurance company. The average law is so trustworthy that it may be
considered predestined that half the children now born
will survive the age of x years. But that does not tell us
whether the span of life of young A. McB. is already
written in the book of fate, or whether there is still time
to alter it by teaching him not to run in front of motor-
buses. The eclipse in 1999 is as safe as the balance of
a life-insurance company; the next quantum jump of an
atom is as uncertain as your life and mine.

We are thus in a position to answer the main argument for a predetermination of the future, viz. that
observation shows the laws of Nature to be of a type
which leads to definite predictions of the future, and it
is reasonable to expect that any laws which remain
undiscovered will conform to the same type. For when
we ask what is the characteristic of the phenomena that
have been successfully predicted, the answer is that they
are effects depending on the average configurations of vast
numbers of individual entities. But averages are predictable because they are averages, irrespective of the
type of government of the phenomena underlying
them.

Considering an atom alone in the world in State 3, the classical theory would have asked, and hoped to answer, the question, What will it do next? The quantum theory substitutes the question, Which will it do next? Because it admits only two lower states for the atom to go to. Further, it makes no attempt to find a definite answer, but contents itself with calculating the respective odds on the jumps to State 1 and State 2. The quantum physicist does not fill the atom with gadgets for directing its future behaviour, as the classical physicist would have done; he fills it with gadgets determining the odds on its future behaviour. He studies the art of the bookmaker not of the trainer.

Thus in the structure of the world as formulated in the new quantum theory it is predetermined that of 500 atoms now in State 3, approximately 400 will go on to State 1 and 100 to State 2—in so far as anything subject to chance fluctuations can be said to be predetermined. The odds of 4 to 1 find their appropriate representation in the picture of the atom; that is to say, something symbolic of a 4 : 1 ratio is present in each of the 500 atoms. But there are no marks distinguishing the atoms belonging to the group of 100 from the 400. Probably most physicists would take the view that although the marks are not yet shown in the picture, they are nevertheless present in Nature; they belong to an elaboration of the theory which will come in good time. The marks, of course, need not be in the atom itself; they may be in the environment which will interact with it. For example, we may load dice in such a way that the odds are 4 to 1 on throwing a 6. Both those dice which turn up 6 and those which do not have these odds written in their constitution—by a displaced position of the centre of gravity. The result of a particular throw is not marked in the dice; nevertheless it is strictly causal (apart perhaps from the human element involved in throwing the dice) being determined by the external influences which are concerned. Our own position at this stage is that future developments of physics may reveal such causal marks (either in the atom or in the influences outside it) or it may not. Hitherto whenever we have thought we have detected causal marks in natural phenomena they have always proved spurious, the apparent determinism having come about in another way. Therefore we are inclined to regard favourably the possibility that there may be no causal marks anywhere.

But, it will be said, it is inconceivable that an atom can be so evenly balanced between two alternative courses that nowhere in the world as yet is there any trace of the ultimately deciding factor. This is an appeal to intuition and it may fairly be countered with another appeal to intuition. I have an intuition much more immediate than any relating to the objects of the physical world; this tells me that nowhere in the world as yet is there any trace of a deciding factor as to whether I am going to lift my right hand or my left. It depends on an unfettered act of volition not yet made or foreshadowed.* My intuition is that the future is able to bring forth deciding factors which are not secretly hidden in the past.

The position is that the laws governing the microscopic elements of the physical world—individual atoms, electrons, quanta—do not make definite predictions as to what the individual will do next. I am

---

* It is fair to assume the trustworthiness of this intuition in answering an argument which appeals to intuition; the assumption would beg the question if we were urging the argument independently.

here speaking of the laws that have been actually discovered and formulated on the old quantum theory and the new. These laws indicate several possibilities in the future and state the odds on each. In general the odds are moderately balanced and are not tempting to an aspiring prophet. But short odds on the behaviour of individuals combine into very long odds on suitably selected statistics of a number of individuals; and the wary prophet can find predictions of this kind on which to stake his credit—without serious risk. All the successful predictions hitherto attributed to causality are traceable to this. It is quite true that the quantum laws for individuals are not incompatible with causality; they merely ignore it. But if we take advantage of this indifference to reintroduce determinism at the basis of world structure it is because our philosophy predisposes us that way, not because we know of any experimental evidence in its favour.

We might for illustration make a comparison with the doctrine of predestination. That theological doctrine, whatever may be said against it, has hitherto seemed to blend harmoniously with the predetermination of the material universe. But if we were to appeal to the new conception of physical law to settle this question by analogy the answer would be:—The individual is not predestined to arrive at either of the two states, which perhaps may here be sufficiently discriminated as State 1 and State 2; the most that can be considered already settled is the respective odds on his reaching these states.

The New Epistemological Outlook. Scientific investigation does not lead to knowledge of the intrinsic nature of things. "Whenever we state the properties of a body

in terms of physical quantities we are imparting knowledge of the response of various metrical indicators to
its presence and nothing more" (p. 257). But if a body
is not acting according to strict causality, if there is an
element of uncertainty as to the response of the indicators, we seem to have cut away the ground for this kind of
knowledge. It is not predetermined what will be the
reading of the weighing-machine if the body is placed
on it, therefore the body has no definite mass; nor where
it will be found an instant hence, therefore it has no
definite velocity; nor where the rays now being reflected
from it will converge in the microscope, therefore it has
no definite position; and so on. It is no use answering
that the body really has a definite mass, velocity,
position, etc., which we are unaware of; that statement,
if it means anything, refers to an intrinsic nature of
things outside the scope of scientific knowledge. We
cannot infer these properties with precision from anything that we can be aware of, because the breach of
causality has broken the chain of inference. Thus our
knowledge of the response of indicators to the presence
of the body is non-existent; therefore we cannot assert
knowledge of it at all. So what is the use of talking
about it? The body which was to be the abstraction of
all these (as yet unsettled) pointer readings has become
superfluous in the physical world. That is the dilemma
into which the old epistemology leads us as soon as we
begin to doubt strict causality.

In phenomena on a gross scale this difficulty can be
got round. A body may have no definite position but
yet have within close limits an extremely probable
position. When the probabilities are large the substitution of probability for certainty makes little difference;
it adds only a negligible haziness to the world. But

though the practical change is unimportant there are fundamental theoretical consequences. All probabilities rest on a basis of *a priori* probability, and we cannot say whether probabilities are large or small without having assumed such a basis. In agreeing to accept those of our calculated probabilities which are very high as virtually equivalent to certainties on the old scheme, we are as it were making our adopted basis of *a priori* probability a constituent of the world-structure—adding to the world a kind of symbolic texture that cannot be expressed on the old scheme.

On the atomic scale of phenomena the probabilities are in general well-balanced, and there are no "naps" for the scientific punter to put his shirt on. If a body is still defined as a bundle of pointer readings (or highly probable pointer readings) there are no "bodies" on the atomic scale. All that we can extract is a bundle of probabilities. That is in fact just how Schrödinger tries to picture the atom—as a wave centre of his probability entity ψ.

We commonly have had to deal with probabilities which arise through ignorance. With fuller knowledge we should sweep away the references to probability and substitute the exact facts. But it appears to be a fundamental point in Schrödinger's theory that his probabilities are not to be replaced in that way. When his ψ is sufficiently concentrated it indicates the point where the electron is; when it is diffused it gives only a vague indication of the position. But this vague indication is not something which ideally ought to be replaced by exact knowledge; it is ψ itself which acts as the source of the light emitted from the atom, the period of the light being that of the beats of ψ. I think this means that the spread of ψ is not a symbol for uncertainty arising through lack of information; it is a symbol for causal failure—an indeterminacy of behaviour which is part of the character of the atom.

We have two chief ways of learning about the interior of the atom. We can observe electrons entering or leaving, and we can observe light entering or leaving. Bohr has assumed a structure connected by strictly causal law with the first phenomenon, Heisenberg and his followers with the second. If the two structures were identifiable then the atom would involve a complete causal connection of the two types of phenomena. But apparently no such causal linkage exists. Therefore we have to be content with a correlation in which the entities of the one model represent probabilities in the second model. There are perhaps details in the two theories which do not quite square with this; but it seems to express the ideal to be aimed at in describing the laws of an incompletely causal world, viz. that the causal source of one phenomenon shall represent the probability of causal source of another phenomenon. Schrödinger's theory has given at least a strong hint that the actual world is controlled on this plan.

The Principle of Indeterminacy. Thus far we have shown that modern physics is drifting away from the postulate that the future is predetermined, ignoring it rather than deliberately rejecting it. With the discovery of the Principle of Indeterminacy (p. 220) its attitude has become more definitely hostile.

Let us take the simplest case in which we think we can predict the future. Suppose that we have a particle with known position and velocity at the present instant. Assuming that nothing interferes with it we can predict the position at a subsequent instant. (Strictly the noninterference would be a subject for another prediction, but to simplify matters we shall concede it.)   It is just this simple prediction which the principle of indeterminacy expressly forbids.   It states that we cannot know accurately both the velocity and position of a particle at the present instant.

At first sight there seems to be an inconsistency. There is no limit to the accuracy with which we may know the position, provided that we do not want to know the velocity also.   Very well; let us make a highly accurate determination of position now, and after waiting a moment make another highly accurate determination of position.   Comparing the two accurate positions we compute the accurate velocity—and snap our fingers at the principle of indeterminacy.   This velocity, however, is of no use for prediction, because in making the second accurate determination of position we have rough-handled the particle so much that it no longer has the velocity we calculated.   *It is a purely retrospective velocity*.   The velocity does not exist in the present tense but in the future perfect; it never exists, it never will exist, but a time may come when it *will have* existed.   There is no room for it in Fig. 4 which contains an Absolute Future and an Absolute Past but not an Absolute Future Perfect.

The velocity which we attribute to a particle now can be regarded as an anticipation of its future positions. To say that it is unknowable (except with a certain degree of inaccuracy) is to say that the future cannot be anticipated.   Immediately the future is accomplished, so that it is no longer an anticipation, the velocity becomes knowable.

The classical view that a particle necessarily has a definite (but not necessarily knowable) velocity now, amounts to disguising a piece of the unknown future as an unknowable element of the present. Classical physics foists a deterministic scheme on us by a trick; it smuggles the unknown future into the present, trusting that we shall not press an inquiry as to whether it has become any more knowable that way.

The same principle extends to every kind of phenomenon that we attempt to predict, so long as the need for accuracy is not buried under a mass of averages. To every co-ordinate there corresponds a momentum, and by the principle of indeterminacy the more accurately the co-ordinate is known the less accurately the momentum is known. Nature thus provides that knowledge of one-half of the world will ensure ignorance of the other half—ignorance which, we have seen, may be remedied later when the same part of the world is contemplated retrospectively. We can scarcely rest content with a picture of the world which includes so much that cannot be known. We have been trying to get rid of unknowable things, i.e. all conceptions which have no causal connection with our experience. We have eliminated velocity through aether, "right" frames of space, etc., for this reason. This vast new unknowable element must likewise be swept out of the Present. Its proper place is in the Future because then it will no longer be unknowable. It has been put in prematurely as an anticipation of that which cannot be anticipated.

In assessing whether the symbols which the physicist has scattered through the external world are adequate to predetermine the future, we must be on our guard against retrospective symbols. It is easy to prophesy after the event.

Natural and Supernatural. A rather serious consequence of dropping causality in the external world is that it leaves us with no clear distinction between the Natural and the Supernatural. In an earlier chapter I compared the invisible agent invented to account for the tug of gravitation to a "demon". Is a view of the world which admits such an agent any more scientific than that of a savage who attributes all that he finds mysterious in Nature to the work of invisible demons? The Newtonian physicist had a valid defence. He could point out that his demon Gravitation was supposed to act according to fixed causal laws and was therefore not to be compared with the irresponsible demons of the savage. Once a deviation from strict causality is admitted the distinction melts away. I suppose that the savage would admit that his demon was to some extent a creature of habit and that it would be possible to make a fair guess as to what he would do in the future; but that sometimes he would show a will of his own. It is that imperfect consistency which formerly disqualified him from admission as an entity of physics along with his brother Gravitation.

That is largely why there has been so much bother about "me"; because I have, or am persuaded that I have, "a will of my own". Either the physicist must leave his causal scheme at the mercy of supernatural interference from me, or he must explain away my supernatural qualities. In self-defence the materialist favoured the latter course; he decided that I was not supernatural—only complicated. We on the other hand have concluded that there is no strict causal behaviour anywhere. We can scarcely deny the charge that in abolishing the criterion of causality we are opening the door to the savage's demons. It is a serious step, but

I do not think it means the end of all true science. After all if they try to enter we can pitch them out again, as Einstein pitched out the respectable causal demon who called himself Gravitation. It is a privation to be no longer able to stigmatise certain views as *unscientific* superstition; but we are still allowed, if the circumstances justify it, to reject them as *bad science*.

Volition. From the philosophic point of view it is of deep interest to consider how this affects the freedom of the human mind and spirit. A complete determinism of the material universe cannot be divorced from determinism of the mind. Take, for example, the prediction of the weather this time next year. The prediction is not likely ever to become practicable, but "orthodox" physicists are not yet convinced that it is theoretically impossible; they hold that next year's weather is already predetermined. We should require extremely detailed knowledge of present conditions, since a small local deviation can exert an ever-expanding influence. We must examine the state of the sun so as to predict the fluctuations in the heat and corpuscular radiation which it sends us. We must dive into the bowels of the earth to be forewarned of volcanic eruptions which may spread a dust screen over the atmosphere as Mt. Katmai did some years ago. But further we must penetrate into the recesses of the human mind. A coal strike, a great war, may directly change the conditions of the atmosphere; a lighted match idly thrown away may cause deforestation which will change the rainfall and climate. There can be no fully deterministic control of inorganic phenomena unless the determinism governs mind itself. Conversely if we wish to emancipate mind we must to some extent emancipate the material world also. There appears to be no longer any obstacle to this emancipation.

Let us look more closely into the problem of how the mind gets a grip on material atoms so that movements of the body and limbs can be controlled by its volition. I think we may now feel quite satisfied that the volition is genuine. The materialist view was that the motions which appear to be caused by our volition are really reflex actions controlled by the material processes in the brain, the act of will being an inessential side phenomenon occurring simultaneously with the physical phenomena. But this assumes that the result of applying physical laws to the brain is fully determinate. It is meaningless to say that the behaviour of a conscious brain is precisely the same as that of a mechanical brain if the behaviour of a mechanical brain is left undetermined. If the laws of physics are not strictly causal the most that can be said is that the behaviour of the conscious brain is one of the possible behaviours of a mechanical brain. Precisely so; and the decision between the possible behaviours is what we call volition.

Perhaps you will say, When the decision of an atom is made between its possible quantum jumps, is that also "volition"? Scarcely; the analogy is altogether too remote. The position is that both for the brain and the atom there is nothing in the physical world, i.e. the world of pointer readings, to predetermine the decision; the decision is a fact of the physical world with consequences in the future but not causally connected to the past. In the case of the brain we have an insight into a mental world behind the world of pointer readings and in that world we get a new picture of the fact of decision which must be taken as revealing its real nature—if the words *real nature* have any meaning.

For the atom we have no such insight into what is behind the pointer readings. We believe that behind all pointer readings there is a background continuous with the background of the brain; but there is no more ground for calling the background of the spontaneous behaviour of the atom "volition" than for calling the background of its causal behaviour "reason". It should be understood that we are not attempting to reintroduce in the background the strict causality banished from the pointer readings. In the one case in which we have any insight—the background of the brain—we have no intention of giving up the freedom of the mind and will. Similarly we do not suggest that the marks of predestination of the atom, not found in the pointer readings, exist undetectable in the unknown background. To the question whether I would admit that the cause of the decision of the atom has something in common with the cause of the decision of the brain, I would simply answer that there is no cause. In the case of the brain I have a deeper insight into the decision; this insight exhibits it as volition, i.e. something outside causality.

A mental decision to turn right or turn left starts one of two alternative sets of impulses along the nerves to the feet. At some brain centre the course of behaviour of certain atoms or elements of the physical world is directly determined for them by the mental decision—or, one may say, the scientific description of that behaviour is the metrical aspect of the decisión. It would be a possible though difficult hypothesis to assume that very few atoms (or possibly only one atom) have this direct contact with the conscious decision, and that these few atoms serve as a switch to deflect the material world from one course to the other. But it is physically improbable that each atom has its duty in the brain so precisely allotted that the control of its behaviour would prevail over all possible irregularities of the other atoms. If I have at all rightly understood the processes of my own mind, there is no finicking with individual atoms.

I do not think that our decisions are precisely balanced on the conduct of certain key-atoms. Could we pick out one atom in Einstein's brain and say that if it had made the wrong quantum jump there would have been a corresponding flaw in the theory of relativity? Having regard to the physical influences of temperature and promiscuous collision it is impossible to maintain this. It seems that we must attribute to the mind power not only to decide the behaviour of atoms individually but to affect systematically large groups— in fact to tamper with the odds on atomic behaviour. This has always been one of the most dubious points in the theory of the interaction of mind and matter.

Interference with Statistical Laws. Has the mind power to set aside *statistical laws* which hold in inorganic matter? Unless this is granted its opportunity of interference seems to be too circumscribed to bring about the results which are observed to follow from mental decisions. But the admission involves a genuine physical difference between inorganic and organic (or, at any rate, conscious) matter. I would prefer to avoid this hypothesis, but it is necessary to face the issue squarely. The indeterminacy recognised in modern quantum theory is only a partial step towards freeing our actions from deterministic control. To use an analogy—we have admitted an uncertainty which may take or spare human lives; but we have yet to find an uncertainty which may upset the expectations of a life-insurance company. Theoretically the one uncertainty might lead to the other, as when the fate of millions turned on the murders at Sarajevo. But the hypothesis that the mind operates through two or three key-atoms in the brain is too desperate a way of escape for us, and I reject it for the reasons already stated.

It is one thing to allow the mind to direct an atom between two courses neither of which would be improbable for an inorganic atom; it is another thing to allow it to direct a crowd of atoms into a configuration which the secondary laws of physics would set aside as "too improbable". Here the improbability is that a large number of entities each acting independently should conspire to produce the result; it is like the improbability of the atoms finding themselves by chance all in one half of a vessel. We must suppose that in the physical part of the brain immediately affected by a mental decision there is some kind of interdependence of behaviour of the atoms which is not present in inorganic matter.

I do not wish to minimise the seriousness of admitting this difference between living and dead matter. But I think that the difficulty has been eased a little, if it has not been removed. To leave the atom constituted as it was but to interfere with the probability of its undetermined behaviour, does not seem quite so drastic an interference with natural law as other modes of mental interference that have been suggested. (Perhaps that is only because we do not understand enough about these probabilities to realise the heinousness of our suggestion.) Unless it belies its name, probability can be modified in ways which ordinary physical entities would not admit of. There can be no unique probability attached to any event or behaviour; we can only speak of "probability in the light of certain given information", and the probability alters according to the extent of the information. It is, I think, one of the most unsatisfactory features of the new quantum theory in its present stage that it scarcely seems to recognise this fact, and leaves us to guess at the basis of information to which its probability theorems are supposed to refer.

Looking at it from another aspect—if the unity of a man's consciousness is not an illusion, there must be some corresponding unity in the relations of the mind-stuff which is behind the pointer readings. Applying our measures of relation structure, as in chapter XI, we shall build matter and fields of force obeying identically the principal field-laws; the atoms will individually be in no way different from those which are without this unity in the background. But it seems plausible that when we consider their collective behaviour we shall have to take account of the broader unifying trends in the mind-stuff, and not expect the statistical results to agree with those appropriate to structures of haphazard origin.

I think that even a materialist must reach a conclusion not unlike ours if he fairly faces the problem. He will need in the physical world something to stand for a symbolic unity of the atoms associated with an individual consciousness, which does not exist for atoms not so associated—a unity which naturally upsets physical predictions •based on the hypothesis of random disconnection. For he has not only to translate into material configurations the multifarious thoughts and images of the mind, but must surely not neglect to find some kind of physical substitute for the Ego.

Chapter XV

SCIENCE AND MYSTICISM

One day I happened to be occupied with the subject of "Generation of Waves by Wind". I took down the standard treatise on hydrodynamics, and under that heading I read—

The equations (12) and (13) of the preceding Art. enable us to examine a related question of some interest, viz. the generation and maintenance of waves against viscosity, by suitable forces applied to the surface.

If the external forces p'_{yy}, p'_{xy} be given multiples of e^{ikx+at}, where k and α are prescribed, the equations in question determine A and C, and thence, by (9) the value of η. Thus we find

$$\frac{p'_{yy}}{g\rho\eta} = \frac{(\alpha^2 + 2\nu k^2\alpha + \sigma^2)\, A - i\,(\sigma^2 + 2\nu km\alpha)\, C}{gk(A - iC)},$$

$$\frac{p'_{xy}}{g\rho\eta} = \frac{\alpha}{gk} \cdot \frac{2i\nu k^2 A + (\alpha + 2\nu k^2)\, C}{(A - iC)},$$

where σ^2 has been written for $gk + T'k^3$ as before. . . .

And so on for two pages. At the end it is made clear that a wind of less than half a mile an hour will leave the surface unruffled. At a mile an hour the surface is covered with minute corrugations due to capillary waves which decay immediately the disturbing cause ceases. At two miles an hour the gravity waves appear. As the author modestly concludes, "Our theoretical investigations give considerable insight into the incipient stages of wave-formation".

On another occasion the same subject of "Generation

of Waves by Wind" was in my mind; but this time
another book was more appropriate, and I read—

> There are waters blown by changing winds to laughter
> And lit by the rich skies, all day. And after,
>   Frost, with a gesture, stays the waves that dance
> And wandering loveliness. He leaves a white
>   Unbroken glory, a gathered radiance,
> A width, a shining peace, under the night.

The magic words bring back the scene.   Again we
feel Nature drawing close to us, uniting with us, till
we are filled with the gladness of the waves dancing in
the sunshine, with the awe of the moonlight on the
frozen lake.   These were not moments when we fell
below ourselves.   We do not look back on them and say,
"It was disgraceful for a man with six sober senses and
a scientific understanding to let himself be deluded in
that way.   I will take Lamb's *Hydrodynamics* with me
next time".   It is good that there should be such
moments for us.   Life would be stunted and narrow if
we could feel no significance in the world around us
beyond that which can be weighed and measured with
the tools of the physicist or described by the metrical
symbols of the mathematician.

Of course it was an illusion.   We can easily expose
the rather clumsy trick that was played on us.   Aethereal
vibrations of various wave-lengths, reflected at different
angles from the disturbed interface between air and
water, reached our eyes, and by photoelectric action
caused appropriate stimuli to travel along the optic
nerves to a brain-centre.   Here the mind set to work to
weave an impression out of the stimuli.   The incoming
material was somewhat meagre; but the mind is a great
storehouse of associations that could be used to clothe

the skeleton. Having woven an impression the mind surveyed all that it had made and decided that it was very good. The critical faculty was lulled. We ceased to analyse and were conscious only of the impression as a whole. The warmth of the air, the scent of the grass, the gentle stir of the breeze, combined with the visual scene in one transcendent impression, around us and within us. Associations emerging from their storehouse grew bolder. Perhaps we recalled the phrase "rippling laughter". Waves—ripples—laughter—gladness—the ideas jostled one another. Quite illogically we were glad; though what there can possibly be to be glad about in a set of aethereal vibrations no sensible person can explain. A mood of quiet joy suffused the whole impression. The gladness in ourselves was in Nature, in the waves, everywhere. That's how it was.

It was an illusion. Then why toy with it longer? These airy fancies which the mind, when we do not keep it severely in order, projects into the external world should be of no concern to the earnest seeker after truth. Get back to the solid substance of things, to the material of the water moving under the pressure of the wind and the force of gravitation in obedience to the laws of hydrodynamics. But the solid substance of things is another illusion. It too is a fancy projected by the mind into the external world. We have chased the solid substance from the continuous liquid to the atom, from the atom to the electron, and there we have lost it. But at least, it will be said, we have reached something real at the end of the chase—the protons and electrons. Or if the new quantum theory condemns these images as too concrete and leaves us with no coherent images at all, at least we have symbolic co-ordinates and momenta and Hamiltonian functions devoting themselves with single-minded purpose to ensuring that $qp - pq$ shall be equal to $ih/2\pi$.

In a previous chapter I have tried to show that by following this course we reach a cyclic scheme which from its very nature can only be a partial expression of our environment. It is not reality but the skeleton of reality. "Actuality" has been lost in the exigencies of the chase. Having first rejected the mind as a worker of illusion we have in the end to return to the mind and say, "Here are worlds well and truly built on a basis more secure than your fanciful illusions. But there is nothing to make any one of them an actual world. Please choose one and weave your fanciful images into it. That alone can make it actual". We have torn away the mental fancies to get at the reality beneath, only to find that the reality of that which is beneath is bound up with its potentiality of awakening these fancies. It is because the mind, the weaver of illusion, is also the only guarantor of reality that reality is always to be sought at the base of illusion. Illusion is to reality as the smoke to the fire. I will not urge that hoary untruth "There is no smoke without fire". But it is reasonable to inquire whether in the mystical illusions of man there is not a reflection of an underlying reality.

To put a plain question—Why should it be good for us to experience a state of self-deception such as I have described? I think everyone admits that it is good to have a spirit sensitive to the influences of Nature, good to exercise an appreciative imagination and not always to be remorselessly dissecting our environment after the manner of the mathematical physicists. And it is good not merely in a utilitarian sense, but in some purposive sense necessary to the fulfilment of the life that is given us. It is not a dope which it is expedient to take from time to time so that we may return with greater vigour to the more legitimate employment of the mind in scientific investigation. Just possibly it might be defended on the ground that it affords to the non-mathematical mind in some feeble measure that delight in the external world which would be more fully provided by an intimacy with its differential equations. (Lest it should be thought that I have intended to pillory hydrodynamics, I hasten to say in this connection that I would not rank the intellectual (scientific) appreciation on a lower plane than the mystical appreciation; and I know of passages written in mathematical symbols which in their sublimity might vie with Rupert Brooke's sonnet.) But I think you will agree with me that it is impossible to allow that the one kind of appreciation can adequately fill the place of the other. Then how can it be deemed good if there is *nothing* in it but self-deception? That would be an upheaval of all our ideas of ethics. It seems to me that the only alternatives are either to count all such surrender to the mystical contact of Nature as mischievous and ethically wrong, or to admit that in these moods we catch something of the true relation of the world to ourselves—a relation not hinted at in a purely scientific analysis of its content. I think the most ardent materialist does not advocate, or at any rate does not practice, the first alternative; therefore I assume the second alternative, that there is some kind of truth at the base of the illusion.

But we must pause to consider the extent of the illusion. Is it a question of a small nugget of reality buried under a mountain of illusion? If that were so it would be our duty to rid our minds of some of the illusion at least, and try to know the truth in purer form.

But I cannot think there is much amiss with our appreciation of the natural scene that so impresses us. I do not think a being more highly endowed than ourselves would prune away much of what we feel. It is not so much that the feeling itself is at fault as that our introspective examination of it wraps it in fanciful imagery. If I were to try to put into words the essential truth revealed in the mystic experience, it would be that our minds are not apart from the world; and the feelings that we have of gladness and melancholy and our yet deeper feelings are not of ourselves alone, but are glimpses of a reality transcending the narrow limits of our particular consciousness—that the harmony and beauty of the face of Nature is at root one with the gladness that transfigures the face of man. We try to express much the same truth when we say that the physical entities are only an extract of pointer readings and beneath them is a nature continuous with our own. But I do not willingly put it into words or subject it to introspection. We have seen how in the physical world the meaning is greatly changed when we contemplate it as surveyed from without instead of, as it essentially must be, from within. By introspection we drag out the truth for external survey; but in the mystical feeling the truth is apprehended from within and is, as it should be, a part of ourselves.

Symbolic Knowledge and Intimate Knowledge. May I elaborate this objection to introspection? We have two kinds of knowledge which I call symbolic knowledge and intimate knowledge. I do not know whether it would be correct to say that reasoning is only applicable to symbolic knowledge, but the more customary forms of reasoning have been developed for symbolic knowledge only. The intimate knowledge will not submit to codification and analysis; or, rather, when we attempt to analyse it the intimacy is lost and it is replaced by symbolism.

For an illustration let us consider Humour. I suppose that humour can be analysed to some extent and the essential ingredients of the different kinds of wit classified. Suppose that we are offered an alleged joke. We subject it to scientific analysis as we would a chemical salt of doubtful nature, and perhaps after careful consideration of all its aspects we are able to confirm that it really and truly is a joke. Logically, I suppose, our next procedure would be to laugh. But it may certainly be predicted that as the result of this scrutiny we shall have lost all inclination we may ever have had to laugh at it. It simply does not do to expose the inner workings of a joke. The classification concerns a symbolic knowledge of humour which preserves all the characteristics of a joke except its laughableness. The real appreciation must come spontaneously, not introspectively. I think this is a not unfair analogy for our mystical feeling for Nature, and I would venture even to apply it to our mystical experience of God. There are some to whom the sense of a divine presence irradiating the soul is one of the most obvious things of experience. In their view a man without this sense is to be regarded as we regard a man without a sense of humour. The absence is a kind of mental deficiency. We may try to analyse the experience as we analyse humour, and construct a theology, or it may be an atheistic philosophy, which shall put into scientific form what is to be inferred about it. But let us not forget that the theology is symbolic knowledge whereas the experience is intimate knowledge. And as laughter cannot be compelled by the scientific exposition of the structure of a joke, so a philosophic discussion of the attributes of God (or an impersonal substitute) is likely to miss the intimate response of the spirit which is the central point of the religious experience.

Defence of Mysticism. A defence of the mystic might run something like this. We have acknowledged that the entities of physics can from their very nature form only a partial aspect of the reality. How are we to deal with the other part? It cannot be said that that other part concerns us less than the physical entities. Feelings, purpose, values, make up our consciousness as much as sense-impressions. We follow up the sense-impressions and find that they lead into an external world discussed by science; we follow up the other elements of our being and find that they lead—not into a world of space and time, but surely somewhere. If you take the view that the whole of consciousness is reflected in the dance of electrons in the brain, so that each emotion is a separate figure of the dance, then all features of consciousness alike lead into the external world of physics. But I assume that you have followed me in rejecting this view, and that you agree that consciousness as a whole is greater than those quasi-metrical aspects of it which are abstracted to compose the physical brain. We have then to deal with those parts of our being unamenable to metrical specification, that do not make contact—jut out, as it were—into space and time. By dealing with them I do not mean make scientific inquiry into them. The first step is to give acknowledged status to the crude conceptions in which the mind invests them, similar to the status of those crude conceptions which constitute the familiar material world.

Our conception of the familiar table was an illusion.

But if some prophetic voice had warned us that it was an illusion and therefore we had not troubled to investigate further we should never have found the scientific table. To reach the reality of the table we need to be endowed with sense-organs to weave images and illusions about it. And so it seems to me that the first step in a broader revelation to man must be the awakening of image-building in connection with the higher faculties of his nature, so that these are no longer blind alleys but open out into a spiritual world—a world partly of illusion, no doubt, but in which he lives no less than in the world, also of illusion, revealed by the senses.

The mystic, if haled before a tribunal of scientists, might perhaps end his defence on this note. He would say, The familiar material world of everyday conception, though lacking somewhat in scientific truth, is good enough to live in; in fact the scientific world of pointer readings would be an impossible sort of place to inhabit. It is a symbolic world and the only thing that could live comfortably in it would be a *symbol*. But I am not a symbol; I am compounded of that mental activity which is from your point of view a nest of illusion, so that to accord with my own nature I have to transform even the world explored by my senses. But I am not merely made up of senses; the rest of my nature has to live and grow. I have to render account of that environment into which it has its outlet. My conception of my spiritual environment is not to be compared with your scientific world of pointer readings; it is an everyday world to be compared with the material world of familiar experience. I claim it as no more real and no less real than that. Primarily it is not a world to be analysed, but a world to be lived in."

Granted that this takes us outside the sphere of

exact knowledge, and that it is difficult to imagine that anything corresponding to exact science will ever be applicable to this part of our environment, the mystic is unrepentant. Because we are unable to render exact account of our environment it does not follow that it would be better to pretend that we live in a vacuum.

If the defence may be considered to have held good against the first onslaught, perhaps the next stage of the attack will be an easy tolerance. "Very well. Have it your own way. It is a harmless sort of belief—not like a more dogmatic theology. You want a sort of spiritual playground for those queer tendencies in man's nature, which sometimes take possession of him. Run away and play then; but do not bother the serious people who are making the world go round." The challenge now comes not from the scientific materialism which professes to seek a natural explanation of spiritual power, but from the deadlier moral materialism which despises it. Few deliberately hold the philosophy that the forces of progress are related only to the material side of our environment, but few can claim that they are not more or less under its sway. We must not interrupt the "practical men", these busy moulders of history carrying us at ever-increasing pace towards our destiny as an ant-heap of humanity infesting the earth. But is it true in history that material forces have been the most potent factors? Call it of God, of the Devil, fanaticism, unreason; but do not underrate the power of the mystic. Mysticism may be fought as error or believed as inspired, but it is no matter for easy tolerance—

> We are the music-makers
>   And we are the dreamers of dreams
> Wandering by lone sea-breakers
>   And sitting by desolate streams;

World-losers and world-forsakers,
  On whom the pale moon gleams:
Yet we are the movers and shakers
  Of the world for ever, it seems.

Reality and Mysticism.   But a defence before the scientists may not be a defence to our own self-questionings. We are haunted by the word *reality*.   I have already tried to deal with the questions which arise as to the meaning of reality; but it presses on us so persistently that, at the risk of repetition, I must consider it once more from the standpoint of religion.   A compromise of illusion and reality may be all very well in our attitude towards physical surroundings; but to admit such a compromise into religion would seem to be a trifling with sacred things.   Reality seems to concern religious beliefs much more than any others.   No one bothers as to whether there is a reality behind humour.   The artist who tries to bring out the soul in his picture does not really care whether and in what sense the soul can be said to exist. Even the physicist is unconcerned as to whether atoms or electrons really exist; he usually asserts that they do, but, as we have seen, existence is there used in a domestic sense and no inquiry is made as to whether it is more than a conventional term.   In most subjects (perhaps not excluding philosophy) it seems sufficient to agree on the things that we shall call real, and afterwards try to discover what we mean by the word.   And so it comes about that religion seems to be the one field of inquiry in which the question of reality and existence is treated as of serious and vital importance.

But it is difficult to see how such an inquiry can be profitable.   When Dr. Johnson felt himself getting tied up in argument over "Bishop Berkeley's ingenious sophistry to prove the non-existence of matter, and that everything in the universe is merely ideal", he answered, "striking his foot with mighty force against a large stone, till he rebounded from it,—'I refute it *thus*' ". Just what that action assured him of is not very obvious; but apparently he found it comforting. And to-day the matter-of-fact scientist feels the same impulse to recoil from these flights of thought back to something kick-able, although he ought to be aware by this time that what Rutherford has left us of the large stone is scarcely worth kicking.

There is still the tendency to use "reality" as a word of magic comfort like the blessed word "Mesopotamia". If I were to assert the reality of the soul or of God, I should certainly not intend a comparison with Johnson's large stone—a patent illusion—or even with the p's and q's of the quantum theory—an abstract symbolism. Therefore I have no right to use the word in religion for the purpose of borrowing on its behalf that comfortable feeling which (probably wrongly) has become associated with stones and quantum co-ordinates.

Scientific instincts warn me that any attempt to answer the question "What is real?" in a broader sense than that adopted for domestic purposes in science, is likely to lead to a floundering among vain words and high-sounding epithets. We all know that there are regions of the human spirit untrammelled by the world of physics. In the mystic sense of the creation around us, in the expression of art, in a yearning towards God, the soul grows upward and finds the fulfilment of something implanted in its nature. The sanction for this development is within us, a striving born with our consciousness or an Inner Light proceeding from a greater power than ours. Science can scarcely question this sanction, for the pursuit of science springs from a striving which the mind is impelled to follow, a questioning that will not be suppressed. Whether in the intellectual pursuits of science or in the mystical pursuits of the spirit, the light beckons ahead and the purpose surging in our nature responds. Can we not leave it at that? Is it really necessary to drag in the comfortable word "reality" to be administered like a pat on the back?

The problem of the scientific world is part of a broader problem—the problem of all experience. Experience may be regarded as a combination of self and environment, it being part of the problem to disentangle these two interacting components. Life, religion, knowledge, truth are all involved in this problem, some relating to the finding of ourselves, some to the finding of our environment from the experience confronting us. All of us in our lives have to make something of this problem; and it is an important condition that we who have to solve the problem are ourselves part of the problem. Looking at the very beginning, the initial fact is the feeling of purpose in ourselves which urges us to embark on the problem. We are meant to fulfil something by our lives. There are faculties with which we are endowed, or which we ought to attain, which must find a status and an outlet in the solution. It may seem arrogant that we should in this way insist on moulding truth to our own nature; but it is rather that the problem of truth can only spring from a desire for truth which is in our nature.

A rainbow described in the symbolism of physics is a band of aethereal vibrations arranged in systematic order of wave-length from about ·000040 cm. to ·000072 cm. From one point of view we are paltering with the truth whenever we admire the gorgeous bow of colour, and should strive to reduce our minds to such a state that we receive the same impression from the rainbow as from a table of wave-lengths. But although that is how the rainbow impresses itself on an impersonal spectroscope, we are not giving the whole truth and significance of experience—the starting-point of the problem—if we suppress the factors wherein we ourselves differ from a spectroscope. We cannot say that the rainbow, as part of the world, was meant to convey the vivid effects of colour; but we can perhaps say that the human mind as part of the world was meant to perceive it that way.

Significance and Values. When we think of the sparkling waves as moved with laughter we are evidently attributing a significance to the scene which was not there. The physical elements of the water—the scurrying electric charges—were guiltless of any intention to convey the impression that they were happy. But so also were they guiltless of any intention to convey the impression of substance, of colour, or of geometrical form of the waves. If they can be held to have had any intention at all it was to satisfy certain differential equations—and that was because they are the creatures of the mathematician who has a partiality for differential equations. The physical no less than the mystical significance of the scene is not there; it is *here*—in the mind.

What we make of the world must be largely dependent on the sense-organs that we happen to possess. How the world must have changed since man came to rely on his eyes rather than his nose! You are alone on the mountains wrapt in a great silence; but equip yourself with an extra artificial sense-organ and, lo! the aether is hideous with the blare of the Savoy bands.   Or—

> The isle is full of noises,
> Sounds, and sweet airs, that give delight, and hurt not.
> Sometimes a thousand twangling instruments
> Will hum about mine ears; and sometimes voices.

So far as broader characteristics are concerned we see in Nature what we look for or are equipped to look for. Of course, I do not mean that we can arrange the details of the scene; but by the light and shade of our values we can bring out things that shall have the broad characteristics we esteem. In this sense the value placed on permanence creates the world of apparent substance; in this sense, perhaps, the God within creates the God in Nature. But no complete view can be obtained so long as we separate our consciousness from the world of which it is a part. We can only speak speculatively of that which I have called the "background of the pointer readings"; but it would at least seem plausible that if the values which give the light and shade of the world are absolute they must belong to the background, unrecognised in physics because they are not in the pointer readings but recognised by consciousness which has its roots in the background. I have no wish to put that forward as a theory; it is only to emphasise that, limited as we are to a knowledge of the physical world and its points of contact with the background in isolated consciousness, we do not quite attain that thought of the unity of the whole which is essential to a complete theory. Presumably human nature has been specialised to a considerable extent by the operation of natural selection; and it might well be debated whether its valuation of permanence and other traits now apparently fundamental are essential properties of consciousness or have been evolved through interplay with the external world. In that case the values given by mind to the external world have originally come to it from the external world-stuff. Such a tossing to and fro of values is, I think, not foreign to our view that the world-stuff behind the pointer readings is of nature continuous with the mind.

In viewing the world in a practical way values for normal human consciousness may be taken as standard. But the evident possibility of arbitrariness in this valuation sets us hankering after a standard that could be considered final and absolute. We have two alternatives. Either there are no absolute values, so that the sanctions of the inward monitor in our consciousness are the final court of appeal beyond which it is idle to inquire. Or there are absolute values; then we can only trust optimistically that our values are some pale reflection of those of the Absolute Valuer, or that we have insight into the mind of the Absolute from whence come those strivings and sanctions whose authority we usually forbear to question.

I have naturally tried to make the outlook reached in these lectures as coherent as possible, but I should not be greatly concerned if under the shafts of criticism it becomes very ragged. Coherency goes with finality; and the anxious question is whether our arguments have begun right rather than whether they have had the good fortune to end right. The leading points which have seemed to me to deserve philosophic consideration may be summarised as follows:

(1) The symbolic nature of the entities of physics is generally recognised; and the scheme of physics is now formulated in such a way as to make it almost

self-evident that it is a partial aspect of something wider.

(2) Strict causality is abandoned in the material world. Our ideas of the controlling laws are in process of reconstruction and it is not possible to predict what kind of form they will ultimately take; but all the indications are that strict causality has dropped out permanently. This relieves the former necessity of supposing that mind is subject to deterministic law or alternatively that it can suspend deterministic law in the material world.

(3) Recognising that the physical world is entirely abstract and without "actuality" apart from its linkage to consciousness, we restore consciousness to the fundamental position instead of representing it as an inessential complication occasionally found in the midst of inorganic nature at a late stage of evolutionary history.

(4) The sanction for correlating a "real" physical world to certain feelings of which we are conscious does not seem to differ in any essential respect from the sanction for correlating a spiritual domain to another side of our personality.

It is not suggested that there is anything new in this philosophy. In particular the essence of the first point has been urged by many writers, and has no doubt won individual assent from many scientists before the recent revolutions of physical theory. But it places a somewhat different complexion on the matter when this is not merely a philosophic doctrine to which intellectual assent might be given, but has become part of the scientific attitude of the day, illustrated in detail in the current scheme of physics.

Conviction. Through fourteen chapters you have followed with me the scientific approach to knowledge. I have given the philosophical reflections as they have naturally arisen from the current scientific conclusions, I hope without distorting them for theological ends. In the present chapter the standpoint has no longer been predominantly scientific; I started from that part of our experience which is not within the scope of a scientific survey, or at least is such that the methods of physical science would miss the significance that we consider it essential to attribute to it. The starting-point of belief in mystical religion is a conviction of significance or, as I have called it earlier, the sanction of a striving in the consciousness. This must be emphasised because appeal to intuitive conviction of this kind has been the foundation of religion through all ages and I do not wish to give the impression that we have now found something new and more scientific to substitute. I repudiate the idea of proving the distinctive beliefs of religion either from the data of physical science or by the methods of physical science. Presupposing a mystical religion based not on science but (rightly or wrongly) on a self-known experience accepted as fundamental, we can proceed to discuss the various criticisms which science might bring against it or the possible conflict with scientific views of the nature of experience equally originating from self-known data.

It is necessary to examine further the nature of the conviction from which religion arises; otherwise we may seem to be countenancing a blind rejection of reason as a guide to truth. There is a hiatus in reasoning, we must admit; but it is scarcely to be described as a rejection of reasoning. There is just the same hiatus in reasoning about the physical world if we go back far enough. We can only reason from data and the ultimate data must be given to us by a non-reasoning process—a self-knowledge of that which is in our consciousness. To make a start we must be aware of something. But that is not sufficient; we must be convinced of the significance of that awareness. We are bound to claim for human nature that, either of itself or as inspired by a power beyond, it is capable of making legitimate judgments of significance. Otherwise we cannot even reach a physical world.*

Accordingly the conviction which we postulate is that certain states of awareness in consciousness have at least equal significance with those which are called sensations. It is perhaps not irrelevant to note that time by its dual entry into our minds (p. 51) to some extent bridges the gap between sense-impressions and these other states of awareness. Amid the latter must be found the basis of experience from which a spiritual religion arises. The conviction is scarcely a matter to be argued about, it is dependent on the forcefulness of the feeling of awareness.

But, it may be said, although we may have such a department of consciousness, may we not have misunderstood altogether the nature of that which we believe we are experiencing? That seems to me to be rather beside the point. In regard to our experience of the physical world we have very much misunderstood the meaning of our sensations. It has been the task of science to discover that things are very different from

---

* We can of course solve the problem arising from certain data without being convinced of the significance of the data—the "official" scientific attitude as I have previously called it. But a physical world which has only the status of the solution of a problem, arbitrarily chosen to pass an idle hour, is not what is intended here.

what they seem. But we do not pluck out our eyes
because they persist in deluding us with fanciful
colourings instead of giving us the plain truth about
wave-length. It is in the midst of such misrepresenta-
tions of environment (if you must call them so) that we
have to live. It is, however, a very one-sided view of
truth which can find in the glorious colouring of our
surroundings nothing but misrepresentation—which
takes the environment to be all important and the
conscious spirit to be inessential. In our scientific
chapters we have seen how the mind must be regarded
as dictating the course of world-building; without it
there is but formless chaos. It is the aim of physical
science, so far as its scope extends, to lay bare the
fundamental structure underlying the world; but science
has also to explain if it can, or else humbly to accept,
the fact that from this world have arisen minds capable
of transmuting the bare structure into the richness of
our experience. It is not misrepresentation but rather
achievement—the result perhaps of long ages of biological evolution—that we should have fashioned a
familiar world out of the crude basis. It is a fulfilment
of the purpose of man's nature. If likewise the spiritual
world has been transmuted by a religious colour beyond
anything implied in its bare external qualities, it may
be allowable to assert with equal conviction that this
is not misrepresentation but the achievement of a divine
element in man's nature.

May I revert again to the analogy of theology with
the supposed science of humour which (after consulta-
tion with a classical authority) I venture to christen
"geloeology". Analogy is not convincing argument, but
it must serve here. Consider the proverbial Scotchman
with strong leanings towards philosophy and incapable

of seeing a joke. There is no reason why he should not take high honours in geloeology, and for example write an acute analysis of the differences between British and American humour. His comparison of our respective jokes would be particularly unbiased and judicial, seeing that he is quite incapable of seeing the point of either. But it would be useless to consider his views as to which was following the right development; for that he would need a sympathetic understanding—he would (in the phrase appropriate to the other side of my analogy) need to be *converted*. The kind of help and criticism given by the geloeologist and the philosophical theologian is to secure that there is method in our madness. The former may show that our hilarious reception of a speech is the result of a satisfactory dinner and a good cigar rather than a subtle perception of wit; the latter may show that the ecstatic mysticism of the anchorite is the vagary of a fevered body and not a transcendent revelation. But I do not think we should appeal to either of them to discuss the reality of the sense with which we claim to be endowed, nor the direction of its right development. That is a matter for our inner sense of values which we all believe in to some extent, though it may be a matter of dispute just how far it goes. If we have no such sense then it would seem that not only religion, but the physical world and all faith in reasoning totter in insecurity.

I have sometimes been asked whether science cannot now furnish an argument which ought to convince any reasonable atheist. I could no more ram religious conviction into an atheist than I could ram a joke into the Scotchman. The only hope of "converting" the latter is that through contact with merry-minded companions he may begin to realise that he is missing something in life which is worth attaining. Probably in the recesses of his solemn mind there exists inhibited the seed of humour, awaiting an awakening by such an impulse. The same advice would seem to apply to the propagation of religion; it has, I believe, the merit of being entirely orthodox advice.

We cannot pretend to offer proofs. *Proof* is an idol before whom the pure mathematician tortures himself. In physics we are generally content to sacrifice before the lesser shrine of *Plausibility*. And even the pure mathematician—that stern logician—reluctantly allows himself some prejudgments; he is never quite convinced that the scheme of mathematics is flawless, and mathematical logic has undergone revolutions as profound as the revolutions of physical theory. We are all alike stumblingly pursuing an ideal beyond our reach. In science we sometimes have convictions as to the right solution of a problem which we cherish but cannot justify; we are influenced by some innate sense of the fitness of things. So too there may come to us convictions in the spiritual sphere which our nature bids us hold to. I have given an example of one such conviction which is rarely if ever disputed—that surrender to the mystic influence of a scene of natural beauty is right and proper for a human spirit, although it would have been deemed an unpardonable eccentricity in the "observer" contemplated in earlier chapters. Religious conviction is often described in somewhat analogous terms as a surrender; it is not to be enforced by argument on those who do not feel its claim in their own nature.

I think it is inevitable that these convictions should emphasise a personal aspect of what we are trying to grasp. We have to build the spiritual world out of symbols taken from our own personality, as we build the scientific world out of the metrical symbols of the mathematician. If not, it can only be left ungraspable—an environment dimly felt in moments of exaltation but lost to us in the sordid routine of life. To turn it into more continuous channels we must be able to approach the World-Spirit in the midst of our cares and duties in that simpler relation of spirit to spirit in which all true religion finds expression.

Mystical Religion. We have seen that the cyclic scheme of physics presupposes a background outside the scope of its investigations. In this background we must find, first, our own personality, and then perhaps a greater personality. The idea of a universal Mind or Logos would be, I think, a fairly plausible inference from the present state of scientific theory; at least it is in harmony with it. But if so, all that our inquiry justifies us in asserting is a purely colourless pantheism. Science cannot tell whether the world-spirit is good or evil, and its halting argument for the existence of a God might equally well be turned into an argument for the existence of a Devil.

I think that that is an example of the limitation of physical schemes that has troubled us before—namely, that in all such schemes opposites are represented by $+$ and $-$. Past and future, cause and effect, are represented in this inadequate way. One of the greatest puzzles of science is to discover why protons and electrons are not simply the opposites of one another, although our whole conception of electric charge requires that positive and negative electricity should be related like $+$ and $-$. The direction of time's arrow could only be determined by that incongruous mixture of theology and statistics known as the second law of thermodynamics; or, to be more explicit, the direction of the arrow could be determined by statistical rules, but its significance as a governing fact "making sense of the world" could only be deduced on teleological assumptions. If physics cannot determine which way up its own world ought to be regarded, there is not much hope of guidance from it as to ethical orientation. We trust to some inward sense of fitness when we orient the physical world with the future on top, and likewise we must trust to some inner monitor when we orient the spiritual world with the good on top.

Granted that physical science has limited its scope so as to leave a background which we are at liberty to, or even invited to, fill with a reality of spiritual import, we have yet to face the most difficult criticism from science. "Here", says science, "I have left a domain in which I shall not interfere. I grant that you have some kind of avenue to it through the self-knowledge of consciousness, so that it is not necessarily a domain of pure agnosticism. But how are you going to deal with this domain? Have you any system of inference from mystic experience comparable to the system by which science develops a knowledge of the outside world? I do not insist on your employing my method, which I acknowledge is inapplicable; but you ought to have some defensible method. The alleged basis of experience may possibly be valid; but have I any reason to regard the religious interpretation currently given to it as anything more than muddle-headed romancing?"

The question is almost beyond my scope. I can only acknowledge its pertinency. Although I have chosen the lightest task by considering only mystical religion— and I have no impulse to defend any other—I am not competent to give an answer which shall be anything like complete. It is obvious that the insight of consciousness, although the only avenue to what I have called *intimate* knowledge of the reality behind the symbols of science, is not to be trusted implicitly without control. In history religious mysticism has often been associated with extravagances that cannot be approved. I suppose too that oversensitiveness to aesthetic influences may be a sign of a neurotic temperament unhealthy to the individual. We must allow something for the pathological condition of the brain in what appear to be moments of exalted insight. One begins to fear that after all our faults have been detected and removed there will not be any "us" left. But in the study of the physical world we have ultimately to rely on our sense-organs, although they are capable of betraying us by gross illusions; similarly the avenue of consciousness into the spiritual world may be beset with pitfalls, but that does not necessarily imply that no advance is possible.

A point that must be insisted on is that religion or contact with spiritual power if it has any general importance at all must be a commonplace matter of ordinary life, and it should be treated as such in any discussion. I hope that you have not interpreted my references to mysticism as referring to abnormal experiences and revelations. I am not qualified to discuss what evidential value (if any) may be attached to the stranger forms of experience and insight. But in any case to suppose that mystical religion is mainly concerned with these is like supposing that Einstein's theory is mainly concerned with the perihelion of Mercury and a few other exceptional observations. For a matter belonging to daily affairs the tone of current discussions often seems quite inappropriately pedantic.

As scientists we realise that colour is merely a question of the wave-lengths of aethereal vibrations; but that does not seem to have dispelled the feeling that eyes which reflect light near wave-length 4800 are a subject for rhapsody whilst those which reflect wave-length 5300 are left unsung. We have not yet reached the practice of the Laputans, who, "if they would, for example, praise the beauty of a woman, or any other animal, they describe it by rhombs, circles, parallelograms, ellipses, and other geometrical terms". The materialist who is convinced that all phenomena arise from electrons and quanta and the like controlled by mathematical formulae, must presumably hold the belief that his wife is a rather elaborate differential equation; but he is probably tactful enough not to obtrude this opinion in domestic life. If this kind of scientific dissection is felt to be inadequate and irrelevant in ordinary personal relationships, it is surely out of place in the most personal relationship of all—that of the human soul to a divine spirit.

We are anxious for perfect truth, but it is hard to say in what form perfect truth is to be found. I cannot quite believe that it has the form typified by an inventory. Somehow as part of its perfection there should be incorporated in it that which we esteem as a "sense of proportion". The physicist is not conscious of any disloyalty to truth on occasions when his sense of proportion tells him to regard a plank as continuous material, well knowing that it is "really" empty space containing sparsely scattered electric charges. And the deepest philosophical researches as to the nature of the Deity may give a conception equally out of proportion for daily life; so that we should rather employ a conception that was unfolded nearly two thousand years ago.

I am standing on the threshold about to enter a room. It is a complicated business. In the first place I must shove against an atmosphere pressing with a force of fourteen pounds on every square inch of my body. I must make sure of landing on a plank travelling at twenty miles a second round the sun—a fraction of a second too early or too late, the plank would be miles away. I must do this whilst hanging from a round planet head outward into space, and with a wind of aether blowing at no one knows how many miles a second through every interstice of my body. The plank has no solidity of substance. To step on it is like stepping on a swarm of flies. Shall I not slip through? No, if I make the venture one of the flies hits me and gives a boost up again; I fall again and am knocked upwards by another fly; and so on. I may hope that the net result will be that I remain about steady; but if unfortunately I should slip through the floor or be boosted too violently up to the ceiling, the occurrence would be, not a violation of the laws of Nature, but a rare coincidence. These are some of the minor difficulties. I ought really to look at the problem four-dimensionally as concerning the intersection of my world-line with that of the plank. Then again it is necessary to determine in which direction the entropy of the world is increasing in order to make sure that my passage over the threshold is an entrance, not an exit.

Verily, it is easier for a camel to pass through the eye of a needle than for a scientific man to pass through a door. And whether the door be barn door or church door it might be wiser that he should consent to be an ordinary man and walk in rather than wait till all the difficulties involved in a really scientific ingress are resolved.

CONCLUSION

A tide of indignation has been surging in the breast of the matter-of-fact scientist and is about to be unloosed upon us. Let us broadly survey the defence we can set up.

I suppose the most sweeping charge will be that I have been talking what at the back of my mind I must know is only a well-meaning kind of nonsense. I can assure you that there is a scientific part of me that has often brought that criticism during some of the later chapters. I will not say that I have been half-convinced, but at least I have felt a homesickness for the paths of physical science where there are more or less discernible handrails to keep us from the worst morasses of foolishness. But however much I may have felt inclined to tear up this part of the discussion and confine myself to my proper profession of juggling with pointer readings, I find myself holding to the main principles. Starting from aether, electrons and other physical machinery we cannot reach conscious man and render count of what is apprehended in his consciousness. Conceivably we might reach a human machine interacting by reflexes with its environment; but we cannot reach rational man morally responsible to pursue the truth as to aether and electrons or to religion. Perhaps it may seem unnecessarily portentous to invoke the latest developments of the relativity and quantum theories merely to tell you this; but that is scarcely the point. We have followed these theories because they contain the conceptions of modern science; and it is not a question of asserting a faith that science must ultimately be reconcilable with an idealistic view, but of examining how at the moment

343

it actually stands in regard to it. I might sacrifice the detailed arguments of the last four chapters (perhaps marred by dialectic entanglement) if I could otherwise convey the significance of the recent change which has overtaken scientific ideals. The physicist now regards his own external world in a way which I can only describe as more mystical, though not less exact and practical, than that which prevailed some years ago, when it was taken for granted that nothing could be true unless an engineer could make a model of it. There was a time when the whole combination of self and environment which makes up experience seemed likely to pass under the dominion of a physics much more iron-bound than it is now. That overweening phase, when it was almost necessary to ask the permission of physics to call one's soul one's own, is past. The change gives rise to thoughts which ought to be developed. Even if we cannot attain to much clarity of constructive thought we can discern that certain assumptions, expectations or fears are no longer applicable.

Is it merely a well-meaning kind of nonsense for a physicist to affirm this necessity for an outlook beyond physics? It is worse nonsense to deny it. Or as that ardent relativist the Red Queen puts it, "You call that nonsense, but I've heard nonsense compared with which that would be as sensible as a dictionary".

For if those who hold that there must be a physical basis for everything hold that these mystical views are nonsense, we may ask—What then is the physical basis of nonsense? The "problem of nonsense" touches the scientist more nearly than any other moral problem. He may regard the distinction of good and evil as too remote to bother about; but the distinction of sense and nonsense, of valid and invalid reasoning, must be accepted at the beginning of every scientific inquiry. Therefore it may well be chosen for examination as a test case.

If the brain contains a physical basis for the nonsense which it thinks, this must be some kind of configuration of the entities of physics—not precisely a chemical secretion, but not essentially different from that kind of product. It is as though when my brain says 7 times 8 are 56 its machinery is manufacturing sugar, but when it says 7 times 8 are 65 the machinery has gone wrong and produced chalk. But who says the machinery has gone wrong? As a physical machine the brain has acted according to the unbreakable laws of physics; so why stigmatise its action? This discrimination of chemical products as good or evil has no parallel in chemistry. We cannot assimilate laws of thought to natural laws; they are laws which *ought* to be obeyed, not laws which *must* be obeyed; and the physicist must accept laws of thought before he accepts natural law. "Ought" takes us outside chemistry and physics. It concerns something which wants or esteems sugar, not chalk, sense, not nonsense. A physical machine cannot esteem or want anything; whatever is fed into it it will chaw up according to the laws of its physical machinery. That which in the physical world shadows the nonsense in the mind affords no ground for its condemnation. In a world of aether and electrons we might perhaps encounter *nonsense*; we could not encounter *damned nonsense*.

The most plausible physical theory of correct reasoning would probably run somewhat as follows. By reasoning we are sometimes able to predict events afterwards confirmed by observation; the mental processes follow a sequence ending in a conception which anticipates a subsequent perception. We may call such a chain of mental states "successful reasoning"—intended as a technical classification without any moral implications involving the awkward word "ought". We can examine what are the common characteristics of various pieces of successful reasoning. If we apply this analysis to the mental aspects of the reasoning we obtain laws of logic; but presumably the analysis could also be applied to the physical constituents of the brain. It is not unlikely that a distinctive characteristic would be found in the physical processes in the brain-cells which accompany successful reasoning, and this would constitute "the physical basis of success."

But we do not use reasoning power solely to predict observational events, and the question of success (as above defined) does not always arise. Nevertheless if such reasoning were accompanied by the product which I have called "the physical basis of success" we should naturally assimilate it to successful reasoning.

And so if I persuade my materialist opponent to withdraw the epithet "damned nonsense" as inconsistent with his own principles he is still entitled to allege that my brain in evolving these ideas did not contain the physical basis of success. As there is some danger of our respective points of view becoming mixed up, I must make clear my contention:

(*a*) If I thought like my opponent I should not worry about the alleged absence of a physical basis of success in my reasoning, since it is not obvious why this should be demanded when we are not dealing with observational predictions.

(*b*) As I do not think like him, I am deeply perturbed by the allegation; because I should consider it to be the outward sign that the stronger epithet (which is not inconsistent with *my* principles) is applicable.

I think that the "success" theory of reasoning will
not be much appreciated by the pure mathematician.
For him reasoning is a heaven-sent faculty to be enjoyed
remote from the fuss of external Nature. It is heresy
to suggest that the status of his demonstrations depends
on the fact that a physicist now and then succeeds in
predicting results which accord with observation. Let
the external world behave as irrationally as it will, there
will remain undisturbed a corner of knowledge where
he may happily hunt for the roots of the Riemann-
Zeta function. The "success" theory naturally justifies
itself to the physicist. He employs this type of activity
of the brain because it leads him to what he wants—a
verifiable prediction as to the external world—and for
that reason he esteems it. Why should not the theologian employ and esteem one of the mental processes
of unreason which leads to what he wants—an assurance
of future bliss, or a Hell to frighten us into better
behaviour? Understand that I do not encourage theologians to despise reason; my point is that they might
well do so if it had no better justification than the
"success" theory.

And so my own concern lest I should have been
talking nonsense ends in persuading me that I have to
reckon with something that could not possibly be
found in the physical world.

Another charge launched against these lectures may
be that of admitting some degree of supernaturalism,
which in the eyes of many is the same thing as superstition. In so far as supernaturalism is associated with
the denial of strict causality (p. 309) I can only answer
that that is what the modern scientific development of
the quantum theory brings us to. But probably the
more provocative part of our scheme is the rôle allowed

to mind and consciousness. Yet I suppose that our adversary admits consciousness as a fact and he is aware that but for knowledge by consciousness scientific investigation could not begin. Does he regard consciousness as supernatural? Then it is he who is admitting the supernatural. Or does he regard it as part of Nature? So do we. We treat it in what seems to be its obvious position as the avenue of approach to the reality and significance of the world, as it is the avenue of approach to all scientific knowledge of the world. Or does he regard consciousness as something which unfortunately has to be admitted but which it is scarcely polite to mention? Even so we humour him. We have associated consciousness with a background untouched in the physical survey of the world and have given the physicist a domain where he can go round in cycles without ever encountering anything to bring a blush to his cheek. Here a realm of natural law is secured to him covering all that he has ever effectively occupied. And indeed it has been quite as much the purpose of our discussion to secure such a realm where scientific method may work unhindered, as to deal with the nature of that part of our experience which lies beyond it. This defence of scientific method may not be superfluous. The accusation is often made that, by its neglect of aspects of human experience evident to a wider culture, physical science has been overtaken by a kind of madness leading it sadly astray. It is part of our contention that there exists a wide field of research for which the methods of physics suffice, into which the introduction of these other aspects would be entirely mischievous.

A besetting temptation of the scientific apologist for religion is to take some of its current expressions and after clearing away crudities of thought (which must necessarily be associated with anything adapted to the everyday needs of humanity) to water down the meaning until little is left that could possibly be in opposition to science or to anything else. If the revised interpretation had first been presented no one would have raised vigorous criticism; on the other hand no one would have been stirred to any great spiritual enthusiasm. It is the less easy to steer clear of this temptation because it is necessarily a question of degree. Clearly if we are to extract from the tenets of a hundred different sects any coherent view to be defended some at least of them must be submitted to a watering-down process. I do not know if the reader will acquit me of having succumbed to this temptation in the passages where I have touched upon religion; but I have tried to make a fight against it. Any apparent failure has probably arisen in the following way. We have been concerned with the borderland of the material and spiritual worlds as approached from the side of the former. From this side all that we could assert of the spiritual world would be insufficient to justify even the palest brand of theology that is not too emaciated to have any practical influence on man's outlook. But the spiritual world as understood in any serious religion is by no means a colourless domain. Thus by calling this hinterland of science a spiritual world I may seem to have begged a vital question, whereas I intended only a provisional identification. To make it more than provisional an approach must be made from the other side. I am unwilling to play the amateur theologian, and examine this approach in detail. I have, however, pointed out that the attribution of religious colour to the domain must rest on inner conviction; and I think we should not deny validity to certain inner convictions, which seem parallel with the unreasoning trust in reason which is at the basis of mathematics, with an innate sense of the fitness of things which is at the basis of the science of the physical world, and with an irresistible sense of incongruity which is at the basis of the justification of humour. Or perhaps it is not so much a question of asserting the validity of these convictions as of recognising their function as an essential part of our nature. We do not defend the validity of seeing beauty in a natural landscape; we accept with gratitude the fact that we are so endowed as to see it that way.

It will perhaps be said that the conclusion to be drawn from these arguments from modern science, is that religion first became possible for a reasonable scientific man about the year 1927. If we must consider that tiresome person, the consistently reasonable man, we may point out that not merely religion but most of the ordinary aspects of life first became possible for him in that year. Certain common activities (e.g. falling in love) are, I fancy, still forbidden him. If our expectation should prove well founded that 1927 has seen the final overthrow of strict causality by Heisenberg, Bohr, Born and others, the year will certainly rank as one of the greatest epochs in the development of scientific philosophy. But seeing that before this enlightened era men managed to persuade themselves that they had to mould their own material future notwithstanding the yoke of strict causality, they might well use the same *modus vivendi* in religion.

This brings us to consider the view often pontifically asserted that there can be no conflict between science and religion because they belong to altogether different realms of thought. The implication is that discussions such as we have been pursuing are superfluous. But it seems to me rather that the assertion challenges this kind of discussion—to see how both realms of thought can be associated independently with our existence. Having seen something of the way in which the scientific realm of thought has constituted itself out of a self-closed cyclic scheme we are able to give a guarded assent. The conflict will not be averted unless both sides confine themselves to their proper domain; and a discussion which enables us to reach a better understanding as to the boundary should be a contribution towards a state of peace. There is still plenty of opportunity for frontier difficulties; a particular illustration will show this.

A belief not by any means confined to the more dogmatic adherents of religion is that there is a future non-material existence in store for us. Heaven is nowhere in space, but it is in time. (All the meaning of the belief is bound up with the word *future*; there is no comfort in an assurance of bliss in some *former* state of existence.) On the other hand the scientist declares that time and space are a single continuum, and the modern idea of a Heaven in time but not in space is in this respect more at variance with science than the pre-Copernican idea of a Heaven above our heads. The question I am now putting is not whether the theologian or the scientist is right, but which is trespassing on the domain of the other? Cannot theology dispose of the destinies of the human soul in a non-material way without trespassing on the realm of science? Cannot science assert its conclusions as to the geometry of the space-time continuum without trespassing on the realm of theology? According to the assertion above science and theology can make what mistakes they please provided that they make them *in their own territory*; they cannot quarrel if they keep to their own realms. But it will require a skilful drawing of the boundary line to frustrate the development of a conflict here.*

The philosophic trend of modern scientific thought differs markedly from the views of thirty years ago. Can we guarantee that the next thirty years will not see another revolution, perhaps even a complete reaction? We may certainly expect great changes, and by that time many things will appear in a new aspect. That is one of the difficulties in the relations of science and philosophy; that is why the scientist as a rule pays so little heed to the philosophical implications of his own discoveries. By dogged endeavour he is slowly and tortuously advancing to purer and purer truth; but his ideas seem to zigzag in a manner most disconcerting to the onlooker. Scientific discovery is like the fitting together of the pieces of a great jig-saw puzzle; a revolution of science does not mean that the pieces already arranged and interlocked have to be dispersed; it means that in fitting on fresh pieces we have had to revise our impression of what the puzzle-picture is going to be like. One day you ask the scientist how he is getting on; he replies, "Finely. I have very nearly finished this piece of blue sky." Another day you ask how the sky is progressing and are told, "I have added a lot more, but it was sea, not sky; there's a boat floating on the top of it". Perhaps next time it will have turned out to be a parasol upside down; but our friend is still enthusiastically delighted with the progress he is making. The scientist has his guesses as to how the finished picture will work out; he depends largely on these in his search for other pieces to fit; but his guesses are modified from time to time by unexpected developments as the fitting pro-

* This difficulty is evidently connected with the dual entry of time into our experience to which I have so often referred.

ceeds. These revolutions of thought as to the final picture do not cause the scientist to lose faith in his handiwork, for he is aware that the completed portion is growing steadily. Those who look over his shoulder and use the present partially developed picture for purposes outside science, do so at their own risk.

The lack of finality of scientific theories would be a very serious limitation of our argument, if we had staked much on their permanence. The religious reader may well be content that I have not offered him a God revealed by the quantum theory, and therefore liable to be swept away in the next scientific revolution. It is not so much the particular form that scientific theories have now taken—the conclusions which we believe we have proved—as the movement of thought behind them that concerns the philosopher. Our eyes once opened, we may pass on to a yet newer outlook on the world, but we can never go back to the old outlook.

If the scheme of philosophy which we now rear on the scientific advances of Einstein, Bohr, Rutherford and others is doomed to fall in the next thirty years, it is not to be laid to their charge that we have gone astray. Like the systems of Euclid, of Ptolemy, of Newton, which have served their turn, so the systems of Einstein and Heisenberg may give way to some fuller realisation of the world. But in each revolution of scientific thought new words are set to the old music, and that which has gone before is not destroyed but refocussed. Amid all our faulty attempts at expression the kernel of scientific truth steadily grows; and of this truth it may be said— The more it changes, the more it remains the same thing.

paradox

INDEX